The Homebuyer'$ Guide For The 80'$

Richard W. O'Neill

GROSSET & DUNLAP
A Filmways Company
Publishers   New York

Special thanks for the cooperation and help of James V. Rice of Cincinnati, Ohio, and my wife, Patricia.

Contents

4　　　　　　　　　　　　　　　　　　　　　　　　　　Contents

Contents   5

Preface

This book has a major and a minor purpose. The major purpose is to provide step-by-step guidance on deciding to buy and then completing the purchase of your own home. Although this may sound simple, it is actually a complex process, because the ways we live and work and structure the places where we live are complex. And you yourself are complex, as are those immediately around you. All these factors influence what and where you buy.

The secondary purpose of this book is to show how home-ownership works in this country, to unravel its mystery and mystique. Today, two-thirds of all U.S. households own their own homes, but this is a recent phenomenon. Before World War II, when we had a much smaller population, fewer than a third of us owned our homes. So homeownership is relatively new for most of us.

And, of course, it will be a new experience for millions of young people in the years immediately ahead. Let me give you a brief insight into the magnitude of this future experience. In the decade of the 1950's, about 24 million people reached the age of thirty, and a fairly sizable proportion of them in the years just before or just after thirty bought their first houses. About 23 million people reached thirty in the decade of the 1960's, some 30 million in the 1970's; and 42 million will reach that age in the 1980's. In 1979 American households *bought* almost 6 million homes—a record, in a year when mortgage rates ranged from 9½% to 11%. Those were new homes, used homes, condominiums, townhouses, single-family detached houses, co-ops, and mobile homes—all owned.

So this book is written for the majority of Americans, because a majority can buy houses—for the first or even the tenth time. It is especially intended for those people, families, couples, and single people, who at one time may not have dreamed of homeownership but have since changed their minds. It also provides extensive new knowledge, particularly in mortgage-loan developments, for you who now own homes.

The book should have special meaning for professionals in the housing industry, bringing together as it does the myriad facets of that business in one source. In effect, it details the housing process; for real estate investors, that assures the continuing and rising value of property.

It is necessary to go into technical aspects of law, mortgage financing, and construction, but these sections of the book are written to be easily digested by people who have no knowledge of those underpinnings of the residential housing market.

The complexity of that market is reflected in the host of professionals involved: builders, realtors, lenders, architects, land developers, designers, decorators, landscape architects, building-product manufacturers, engineers, lawyers, retailers, and federal, state, and local officials. All of them, too, may find this book useful.

Foreword
Homeownership—An Affair of the Heart

Almost all of us want our own homes. You can rarely find anybody today in this country who, if given his or her "druthers," would not want to be a homeowner—in town, in the suburbs, in the country. The first reason we want our own homes is not monetary, but rather personal. Our home becomes an expression of ourselves and our families, a place to be ourselves, a place where we feel secure and comfortable. It's an affair of the heart first.

The roots of that affair, if you please, are deep. Famous houses sometimes seem as much a part of our history as were the men who made it—Monticello, Mount Vernon, Abe Lincoln's cabin. Some of our most popular Christmas cards depict houses in country settings—because such pictures mean warmth, family, roots. Currier and Ives prints abound with houses that, somehow or other, we all seem to identify with.

How big a role have houses played in your life? Do you remember the first time you had your own bedroom? How about the first time you had your own "pad"? The new life that a new home can be is stimulating, energizing. So we have developed a whole set of emotions about our own homes.

We do things to our houses that please us. We try to keep them shipshape; we fuss over them ten times more than we'd fuss over an apartment. Our forebears dreamed of country homes when they first came to this continent, even though many of them realized it might be a generation or two before their descendants would own their own piece of land and build their own house on it. It is our dream, too. There is deeper satisfaction in homeownership than just realizing the buildup of equity through mortgage payments and appreciation.

Trying to define the satisfaction a home can give is difficult. There are so many things you can say about how you feel about your own home, or even just the prospect of owning your own home. It's not just heart, it's ego, emotions . . .and those things vary for different people.

This many-sided relationship that people have with their homes is usually most special for women, whether or not they work, whether or not they are married, whether or not they have children. Homes have always been women's worlds. But they are also more men's worlds today in the United States than probably at any time in the history of this or any other country. Which is why so many of us treat our homes almost as if they were our children, at least in the way we fuss over them and create of them a special reflection of ourselves and our life-styles.

Your home is not walls and floors and windows. It's identity, security, romance, savings, where your kids lived or will live. It's a neighborhood, a front yard, a backyard; it's the sure end of a trip to the store, a trip to the movies. Dwell on your thoughts and feelings as you contemplate looking for a house to buy; you're not just thinking about square footage, materials, and dollars. Those things may be farthest from your mind as you set out on a mission to find the house that will be yours.

There is a pleasant excitement in this mission, the excitement of risk taking, maybe gambling; but the odds are heavily weighted in your favor: you know you're going to win, if you're careful, take your time, and act deliberately.

HOUSE HUNTING IN YOUR IMAGINATION

You will find that when you look for a house, your home, you dream and fantasize about it. That's the way it should be, because what you are doing is setting down in your mind's eye all those things that are most important to you in a house. If you can't find some of them in a particular house, you'll make a mental note to change what you buy into what you really want: fireplace, big master bedroom, lots of closets, sunlight in the kitchen, sunlight in the baby's room, TV in the den, a flower garden out front, tulips in the spring, strawberries in the backyard, a swing under the sycamore, maybe climbing roses around the front door, wide floorboards, lots of people in at Christmas.

Why not?

Why not indeed. Millions of other Americans have started out having just such visions and have achieved a great many of them. By fantasizing, you're creating a mind's-eye vision of what you want your home to be, and of what you and your spouse and your friends will do in this home.

How would it feel to cut down a tree on your own property, to swing your ax and work up a sweat on your own turf? Or play touch football with the kids, or till your new garden patch, or get sawdust in your hair in your own workshop? You can develop a sense of dedication about your home which comes about just from physical activity, from playful violence. It's an atavistic feeling that may take you back to how your forebears might have felt about their land, their place.

That's fine, you say, but that kind of daydreaming can be dangerous; it can be a source of big disappointment. A lot of people would disagree with you if you take that position. If you don't know what you want (one of the results of daydreaming), looking for a house will produce anxiety. You may be too hesitant and miss the deal that would have been best for you because of indecision.

When you talk to your friends about buying a house—and you should, for they often can give you ideas and information—you will undoubtedly hear about people who bought lemons, or who didn't buy because the price was a few thousand too high or some detail wasn't the way they would have liked it. But if you recognize that the home you love is an affair of the heart first and foremost, you won't buy what you shouldn't, and you won't let a few details or even a few thousand dollars stand in your way. Love really does conquer all.

I'm not suggesting that you take on more than you can handle in a house. That's what much of the rest of this book is all about. You don't want something that's beyond your grasp economically or in maintenance, remodeling, or whatever. Just remember to consider how you *feel* about the house.

Very likely you know some people for whom life is very grim. They may have a lot of reasons for feeling that way, but almost always one of the reasons is that they don't like their homes. The places they live make them feel bad, inadequate, uncomfortable. You don't have to be a psychiatrist to understand this.

I'm not implying that there must be a "perfect" house for everybody. Nothing in or for the human condition is absolutely perfect. But we try to get close, and we often succeed.

If you're married, be sure that you and your spouse can agree, if not fully at least almost fully, about what you need in a house. If you have different images of your house, if your life-styles differ, there can be trouble. Suppose one of you likes gardening, informality, and no big parties, and the other's tastes are just the opposite. One will want to look at houses with large yards and gardens, while the other will consider only houses with large formal dining rooms. Work out all your compromises before you start looking; otherwise, you really won't know what to look for. That's where the anxiety and the cold feet come in.

Let me just take you briefly through some of the thought processes that your imagination can conjure up to help you write, in your mind, your specifications for your house.

How does the house work for you? Where do you shop, where do you work, where do you go to church, where do you play, how do you travel? Are restaurants close by? What friends are close by? What schools are there, what financial institutions and other facilities? Think about eating, sleeping, reading, watching TV, listening to radio, recreation, caring for children, entertaining, studying, working, what to do when there's little that actually needs to be done.

The decision to buy is really a whole series of decisions concerning the way you live, your desires, the future of the community around you, the value of your time and money, and so forth. If all those decisions are made properly, the final decision to buy a particular house is easy. It will come almost automatically, because you have gone through a careful thought process, have weighed all the variables, to the point that when you come up to the closing table, that final signature, that final check, is really anticlimactic. You just want to get in the house—you want it right now, because in your imagination you have already occupied it for weeks.

A VOICE OF EXPERIENCE

John L. Schmidt is an Illinois architect and a vice-president of the Institute of Financial Education. He's had years of experience in teaching, designing, and building (including his own houses over the years) most of it residential work. This is what he told me about finding a house:

"Your first impression of a house, or just a lot, is usually your best test, emotionally. If the property moves you, don't worry about the little things that may be wrong. An awful lot can be fixed. So you should weigh this first impression heavily. If you're married, be sure the house rings both your bells, and see it and the neighborhood both in daytime and at night.

"That first impression is like the first few minutes of a job interview, or the first impression your kids make, or the opening moments of a football game. It's a legitimate measure. It's that opening point where you will sell yourself. If the salesman has to sell you after the first impression (which was bad for you), forget it ninety-nine times out of a hundred. It'll be like that new suit that some hotshot salesman 'forced' on you. You'll hate it.

"But now, having said that, let me back up. You've got to examine very carefully your mind's-eye vision of what you want. I'm very wary of the dream-house image, or concept. Too often it is made up of symbols that can be misleading, that can lead to disappointment, that may have to do only with the front elevation of the house and have nothing to do with the lot, the floor plan, how the house is oriented, how it works with the lot.

"The dream house, when you spot it, often hides a fraudulent design, a design that's awkward to live with or maybe doesn't work at all. You have to know how the house will work for you and your family.

"The symbols that make up the dream house are often nothing more than appearances. A spiral staircase coming down into the front hall—you see your daughter on her wedding day coming down those stairs. Nice and romantic, but it has little to do with the way the house will 'live' for you every day.

"Most of the usual symbols that make up the dream house are ones of familiarity and status. Familiarity: panel doors, seven-by-ten-inch glass panes (all they could make two hundred years ago), shutters that once had a number of functions but now are purely decorative, like the vinyl photo of wood grain on the side of a station wagon harking back to the 1930's when carriage makers made station-wagon bodies. Those things are emotionally comfortable, and there's nothing wrong with that, but they're just symbols, not the elements of daily living and working.

"Status symbols. Those spiral stairs. Traditional design—all the houses on the right side of town when you grew up may have been traditional in style; hence status. Nothing wrong with this either, but it can prevent an understanding of what contemporary design is all about. A two-story colonial, with living room on the right, dining room on the left, center hall, twin fireplaces back to back in the center of the house, little windows, two stories stacked, was built that way to stand the rugged winters when two fireplaces, a stove, and a dutch oven provided all the heat there was.

"In the South, curving driveways are very popular, but they may not make any sense. A curving driveway provided room for everybody to park his carriage (or car) when they all came to the June wedding. Or big columns on the front portico. When it was a porch, and you needed a roof over it for when it rained, okay. But today all that stuff is just decoration—and pretty expensive at that.

"We can do a lot more for your money today, so take that first impression, make note of it, and then be prepared to match it against all the rational (as opposed to emotional) decisions you're going to make. First; the lot and how it works; then the floor plan and how it works; how the house is oriented to the sun, to the view, to the street. Then consider the elevations and all the symbols. They are properly last in the long-run considerations, even though they may have been first in your initial impression. I'm not discounting the importance of symbols to you; they can be very heavy. But you've got to live with your house.

"I don't want to dampen that emotional yen. It's important, but you don't marry the best-looking girl you see (if you've been around) or the best-looking man, if you're a girl. You've got to know the person. Good looks are nice, like symbols that are important to you, but that's all."

You're going to make a decision about a house that you may live with for a long time. It will be a good decision and an *easy* decision if you observe all the steps along the way. The sequence of those steps is the way I have organized this book.

HOMEOWNERSHIP IS FOR ALMOST EVERYBODY

What chance do you have to buy a house, a new house, another house? If you already own a house, you have every chance in the world. If you don't own a house right now, the chances are at least as good as two out of three, for most of us better—and that's for all Americans.

Your first decision is whether or not you can buy any house. Today, two-thirds of all U.S. households—that includes families and single people or just people doubling up—own their own homes. Before World War II, only one-third of us did.

Look at your personal possibility of homeownership this way. In the past decade or so, partly because of inflation, homeowners have found the effective cost of homeownership to be almost zero. Market values for houses have appreciated; income tax laws provide that interest paid on mortgages and property taxes may be deducted from taxable income. This slows the shift into higher tax brackets as personal income increases because of inflation. It also explains why interest rates for home mortgages are actually below the stated rate. (See the table "After-Tax Cost of Mortgage Interest Paid" in Chapter 10.)

We're becoming a nation of homeowners at the fastest rate in history. One of the best surveys of recent home-buying patterns ever done bears this out by implication. A survey of 8,500 buyers of new and used houses in 1977, by the U.S. League of Savings Associations, showed that 18.2% of first-time buyers were single people and 6.6% were unmarried couples. Among those repurchasing houses, or buying their second, third, or fourth house, 10.1% were single people and 2.4% were unmarried couples. About half of those single persons were women. Roughly the same figures held for 1979.

What has happened is that everyone, not just married couples, is now considered a potential homebuyer. And as more kinds of people buy houses, the more houses will be bought.

HOMEOWNERSHIP IN HISTORY

The relationship of U.S. family incomes to house prices has been and still is steady and strong—and in some ways even improving—in spite of inflation. Contrary to the popular belief that the American consumer is being priced out of the new-house market, U.S. Census data show that hardly any greater proportion of the population is priced out of the housing market today than was priced out in the late 1940's. Those data show that the median new-house price was 2.85 times median family annual income in 1949 (the first year of such data collecting) and 2.87 times annual income in 1975 (the latest complete year)—a remarkably stable relationship except for three years, 1970 through 1972, when the Department of Housing and Urban Development's subsidized housing skewed the figures a bit. Relationships of price to after-tax income also remained stable, in a range of from 3.1 to 3.2 times annual income.

A survey in 1976 by Data Resources of Lexington, Massachusetts, found, using a rule of thumb of house price at 2.5 times annual family income, that 35.9% of all families in 1955 could afford a new house at the median price, and that in 1976, 38.4% could afford that new house. Further, Data Resources forecast that within that rule of thumb, the proportion of families who could afford a median-priced new house would grow from 39.9% in 1977 to 43.8% in 1980.

New-house pricing is often viewed as pushing the new single-family house beyond the reach of the first-time buyer. It's true that most new single-family houses are purchased by second-to-fourth-time buyers. That has been the case for about the last twenty years (and will probably be so in the future). But about a third of new houses are purchased by first-time buyers.

A closer look at American family incomes is useful. As recently as the first half of 1977 the median family income slightly exceeded $16,000. That was sufficient income to purchase one-third of all new houses sold in that first half of 1977 and almost one-half of all existing houses sold—they were priced under $40,000.

Thirty million married-couple families in the United States have incomes over $20,000 a year, enough to purchase a $50,000 house using a rule of thumb of 2.5 house price times income.

In the growing affluence of American families there are some encouraging figures. In the family income bracket between $15,000 and $25,000 there were in each year from 1970 through 1977, a million more families. For the family income category above $25,000, there were also a million more families each year for the same period. These incomes as they relate to home-buying ability involve a new dimension: women's income. Monthly amortization payments, energy costs, and property taxes in general take a larger proportion of income than they did ten or twenty years ago, but the way the American family keeps pace with this heavier financial burden is for wives to go to work: almost 55% are employed full-time. They have swelled the work force some 30% in the last sixteen years when our population increased only about 15%.

Advance Mortgage of Detroit points out that one of the results of the equal-rights movement was the passage of the Equal Credit Opportunity Act of 1975. One of its provisions requires that a working wife's income be counted toward mortgage eligibility according to the same standards as her husband's. That, at a stroke, increased the mortgaging power of millions of two-income families by 40% to 60% and, in many cases, by much more.

It also made mortgages much more readily available to single women, although the impact of this change is hard to quantify. (More than 7 million single women, or 40% of the 17 million nonfamily households, own the houses in which they live, and 86% of those are single-family houses.)

Of course, you should look at homeownership in the context of comparison shopping. In many metropolitan areas today, monthly rent for an apartment with, say, two bedrooms can be lower than the monthly housing expense for some houses with two bedrooms, even when the apartment tenant pays utilities separately. But in the case of homeownership there is equity buildup and real estate appreciation. That's money in the bank, so to speak. In tenancy, after all those rental payments, there's nothing.

And you will find that the rents in a brand-new apartment

house (if it's not a subsidized project) are considerably higher than the monthly housing expense of most same-sized houses, new or old. In rent-controlled areas, no new apartments are built unless the landlord can get luxury rents, except for subsidized projects, which you probably can't qualify for anyhow.

Where apartment rents are equal to monthly housing expenses, or lower, the apartments are in older buildings and/or rent-controlled. Chapter 10 takes you through the arithmetic of rental versus ownership.

Bear in mind, too, when somebody tells you about the good deal he has out in Big Sandy, Montana, say, that rents and expenses differ widely from place to place and for all kinds of circumstances. There are few rules of thumb about the components of the total rent or monthly housing expense.

Also, when you think about the purchase price of a home, don't try to relate it directly to the monthly housing expense. The two bear little relation to each other. A fraction of the purchase price is in the monthly expense, to be sure. But taxes, energy, interest rates, and insurance make up the largest proportion by far. And if you could subtract the cost of the improved lot your new home sits on and the cost of government regulation in the building process, you would find that the cost of construction— just the labor and materials in the house—would represent less than 10% of the monthly housing expense.

In sum, you have to look at the possibility of homeownership very carefully. Your chances to own are better now than at almost any other time in history. One of the most important reasons, and I know I'm repeating myself, is that women can now qualify for a mortgage, and their income must be counted when a married couple, both working, apply for a loan.

Another very important reason lies in the present structure of the mortgage market (see Chapter 13). Until October 1979 there was plenty of mortgage money available to would-be homebuyers. In October 1979 the Federal Reserve Board raised interest rates to the highest levels in history, and many lenders simply stopped lending. In some states usury rates precluded lending; in most states savers took money out of thrift institutions to find better returns on savings elsewhere, so money to lend for mortgages became very scarce. And at 12% to 14% interest rates, many hopeful buyers could not qualify for a mortgage loan.

But until that fateful month, the funds available for mortgages had at least doubled since the early 1970's. What had changed the market was the creation of an active secondary market in mortgages made possible principally by the Emergency Housing Finance Act of 1970. A secondary market is one that buys pools of mortgages already made on individual houses by, let's say, a savings and loan association. It draws its money to buy those pools of mortgages from investors who might otherwise buy stocks and bonds—the secondary market sells negotiable securities backed by those pools of mortgages.

The actions of the secondary market, as a result, provide new funds to the savings and loan association to make more mortgages with. In this way, homeownership competes effectively with stocks and bonds for the investor's funds. In the past that was not true. And houses have always been a great hedge against inflation, so investors find investing in the secondary market easily as desirable as investing elsewhere.

The secondary mortgage market is still a very strong factor in the supply and availability of mortgage money, and it will be even stronger in the 1980's. We have been drawing about 25% of our mortgage money from the secondary market in the United States. That percentage is likely to increase in the decade of the 80's. There will be plenty of mortgage money around in the coming decade—at a price, but there will be plenty.

Section I.

Choosing the Right House

When you were a child and someone asked you, along about Thanksgiving, what you wanted for Christmas and asked you to make a list, you probably came up with a list as long as your leg. This section is a little like that. In a perfect world, and if you were rich, the house you want might meet every criterion here, specific or implied. But that's almost impossible.

So perhaps you might ask yourself, "How do I form an opinion about what I want in a house?" How do you select those things that are important to you, from a whole range of things that you might consider?

This section gives you a procedure by which to choose those things that are most important to you about a house. The section is not a recipe or set of instructions; it's a guideline. You may want a regular "turkey" of a house because of its location, and you might be very right to take it. But, in general, you should try to hedge your bet by checking your heart's desire against most of the points and questions raised in these chapters.

Chapter 1

What Makes a House Look Good

At one time or another you've looked at enough houses to realize that there is a certain proportion to a house that makes it pleasing. When a house is not in proportion—width to height, for example—it looks odd and ugly. Good proportions are one of the first rules of a good-looking house; and it's your judgment, not somebody else's.

The front of the house (front elevation) is another factor that contributes to the way a house looks. It should not be broken up with windows that don't seem to match, doors in odd places, and a wide variety of materials. Houses that mix three or more exterior materials, such as wood siding, brick, and maybe some kind of stone or glass block, obviously look a little bit slapped together.

Something else you may notice when comparing good-looking houses and bad-looking houses is that the outside walls of a good house—the front, sides, and back—do not have a lot of ins and outs. Walls don't jut out or jog back and then forward. The same is true of the roofline. Most houses look better if they don't have a lot of "roofs," all joined together as though they were many buildings stuck together like a cluster of woodsheds.

Poorly designed houses, the ones that don't look good and don't have the value that derives from looking good, often are a jumble of design ideas with no theme that ties the whole house together. A "no-theme" house has doors and windows that are all different sizes, like decorations that might be hung haphazardly on the front or sides of the house, as an afterthought. Lots of gingerbread work from the Victorian era is a giveaway. Some of those old Victorian houses are real beauties, but gingerbread on a house built since 1940 does look out of place to most buyers and to most people who lend money for houses.

Of course, there are personal tastes involved in houses. Contemporary or modern houses, traditional or colonial houses—obviously each style has its fans. We know that a lot of people react coolly to certain types of exteriors.

Generally, all kinds of wood sidings, stone, and brick give a traditional feeling of warmth. Wood, for instance, has wide acceptance because it has a traditional association. If, in fact, most people associate wood with warmth, wood should have a better perceived value for you, and for the person who might buy the house from you five years from now. And, of course, it means the same to the lender. Those considerations are almost as important as your taste.

Ideally the exterior of the house should not have more than two or three sizes of windows, apart from sliding glass doors, and it should not have many more than two or three types of exterior claddings, or sidings, so that the whole works together, giving the house a theme.

Scale and proportion are a bit harder to define. In general, the house should have proportions like other houses that do indeed fit the human functions houses were built for; doors need not be like barn doors, and windows need not be like storefronts. They are for people, not for wagons or horses or displays of merchandise. Look at the houses you like in any given neighborhood, and you will see what I mean about scale and proportion. The ones you like are the ones that have human scale and good proportion; the ones that repel you are the ones that seem out of line, a little grotesque, too big or too small in detail or in overall size.

Color and the number of colors can be both subjective and objective. There are colors you like, colors you have seen on houses that you like; that is your taste. On the other hand, you know that too many colors on the exterior of a house look odd. Even though the house may not look too odd to you, it will to most other people—including those whom you may approach to lend money on it.

The same goes for style. You know what kinds of houses you like, and your best bet is to pick those houses that seem to look, or do look, like houses that most other people would like. Not that you are following the herd, but you must keep in mind that something that is wildly out of line, that isn't a good contemporary or a good colonial, may be the kind of house that most people would reject. At all times you should consider the resale value of the house, even though you expect to spend the rest of your days in it.

A word about architectural style. You have often heard people talk about colonials, Cape Cods, contemporaries, and other styles.

Don't worry too much about those distinctions if they don't mean much to you. If you do want to find out about them, there are plenty of books available that define these various architectural styles at great length.

The fact of the matter is that in today's market, while one house may be a Cape Cod and another a Garrison colonial, both exact copies hewing directly to their respective traditions, it usually doesn't make that much difference to you or to other people in the market, now or in the future, as long as a house seems to have the proportions and the looks (for that general style) that have the stamp of approval of an awful lot of us. In the shelter magazines, such as *House & Garden* and *Better Homes and Gardens,* you have seen these houses identified again and again. It isn't something that you need to spend a lot of time on before you are ready to buy, which is probably right now. You already know what kind of house you like and you know what style it is.

Apart from the house itself, there are two other very important factors that can make a property look good. One is the homesite and how it sets off the house. I deal with that a bit later in this chapter, and you should also see in Chapter 3, "How to Consider Property and Its Value." The other is the nature of the neighborhood—its natural amenities and how they have been preserved or treated. See also Chapter 5, "What to Look for in a Community."

In older areas of almost any town or city, neighborhoods simply grew like Topsy. If an old neighborhood is especially attractive to you, and to other people, it's usually because the property owners there have always cared for their neighborhood, just as they cared for their houses. Often, natural amenities—ravines, sudden outcroppings of rock, streams, big old trees—have had a strong influence on how good a neighborhood looks, if it all has been preserved.

And in those older neighborhoods, the adoption of zoning ordinances (almost all of them in this country came into being after 1926) brought a good deal of order. A gas station couldn't be built on a corner in a residential area, for instance. Deed restrictions in cities that have no zoning, such as Houston, accomplished the same thing. But zoning is not always an unmixed blessing (see Chapter 5). It is often used as a political tool, or as something to curry special favor, and then the consequences can be less than desirable.

In a great many neighborhoods built within the last twenty or so years, land-use planning has been as important to the developer as house design. Some of these newer neighborhoods can be very attractive, even without any special natural amenities. This is usually accomplished with trees, landscaping, and signs. Good new neighborhoods are as carefully designed and laid out as are any of the new houses in them. And you'll be able to spot this care and attention to detail as soon as you drive through a good newer development. If it looks haphazard to you, or grubby, keep right on driving—the value isn't there.

Bear in mind that the preservation of natural amenities, usually most desirable, is an expensive process in most cases and often prevents a more efficient and economic land use. So you will probably pay more for a house in a good neighborhood, new or old, but it will almost always be worth the extra cost.

Let me remind you of what I wrote at the beginning of this chapter: by thinking along the guidelines suggested here about exterior appearance, color, style, and natural amenities around the house, you will form an image of what you want in a house: the way it looks, and how it sits on its lot and in the neighborhood. But that is really only the beginning of the home-buying process.

WHAT TO LOOK FOR IN A HOUSE

One of the great things about home buying today as compared with a generation or two ago is that there are thousands of different kinds of homes on different kinds of homesites available in almost any metropolitan area: old houses, antique houses, and brand-new houses; detached houses, attached houses, and all kinds of newly planned neighborhoods (planned unit developments); and wonderful houses in older neighborhoods.

What are your special needs in a house, what are your requirements for yourself and your household, or if you are married with children, for your family? The problem is identifying the requirements for your life-style, then deciding what it will take to meet them.

You are going to look at many houses that may not have everything you want. Bear in mind that most dwelling units in this country can be expanded. Attics can be finished for bedrooms; lower-level space, as in split-level houses, can be used for bedrooms, family rooms, or game rooms; basements can be finished for family rooms; bathrooms can be built; porches can be enclosed; terraces can be added. There are all kinds of possibilities, especially if you are a do-it-yourselfer. (See Chapter 17, "Some Bargains.")

Everyone agrees that all houses seem to be expensive these days. But we do know that the majority of American households can afford to own their own homes. When you add to that the fact that most Americans improve their homes, either by additions or simply by renovating what is already there, you know that you can take whatever house you can afford and make it worth much more.

Older house or new house? This choice is nearly always resolved by selecting a community or neighborhood first. The turmoil caused by inflation on the market values of houses has destroyed any traditional patterns in the relative sales price of old and new houses. While the new house is usually easier to buy—that is, has a lower proportionate down payment and more liberal financing terms—older houses often have nooks and crannies that can be turned into great little sewing rooms, workshops, and the like. Furthermore, older houses already have a certain amount of character—architectural richness, if you will—as well as landscaping that might take years to develop in a new house. On the other hand, older houses may have bigger problems in plumbing, heating, wiring, and necessary repairs.

Townhouses or attached dwelling units do not have their own side yards, but they do have their own front yards and backyards. They are usually less expensive for the same amount of interior space than a comparable detached house on its own lot that completely surrounds the house. The reason they are less expensive does not lie in the cost of construction itself, but rather in the smaller share of land and land improvements used for the individual townhouse.

Townhouses are increasing in popularity across the country, particularly in condominiums (see Chapter 6), because they offer a good way around today's inflated prices. These attached houses offer the same benefits of homeownership as detached houses— namely, appreciation, equity buildup, and deductibility of interest on mortgage and property taxes—which can give you, in sum, almost an effective zero cost of living in an inflationary economy. (See the example in Chapter 10.)

Perhaps now you have a mental picture of your house. You can envision your family living there, kids coming home from school, dinner being prepared, everybody getting together at Thanksgiving . . . all the events and activities you expect your house to envelop, as it embraces your life-style.

A HOMESITE'S VALUE, USE, AND MAINTENANCE

What is the property around your house going to look like? That is a tough question, because you don't have a particular property yet in mind. But you should have an imaginary view of a piece of land on which you can position a patio, shrubs, trees. Your mind's-eye view is a transferable vision—it is movable—and when you see a particular property in your search, you may be able to close your eyes and see the trees and the patio, the fences and other things you have thought about, transplanted to that property.

What's outside the house is a major attraction. The look of the lot from the street is your first introduction to the house. Walk over the grounds, looking at all the views. What view do you have from this room or that door? What trees are there, and what condition are they in? What gardens or flower beds are already there? Is that a consideration in your life-style? Is there anything about the property, such as power lines and easements to other property, that might detract from its aesthetic or economic value? Does the property seem big enough for what you envision? If the lot is an odd shape, can you make good use, recreationally or with landscaping, out of all of it?

See what shade and sunshine the lot gets. Older houses are often surrounded by heavy trees; in the winter months and during rainy seasons, their deep shade and dankness can create a depressing mood. A house built in a small hollow or a ravine may get the same effect. Take into consideration how you will feel about too much sunshine or too much shade.

What will happen in the winter when it snows and you have to go to work? What will happen in very heavy rainstorms, as in hurricanes in the South or Northeast? Is there good drainage and a natural slope of the ground away from your house and property to streambeds?

If you're not happy with the look of the property, how much landscaping will you want to do and at what cost or effort? The amount of maintenance necessary for your lot may not be readily apparent. Large lawns and particular types of shrubs and flowers can require a great deal of attention. In the so-called public areas of the lot (a front yard on the street, which you may not use) you don't want to have to do a lot of mowing, weeding, and clipping. In the private areas of your lot, where you may use a lot of outdoor living space, maintenance can be cut down drastically by patios and terraces.

A LANDSCAPE ARCHITECT CAN HELP

You will probably not see any properties in your search that satisfy you completely. That's to be expected. But if you have a strong imagination, even the worst lot you see can demonstrate, in your imagination, a great deal of potential. As a buyer, you don't want to be thrown off by the things that can be corrected relatively easily, and in most instances where the ground will grow things, you will be able to change the aspect of your lot readily. With the basics of good ground and good slopes, and your imagination, you can spot some lots that have potential that may not be visible to most people. What do people do about making their homesite into what they want? They usually do little more than plant a couple of things the first year, making the landscaping of the property haphazard. It is useful for you, as a buyer, to know how a landscape architect might work with you to make a master plan for your property, one that you can carry out over a number of years if you don't have the money immediately available for landscaping. The money that you will spend initially for a landscape architect will be well worth it. Over time, it may even save you money.

Fort Lauderdale, Florida, landscape architect Raymond Ueker, who trained at Michigan State University, described the process this way:

"I visit the family two or three times, at their property, while developing the master plan. I literally take a specification on their life-style—outdoor living, entertainment patterns, hobbies, kids' pastimes, all the family interests, how much they like to garden, how much maintenance they expect and want to do, how much time they have at home, if vacations are spent in part or fully at home, and so forth.

"Climate, soil type, shade, house orientation for summer cooling and winter heating—all affect the landscape design as well as how the site is going to be used.

"The final result is the master plan calling for specific types of plants, trees, shrubs, planting dates, fertilizers, and the whole rundown on how to care for the plants. This costs $500, and that's about standard all around the country today.

"The justification for that fee lies in the fact that the buyer won't go out and buy the wrong things, things that might die, might grow so big they have to be dug up in a few years, might throw too much shade in the winter or let in too much sun in the summer. The master plan does away with the helter-skelter, the 'let's try it anyway and then see if you like it.' It eliminates dressing up your property so it looks great to the neighbors, but does nothing for you because maybe you can't even see it from inside the house.

"Now, if the buyer has a lot of money, he can get the whole thing done to a specification that fits his family right off the bat. But if his budget is tight, he can just get the professional advice he needs for the master plan and then do it all himself over time, whenever he gets the money for fixing up his property that his family budget should be designed to provide. That landscaping is as important to the value of the property as the house itself."

Chapter 2

Personal Requirements— How Does the House "Live"?

Now try to visualize the inside of your house and the floor plan that would "live" best for you and your family, one that fits your life-style and your daily needs.

The best floor plan makes no room a hallway. When you enter a house you should not have to walk directly into the living room to get to any other room. Obviously, this is not always possible, but the ideal floor plan does not have a continual traffic pattern through a room.

When you look at the floor plan of a house, figure out how your daily routine would work with that layout. Will the children disrupt daily activities or entertaining in the living room? Can you get to the bathroom without going through the living room, the kitchen, or another room? Is some key area isolated, such as a laundry in a basement, so that you might have trouble answering the phone or getting to the stove in time to turn off the burner?

A house should be made for the family to live in with the greatest convenience and without disruption of other activities going on at the same time. For instance, if the kids come in from outdoors all covered with snow or mud, can they get to where they can clean up without running through some area that you don't want messed up or will immediately have to clean?

Another way of looking at the problem—and this is a traditional way used by architects and builders—is to consider whether there is proper zoning between living areas, sleeping areas, and working areas such as the kitchen. If so, each has its own space in the house.

Here are some key floor-plan considerations:

The main entrance should lead to the living room, but people shouldn't have to walk through the living room to get to any other room. To prevent the living room from becoming a traffic corridor, it should be in a dead-end location with really only one entranceway to the rest of the house, although it might have outside openings such as patio doors to a terrace.

Ideally, there should be a separate family entrance, or grocery-shopping or back-door entrance, for people on their daily rounds, such as coming from and going to school. A garage entrance should be near the kitchen, not at the opposite side of the house.

Obviously, the kitchen should have a "command post" or central location in the house if at all possible and should not be at some remote area of the house—because a great deal of all the family's time will be spent there, cooking, eating, cleaning, talking, or just visiting.

Keep in mind that you may not live forever in this house. If you're like most Americans, you will live there only a few years, so you don't want a floor plan that will be an obstacle to the next buyer. It should work well for most families, and the two key elements in that floor plan are a traffic pattern that doesn't take people through other rooms to get to their destination—which has already been discussed; and a good kitchen.

There are plenty of books that discuss kitchens and the work triangle, an arrangement of appliances such that the distance between the central cooking area (the range), the preparation and cleaning area (the sink), and the food-storage area (the refrigerator and/or the pantry) is no more than seven feet. Also, the orientation of kitchens with outside windows is very important; windows should face south, west, or east to get some sun. A north-facing kitchen is one of the toughest for people to accept because it gets no sun although it is the coolest in the hot summer months.

Obviously a bathroom should be located near the bedrooms. If there is a second or third bathroom, one should be within easy reach of the front entrance and the living room.

How does your furniture fit in the house? This is a matter for your lively imagination when you contemplate a floor plan. Where will the things you have or want to get fit in this house? Is there sufficient wall space? You need to develop a sense of scale and dimension that will be particularly useful as you evaluate room sizes and window and door locations.

A GOOD DECORATOR CAN MAKE A DIFFERENCE

No doubt you know some people who entertain in the den when they have company, never or rarely using the living room. Have you ever wondered why? It's usually because they aren't as comfortable in the living room as they are in the den; the living room is not decorated to fit their life-style. A good decorator would have changed that.

As you shop for a house, you may be thrown by the way someone else has decorated the interior of one that you might buy. Their taste may not be yours. Again, use your imagination. Gauge the walls, the ceiling heights, the floor area, and try to visualize how you might decorate the same spaces to please you.

One of the greatest aids in that regard can be the ideas and services of a good interior decorator. Just as a landscape architect can help you see the potential in a lot, an interior decorator can give you ideas that may help you decide to purchase.

No doubt you have heard horror stories about some decorator or other who made somebody's living room look like a hotel lobby and cost an arm and a leg. But a good decorator, like a good landscape architect or a good architect, will do his or her work to suit your life-style and your budget and will expect to be paid only for his or her time and design efforts. A good decorator will not earn his or her fee by taking a cut of the total furnishing package. You can easily get gouged that way. You want somebody's brains and ability. The decorator can get it for you wholesale, but a good one will not take any cut from the price of furnishings to reimburse himself.

A good decorator may charge you $50 an hour and spend eight to twelve hours on your design problem, half of it learning about you and your life-style. That fee is easily covered by the 40% off most furnishings you can buy through the decorator. But anyway, a good decorator's advice to you is easily worth that kind of money in the long run simply for your comfort and happiness in your house.

Peggy Walker of New York City is one such decorator. Here is how she described to me the design procedure she likes to use:

"First, I have to get to know the people well—have dinner with them and talk at length about how they live, what they like to do, what kind of environment they like and that they'd like to live in. And everybody's different. Some people want to live in a garden-type environment, some are happier in something darker and closer.

"I have them cut out pictures of rooms they like, from all kinds of magazines, and without paying any attention to what the room pictured might have cost. Cost of furnishings at this point is unimportant. What is important is knowing what they like and how they like it arranged.

"This brings the process down to the types of rooms they'll be happy in. Then we can start analyzing how to get there money-wise, what kind of budget. People may like framed pictures, but if they're young, with a baby or two, a tight budget, attractive posters on the wall can give the same finished look to a room. And that's very important: finished rooms. Nobody's happy with a room that's half finished. You can finish the whole room, and should, without spending a lot of money.

"But before we settle on a room, we work out an overall plan for the house, a plan that can be done over time, in stages, depending on the family's budget.

"So the first thing is the plan of the overall environment to fit the family and their life-style. The second thing is the scale of furnishings. The stuff they'll buy should fit in with the things they have, as to scale, style, colors, and textures, complementing or supplementing, but not clashing or looking out of proportion.

"And the third thing is comfort. When they have finished the job, that's the place they want to be. The house should 'look' like them. That takes some careful study on the decorator's part, getting to know the people well. And decoration should be exciting, have a sense of humor, so to speak, that goes with the people.

"I give them an overall plan and sketches that can be carried out right now, or done by themselves over a period of time. And I've worked with a lot of people who only really needed me the first time—for the next house or apartment they really did the designing themselves because I'd shown them how to do it."

Investing in the services of a good decorator can be valuable to you both now and in the future.

Chapter 3

Choosing a House for Economy and Investment

You can determine pretty quickly how a floor plan might make your life-style easier or more difficult. But there are aspects of a house's livability that may be hidden until you actually live there.

A partially hidden factor can be energy use; there's a lot more on that in Chapter 22. You'll want to know all about the energy-efficient features that can affect energy bills in January and February.

For example, a house can be placed various ways on a building lot, and the way it is placed can make a profound difference in your energy bills in winter, and in summer, too, if the house has central air conditioning. How it is sited is not necessarily immediately visible to you, but if the house is oriented with most of its windows to the south, and with a long roof overhang, the house gets the warming effect of the low winter sun shining below the overhang. In the summer when the sun is high, the eave shades the window area and helps reduce the cooling load. Trees can also make a substantial contribution to controlling the costs of heating and cooling.

Another "hidden" aspect is maintenance. Keeping all the surfaces, inside and out, spick-and-span and keeping all the appliances, hardware, heating and cooling equipment, and plumbing up to snuff can be a chore—a chore that's partly hidden when you first look at a house. Chapter 4 gives you some pointers in that regard. And you'll want the seller to tell you all about the maintenance aspects of any house you get serious about.

How much can you repair and maintain yourself? Probably a great deal more than you may imagine. I know one little lady (she weighs 110 pounds) who stripped most of the downstairs of an older home of two and three coats of wallpaper in five working days. (At the same time her husband was gutting four pantrylike rooms and a kitchen to make one big eat-in kitchen.) She had never done that sort of thing before. The biggest obstacle is really the bother of it all. But home maintenance and repairs, if they are done by professionals, are costly considerations. A good carpenter, electrician, or plumber charges $10 to $25 an hour. So it pays you to try to do much of the maintenance of your house yourself.

Aside from the economic factor, there is a great personal bonus in maintaining your property yourself: the satisfaction that you can derive from your own care and attention to your property. Doing a job well, even if it takes a lot of time, is to many of us worthwhile and rewarding.

As to the mechanics of how to take care of things around the house, decorate them or redecorate them, and repair them, there is a huge variety of how-to books and booklets in bookstores and at your hardware store, lumber dealer's, handyman store, or home center. You can get this kind of information free or for a nominal price. For yardwork, there are many excellent garden books about maintaining your shrubbery, bulbs, roses, herbs, and vegetable gardens. And you can get all kinds of advice for nothing at a good nursery.

Anyone who is not ready to accept the responsibility of home maintenance is not really ready for homeownership. No house can maintain itself, and in these times you would have to be rich to have others maintain your property for you. Further, there is that element of satisfaction in doing a good job yourself.

WHEN TO CALL A PROFESSIONAL

If you don't feel confident about repairing something, you should probably call in a professional. You don't want to do any work that might not meet building-code inspection: you may want to sell the house someday, and to do that everything should be according to code.

One thing you should remember is that the wage rates of carpenters, electricians, plumbers, and the like are lower on *new* building projects than for "house calls" for a maintenance job, or even small remodeling jobs such as those discussed in Chapter 7. I know that sounds odd in these inflationary times, but an electrician or a plumber making a house call must charge for all of the time involved. If he is in the business of home maintenance and remodeling, he probably does not work year-round the way he would on a new building project and therefore must charge more per hour. Skilled tradesmen or journeymen cannot jump into another line of work overnight; they must stay on tap for their kind of work.

How about things like heating equipment and appliances? If you don't contemplate having a service contract for heating and central cooling, with either your fuel supplier or some other professional, you had better be prepared to call in professional service in the event of breakdowns or needed repairs. A basic rule is that if you are not already in the habit of repairing your own heating and cooling systems, you had better not try—you could ruin them, and replacement would be very costly.

If you have or contemplate getting good new appliances, you may want service contracts on those. But calling a qualified repair service every time you need one may not be any more expensive in the long run than a service contract. Generally, except for dishwashers and clothes washers, which have the most moving parts of all big appliances, appliance breakdown is rather rare, unless you're using very old appliances or unknown brands.

Plumbing is not as complex as heating and cooling equipment, and you can get good manuals and booklets on how to fix clogged drains, leaky faucets, and the like. Just take it slowly, think carefully of each step, and you'll find that you can do most plumbing repairs yourself. Broken pipes usually need the attention of a plumber, unless you have the knowledge and equipment to work in copper, plastic, cast-iron, or galvanized pipe. The same can be said of light electrical work—but if you're not confident that you can do the work easily, it's better to call a pro.

You may have some guarantees of various elements in the house that you have forgotten about (see Chapter 4). Many new houses today carry two-year guarantees of just about everything. So when something stops working right in a new house, the only thing you may have to worry about is how long it will take the serviceman (paid for by the guarantee) to get there.

To preclude trouble, if you're not already an expert, it is well worthwhile to hire an expert to survey the house's condition before you buy it (see Chapter 4).

HOW TO CONSIDER PROPERTY AND ITS VALUE

A house and its site are the most lastingly valuable things most families ever have. Economists tell us that the equity that a majority of American families have in their homes is greater than all of their holdings in savings accounts, stocks, bonds, and life insurance put together.

But just as important, and often even more important, house values exceed monetary considerations, because of our emotional feelings about home, place, warmth, and family.

A case in point is Walt and Marge Brown and their two children, ages fourteen and eleven, both boys. Marge is active in local affairs. Walt makes a good living selling electronic parts. They have a pleasant suburban house on a half-acre lot outside Hartford, Connecticut. They have obviously taken some pains to keep both house and lot in excellent condition. The lot is well landscaped and the house is in good reapir.

The house itself could best be described as generous for the family and its location: three bedrooms, two and a half baths, two-car garage, basement with workshop, den that can be used as a fourth bedroom for guests. The place is neat and tidy but also looks lived-in and enjoyed.

I visited the Browns, and after a look around the house we went outside to a small terrace paved in patio block.

Walt said they had moved there five years before because they liked the school district. They also liked the property taxes; they didn't seem to be too high for a nice suburban area. They knew some other people who had moved there. And they liked the house.

Marge has nearly everything she wants in a house, but there are some remodeling jobs she wanted done that Walt was still thinking about. Marge said, "I had wanted a fourth bedroom when we first looked at the place, though I wasn't in any rush for it. Now I am not so sure that I want one. What I really would like is a screened-in porch in the back where I have my flower garden and my vegetable garden."

On the issue of property taxes, Walt and Marge were a little sensitive: they could handle the present load without too much grief, they said, but were afraid that the mil rate was inevitably going to go up and that appraisals would eventually rise to 100% of what the assessor's office thought was market value. (Walt and Marge have always done all their own tax returns, so local municipal finance is no mystery.)

They thoroughly approved of Proposition 13 and believed strongly that every state in the Union in the next ten years would have some kind of similar adjustment to the local tax load.

Well, how about the economy in general? Marge said that one trip to the local supermarket that very morning had cost her $83.75 and that the Sunday roast beef had been $1.89 a pound—so saving money was another reason for her gardening efforts.

Back to the house. They really like it, lavish care and improvements on it all the time. Walt wished he had made the terrace out of flagstones, but they were almost three times the cost of patio blocks.

They try to keep ahead of maintenance. Walt does most of the necessary repairs, both take care of the outside, and Marge does a lot of the interior decorating. Actually, said Walt, they didn't redecorate the place as much as talk about it. They'd redecorated maybe one time in the five years they'd been in the house, mostly in the first year and a half. They had repainted the outside the same battleship gray with black shutters just the fall before, but they'd had a contractor do that.

How about value? Walt said they had paid $64,500 for the house in early 1973. He had put another $14,500 into it, which he could prove by canceled checks, and he knew that if he had to sell today he could get maybe $120,000 or more for the place. I felt he was probably on the low side, and Walt asked where else he could do as well with his money. I told him no place else.

PERFORMANCE AND PRICE

Appreciation in house value relates directly to community. But there are two other components that contribute to value: performance and price. A house's performance means how it functions for you and your family as a living unit. That takes into account the cost of maintenance, repair, energy, and the like. Price has to do with the level of amenity, the size of the house, the size and condition of the property, and so on.

Realtors and builders, and knowledgeable consumers, often try to compare houses by comparing the price per square foot of living space on a house-to-house basis. This price includes a developed or improved lot, the garage, utility room, basement, and so on, but it measures just the livable space within the house.

In metropolitan Phoenix, in 1978, sale prices on new houses were running from $22 to $80 per square foot of living space, for noncomparable houses including their lots. Apart from their locations (value of community), the difference in price related to the level of amenity in the house as well as the size of the lot and the cost of improvement to those lots. Improving a lot that is almost flat is considerably less expensive than trying to improve and build on a lot that is on a mountainside.

The things that a builder can put into a house—every appliance you might think of, expensive lighting fixtures, expensive finishes such as parquet oak flooring and walnut wall paneling— can make all the difference in the world, a difference as great as that between a used 1968 small automobile and a brand-new Cadillac limo.

You will want to know whether or not the price put on a house is right for that market or was simply pulled out of thin air. Does that house price, in fact, conform to other prices in the area? Your realtor should be able to answer that question adequately; if he can't, he doesn't really know the community.

The character and the design itself of the neighborhood are of intrinsic value and are reflected in the house price. Contiguous-land uses, or the uses of the land right next door to your lot, have an awful lot to do with the value of your house and your lot. For instance, in exurban or semirural communities, you can find small houses on small lots going for what you might consider astonishingly high prices. But when you look at those small houses, you may find that they are entirely surrounded by larger houses on much larger pieces of land, what the realtors might call "estate" quality. In other words, a house on a half-acre lot may be priced completely out of range of other houses on half-acre lots within the same community. The reason lies not in the house and its lot, but in what surrounds them. The contiguous-land use can make a small house on a small lot look as though it were an estate surrounded by fields and woods.

The view from the house may contribute greatly to its attraction and its value. The view is not necessarily immediately visible, and it cannot be described as a physical attribute of the house. But if there is a view, it may be more important than whether the house is oriented to take advantage of the sun in the winter and overhang shade in summer.

Next, the house can have something called privacy outdoors as well as the public view outdoors. There are areas on the site on which the house sits that afford family privacy from the street, and there are areas that set off the house like a stage setting. That's the public area of the house. The accent for most families is on the private areas of the lot and how much privacy that lot and the positioning of the house on the lot give them for outdoor time, especially in the summer. What the public sees of the house or the lot should ideally be minimized.

FUTURE VALUE OF A HOUSE

Anyone buying a house should want to anticipate its future value, not necessarily for sale, but for equity and appreciation and what it means to the buyer's future estate. At the time of purchase a given house may not be all that special. But repairs, remodeling, the addition of a half-bath or family room or extra bedroom, and other improvements, can make a profound difference over the long run.

If energy consumption can be cut considerably—and it is possible to cut it as much as 40% in existing houses by improving ceiling and wall and insulation (see Chapter 22)—the work and effort will be more than repaid either in future value or upon resale some three to five years down the road, and this is in addition to the fuel savings you will enjoy while you own the house.

Property taxes and their potential increases in the community have to be looked at, as either a deterrent or an increment of value (see Chapter 5).

On the other hand, costly additions or remodeling don't mean very much to future value if the building or the property is not right. If the property is right—good neighborhood, good town— the value will last in years to come.

You need to know the general condition of the house itself: structural condition, mechanical elements, drainage conditions, energy consumption, condition of the landscaping, what you will need for repairs and improvements to make it livable for your family. If you can't make such evaluations yourself, you should obtain professional help.

In that regard you will want to know how long the house has been up for sale. If it has been on sale for a long time, there might be something wrong with it, or the price may be all wrong. You do not necessarily get a price break when you are buying directly from an owner simply because the owner does not have to pay a realtor's commission. The owner can put the wrong price on the house as easily as anyone.

Chapter 4

Good Workmanship, People, and Products

While looking for a house you may have noticed a subdivision out in the weeds, so to speak—neglected, perhaps few or no people living there, and no activity. Yet at the same time, in the same community, you may find a project of houses being built, with buyers moving in every day, obviously something attracting them. What is the difference between the flourishing project and the subdivision that has weeds all around?

The difference usually has to do with the professional skills that have been assembled to produce the project. The project in the weeds probably was started by a builder, or a land developer, who did not call on all the necessary skills for a successful project, beginning with good basic market research (to find out where people wanted to live and how) and using a good architect, landscape architect, decorator, lender, appraiser, real estate marketing staff, and the like.

The successful project is one put together by a developer-builder who uses this team of professionals with an eye to pleasing and attracting you, the buyer. The first step for the professional is to determine what you want and where you want it. That determination is complex, and it really constitutes the builder's market opportunity.

Everybody can't live in the most desirable section of town, because first, there isn't room, and second, not everybody has that kind of money. The professionals who operate within the real estate industry are those few people, not a majority, who can single out market opportunities that will attract people at various income levels, to give them a choice. Those professionals do provide a host of alternatives in housing, as I described in the Foreword. Those professionals do not disqualify any buyer who has the means to own a home.

Without that professional attention to detail, starting with market research and ending with the professional real estate marketing program, those houses in the weeds will never appreciate as houses in a good attractive project will.

The vision of a successful community or neighborhood that is about to be developed and built is the result of a keen marketing awareness of what you, the buyer, expect of a new community.

Market research reveals the way a community will grow, who will live in the project, and what kind of housing styles will be most desirable, most useful, and most attractive to them. This research measures tastes of potential buyers, their economic base, and their income levels.

The design of the neighborhood and its community services—recreation, shopping, schools, and so on—develops initially from good land planning, which includes such things as drainage, preservation of natural amenities, and the like. Land planners are aware of details like the view a future street may offer.

Next are the landscape designers, who are involved in the arrangement on the land plan of trees, signs, light signals, curbs, gutters—all of the natural amenities and the man-made ones apart from the houses themselves.

At this point the engineer translates the landscape plan into the technical design for roads, drains, sewers, electricity, telephones, gas—all the facilities that make a community a living thing.

Next comes the architect, who designs the housing styles within the functional needs defined in the marketing-direction report prepared by the market researcher. When the response is accurate and carefully considered, the plans will be in accordance with the dominant housing desires of the community.

Behind all this is the builder and his subcontractors. He must bring the whole thing into being and do a competent job that will satisfy not just the buyer but the lender, the zoning board and the building department, and the city council so that health, safety, and the tax base are all protected.

Next comes the interior designer, who makes the model houses attractive enough to get you interested in the project.

Finally we come to the professional salesperson, the real estate marketer who brings you, the buyer, together with the house you want.

A BUILDER AND HIS REPUTATION

A key element in this whole process is the builder and his degree of professionalism. I don't mean his degree in engineering, or master building, or really a degree in anything; I mean his competence, experience, and honesty.

How can you be sure of a builder's professionalism and dedication to his business? First of all, most builders who are competent and honest identify themselves with their own name as the builder, or part of the corporate title, of a particular project or house. If the builder's name does not appear in his advertising or his promotional material, you need to look more carefully at the product being sold. This is not to say that big building companies use the name of their top corporate officers in their advertising—they usually don't. But there are many ways to check on the professional ability and responsibility of a big corporate builder. One of the easiest, of course, is to check with your mortgage lending officer. Big corporate builders do not hide behind anything, and smaller individual builders use their own names.

Another way to find something out about a good builder is to inquire how long he has been in business. This does not necessarily prove anything, but those who have been steadily in business in a particular community or region for some time usually are people who do top jobs and stand behind their products.

Another way to check out the builder is to find out what else he has built and take a look at it. Often a builder has in his office pictures of the various houses he has built, along with the names of the owners. You might call on them and ask them a few questions about the builder. You could also ask the builder who some of his suppliers and subcontractors are, and talk to them, if you have any doubts at all about his trustworthiness and competence.

If the builder is a member of the local homebuilders' association, is a registered builder in that association, and is a member of the Home Owners Warranty Program, discussed later in this chapter, you have probably found a reliable and competent builder you can trust.

You can also check the Better Business Bureau, find out if he has a listed telephone number, and talk to local realtors.

BUILDING PRODUCTS

A good builder selects the best building products he can get his hands on within the economic envelope that limits his house product. In lower-priced houses, he uses products that fulfill the specifications (such as what FHA calls for), but he may not be able to use the most expensive styles available because they would push his budget over the limit of what his prospective customers can buy or qualify for. At the same time a good builder cannot afford to use the cheapest products, because that only leads to trouble in each house, and long-range business trouble for the builder himself.

In considering building products, it may be useful to understand that the only people in the housing business, other than the purchaser, who have any substantial capital investment in the business are the manufacturers of building products. The manufacturer therefore has a long-term commitment to do the best job he can within the constraints of the marketplace—which puts the distribution of most of his products in someone else's hands, and the installation of those products in someone else's hands, and the sale of those products to you in someone else's hands.

What that all adds up to is that building products with recognizable brand names—and you see them advertised on television and in newspapers and magazines all the time—are trustworthy products if the distribution, installation, and use of those products follow the manufacturers' specifications and ideas.

So if you are concerned about the building products and materials used in a particular house, ask the salesperson, if you cannot determine easily yourself, the brand names of appliances, for instance. If the salesperson can't answer the question, he has not done his homework, and maybe you should look at some other houses and talk to some other realtors.

ADVICE FROM A CONSUMER MARKET RESEARCHER

Laurin Magee of Washington, D.C., heads a nationwide market research firm retained by homebuilders to determine what consumers want and need in new housing. Here is Laurin's advice to prospective buyers on how to be sure about good products and good people in housing:

"First, look for a house with an insured warranty on it, like the HOW program [see the section on home warranties in this chapter], or an equivalent guarantee or warranty. People are insurance-conscious these days, and in a great many cases, unless you already know a lot specifically about a particular builder, the warranty is your real insurance.

"Next, ask the salesperson who, other than the builder, was involved in producing the house: architect, land planner, market researcher, landscaper, and the like. You don't have to recognize their names, but you want to be sure that the builder had a team of professionals helping him, guiding him, before he built a bunch of houses—if not, why did he build the houses he built, and for whom? The team approach is as important to the big builder, who may have a lot of those people on his payroll, as it is to the smaller builder. They both have to sell, which means knowing their market and building to it, or they'll go broke, and then everybody suffers.

"Now, if you run into a salesperson who can't answer those questions, and gives no indication he intends to find out for you, or one who tries to bluster through a half-baked answer, you have before you a poor sign of professionalism and you had better beware.

"To be even more sure about the people and the products, knock on a few doors of other buyers in the project and ask them how they like their houses, how they perform, whether everybody did everything he said he would do, things like that. If your builder is a custom builder, he can give you some names and addresses of satisfied customers. Go and talk to a few.

"Manufacturer's names, or brand names on products, are another essential. You should have heard of most of them. But if you haven't, don't take that as a sign that some product or material isn't good. If it's an unknown brand name, on say a range top, go to a local retail outlet and check all the builder's appliance brand names, get the price range, and ask if a warranty comes with the appliance. If nobody's ever heard of the name, watch out. Watch out doubly if the builder doesn't have a service contract on all the appliances.

"You usually expect a house to perform better than a new car, so you should want equivalent guarantees. Some builders have both buyers and their salespeople initial a service policy when a house is sold so that everybody understands thoroughly whose responsibility is what. It lets the consumer really know exactly where he stands. You should want that.

"In a lot of new houses, the builder offers two lines on a lot of products. Sometimes the few extra thousand dollars on the better line are well worth it. It doesn't mean that an elaborate line of appliances is better than a simple line in the way it functions, but there are better appliances and they are worth the money, whether you're buying them yourself to put in an old house or specifying them for a new house."

Obviously, when you look at a house you are quite serious about, you want to try out everything you possibly can before you sign anything or give anybody money. Turn on faucets to check the water pressure, check for leaks; examine basins and tubs to see if they are chipped or stained, turn on ovens and ranges to see if they register and perhaps check their temperature to see if they work right, flush toilets and test drains to see whether they work all right, check whether toilet tanks weep, determine if there are water-reducing sink spray heads on faucets and shower heads, and so on.

Check on the heating and cooling system to see if it responds to thermostatic settings as it should. These may need adjustment, but you want to be sure that the basic apparatus works and responds readily.

Look at all appliances offered with the house to see if they are in good working condition. Check dishwashers, garbage disposals, and garbage compactors to see if they all work. If things like washers and dryers are part of the package, try them out, too. Turn them on to see if they go, to see if they fill up. The same with refrigerators, freezers, countertop built-in mixers, and the like.

SHOULD YOU GET A PROFESSIONAL INSPECTION?

It is often difficult to determine the value and durability of the various elements of a house. Most often, you should try to get the opinion of a third party on the house. Experts do this kind of work for relatively modest fees ($100 to $300), but they should be recommended by your mortgage loan officer, who knows the area well. Such work can save you hundreds and maybe thousands of dollars in the long run.

A good choice of expert is an experienced architect or builder. He is familiar with construction, the materials used, and the workmanship. But even the best architect or builder will usually tell you that you need a separate technical expert to judge such things as heating, plumbing, and wiring. If in doubt about these things, you should call in a reputable heating dealer, plumber, or electrician.

It is even more important, particularly when you are buying an existing house, to get evaluations by a termite expert and, if appropriate, a septic-tank expert. These are just about mandatory in many parts of the United States. Both VA and FHA often require one or both, depending on geographical location. If your mortgage loan officer originates FHA loans, he can provide the names.

The person who may do more harm than good is your brother-in-law, a friend of a friend, or a carpenter acquaintance who will as a favor "be glad to look at that house for you." This can be risky, experience shows, because such people often feel compelled to find something wrong in order to justify their status as experts.

This puts you on the spot. The house may be perfectly good except, like most houses, for a minor flaw or two which the "expert" proceeds to blow up way out of proportion. If you go ahead and buy the house, you fly in the face of a personal relationship. It's therefore best to steer clear of your buddies and relatives. And don't accept *subjective* judgments, such as how the "expert" feels about the design or the color. Just consider *objective* judgments.

HEATING—A SPECIAL PROBLEM

If you don't know much about heating systems for houses, get some expert advice. Ask a professional house inspector, or see a good heating contractor or a fuel supplier you know and trust. Old heating systems can be a disaster—like coal-fired hot-water heat in an old Victorian house, which might have to be torn out and replaced these days—but they can often be modified to be quite satisfactory.

Find out what consumer services your local utilities offer. The local electric or gas utility has a consumer-service department and will be happy to answer all kinds of questions. If the house you are considering is heated by oil, call the fuel supplier who supplies the fuel to give you information and advice about the house's systems.

You want your house to be energy-efficient, so there are several things you should find out about a house you are considering to discover potential problems.

Infiltration can be the greatest offender in pushing up your monthly heating costs. Infiltration lets warm air flow out of the house in the winter and hot summer air seep into the house when you're trying to cool it. Heat or warm air will flow out to cold air through any kind of a hole or crack, and the colder the weather, the greater the outward heat flow. A few small holes in an exterior wall, say two inches by two inches, can almost negate the effect of insulation in the rest of the wall on a very cold day when the wind is high.

Good builders use a four-step process during construction to ensure that there are as few holes and cracks in their houses as possible.

1. They inspect to make sure that every building part meets every other part just so, with no open cracks.

2. They correct on the spot all holes and damage (in things such as wall sheathing and window frames).

3. They caulk in the following places:

between window drip caps (tops of windows) and siding
between door drip caps and siding
between window sills and siding
at joints between window frames and siding
at joints between door frames and siding
at sills where wood structure meets the foundation
around outside water faucets or other special breaks in the
    outside house surface
where pipes and wires penetrate the ceiling below an un-
    heated attic
where chimney or masonry meets siding

    4. They make certain that the edges of doors and windows are properly weatherstripped so that when they close there are no leaks between the operating part and the fixed frame. (The functional difference between caulking and weatherstripping is that the first is used to seal a permanent joint between two fixed parts, the second to seal those points or edges where an openable door or window meets its frame or casing.)

At the eave or the edge of the roof, there is often a gap left open so that outside air can flow directly into the attic above the upper-story ceiling and above the insulation. The flow of this outdoor air directly into that attic space can use up or take away a lot of heat. If that space is closed off by an "eave baffle," the attic temperature in the winter is warmer than the outside temperature, particularly at the eave, and the insulation above the ceiling functions a lot more efficiently, holding what heat there is inside the house.

    It is easier to check the foregoing points in a new house than in an existing one, but you should consider carefully the many things you can do to an existing house to make it warmer, particularly using the tax-deductible $300 that the IRS now lets us have. Approach this problem the way an engineer, architect, builder, or owner would when building a new house to keep his customers' energy costs as low as possible.

    Here are some insulation and atmospheric-flow-control definitions that should be useful:

    R-value (thermal resistance). Thermal resistance is an indication of ability to *retard* heat flow. R-values make it possible to add the insulating properties of a whole series of materials, such as the siding, sheathing, insulation, and interior drywall that make up a typical wall. The higher the R-value, the higher the insulating value.

Fiberglass. This consists of manufactured filaments of glass formed by pulling or spinning molten glass into random links gathered in a woollike mass. Fiberglass is both fire- and moisture-resistant and is a good insulator.

Vapor barrier. A vapor barrier prevents humidity from inside the house from moving out through an insulated wall, floor, or ceiling. If humidity could penetrate a wall, which it would do in the heating season without the presence of a vapor barrier, it would condense inside the wall, and if insulation was in the wall, the resulting wetness would render the insulation useless and could rot the structure. Vapor barriers, usually polyethylene films, are installed on the warm side of walls, floors, and ceilings.

Here is how one good builder, Glenn Cardoso, president of LTC, Lakewood, New Jersey, describes this practice:

"We use friction-fit insulation—it's like a big sponge which must be slightly compressed to be installed and then springs back to hold itself in place and fill every nook and cranny. Vapor barriers are carefully installed on the warm side of all insulation batts.

"We use six inches of fiberglass-batt insulation in the ceiling (R-19) and three and a half inches in walls (R-11).

"We make sure all insulated areas are completely covered. We extend the ceiling insulation over the top of the top plate so that it is covered with insulation. We stuff all cracks around doors and windows and small odd-shaped cavities with insulation.

"We cut batts to fit narrow spaces between framing members, butt the ends of batts tightly against each other, and shove batts tightly against the top and bottom plates in wall cavities.

"We use rigid foam insulation under the edges and around the perimeter of our floor slabs in colder regions.

"Even with insulation and a vapor barrier in the ceiling, good practice calls for attic ventilation. Ours is more than adequate and for a special reason: increased ventilation of the attic space can reduce air temperatures during the summer and so decrease air-conditioning loads. We also insulate all ducts in unheated or non-air-conditioned spaces."

In an old house, insulation can be critical. It's easy to check for ceiling insulation or the lack of it in an old house. Go up to the attic and look. The insulation should be between the beams at the attic floor. If it is installed overhead between the sloping roof rafters directly under the roof, it does not do much good.

Determining the presence of wall insulation is harder. While in the attic of an older house you may be able to see down into the cavities of the outer walls, or from the basement look up into them. If you cannot see because of obstructions, try the touch test, which works if the weather is cold and the heat is on. Inside the house, put the palm of your hand flat against the exterior walls in several rooms, especially the walls on the north. The walls should feel as warm, or almost as warm, as an interior wall in the middle of the house. If the outside wall is cold or downright chilly, there's little or no insulation. Also, remove the covers from a few electrical outlets in the outside walls, shine a flashlight inside the wall, and you will be able to see if there is insulation. Use the palm test to check for floor insulation in a house with no basement. Do it at the outer perimeter on the floor—in other words, near the exterior walls. If the floor there is cold, there's little or no insulation. The palm test does not work during mild or warm weather; then you must rely on the owner's word when you ask if the house is insulated.

The age of a house can also be a clue to the presence or absence of insulation. Insulation generally was not put in houses built before the late 1940's. A house built earlier probably lacks it, particularly in the walls, unless, of course, the owner had it put in. Some older types of insulation, such as blown paper, have been discredited. If you have any doubts about the quality of insulation, seek professional advice.

WARRANTIES OR DO IT YOURSELF?

It's going to take a bit of both, and happily today there are warranties available that really mean something. What really counts is whether the house is a sound product, easy to maintain and operate, rather than one for which a builder has to be called back for fix-up.

One of the little-discussed but most important aspects of homeownership is that the basic construction and finish systems used in our housing lend themselves to repair and remodeling by the occupant more than do the building methods in most other nations. But the first-time buyer must have a strong, positive attitude toward doing his or her own repairs; otherwise he or she should not buy. Actually, such an owner in this country is fortunate: a wood-frame structure is easy to work on, compared with the complexities that most of the rest of the developed world faces in high-density masonry construction.

Most Americans are exposed early in life to various aspects of the building trades, so homeownership has always involved a high degree of care by the occupants. This is one of the principal reasons why frame housing in this country, outside of decaying urban areas, has an average life span of two-thirds of a century; there are even examples that are still habitable after 250 years.

If you're considering buying a house more than ten years old, expect something to go wrong. Maintenance records of the vital systems in older houses usually are nonexistent. If you are a typical buyer of one of these, you'll be virtually ignorant of how long the heating, plumbing, wiring, and built-in appliances will last.

How, then, can you, an uninformed consumer, protect yourself against the future likelihood of costly repairs?

Since 1971, more than a hundred companies have emerged from coast to coast, offering warranty plans that cover the cost of home repairs—and today warranties on resale homes are available in thirty-five states. You, the homebuyer, may sign a contract calling for a fixed annual fee and deductible clause. In return, the company pays the cost of your home repairs.

As an illustration, American Home Shield Corporation of Dublin, California, the largest company in the United States selling comprehensive home service contracts, charges an annual fee of $220 to $250 with a deductible of $25 or $50, respectively. Under its plan, the company services, repairs, or replaces the heating, air-conditioning, electrical, and plumbing systems, as well as built-in appliances (such as oven or dishwasher). Some plans also cover certain structural defects in floors, walls, ceilings, and foundations, at extra cost.

The basic AHS plan is for one year, but you can also get two- and three-year plans. Condominiums as well as single-family houses are covered. The plans are marketed exclusively through real estate brokers, who do not receive a fee.

Brokers, AHS claims, have found that the warranty plans are an effective selling point and that they enhance the chances of a marginally financed buyer to get a mortgage because the lender feels the new homeowner is protected against the cost of high repairs.

The National Association of Realtors has made available home repair insurance that requires no home inspection; the first to date. The company issuing it won't even look at the condition of the mechanical elements, such as the furnace, plumbing, water heater, and wiring. Three companies now selling it: the Minnehoma Insurance Company of Tulsa, Oklahoma; Homestead Inspection Warranty of Camden, New Jersey; and Pacific Cal-West Insurance of Walnut Creek, California.

The noninspection insurance carries a flat fee, usually around $250, with a $50 deductible. With an inspection the insurance cost is geared to the selling price of the house. Most realtors point out that relatively few houses sold today carry home repair insurance because it is a relatively new field. But it is beginning to expand.

The key question is this: If you are offered a repair warranty by a responsible company in the field, should you rush to buy?

The answer is no. First, consider how handy you are around the house as well as the house's age and condition, and decide whether you really need a plan of this sort. Then carefully investigate the company.

Read your contract with utmost caution to make sure it spells out precisely what the warranty covers, the cost of service calls for your area, whether they are deductible, if you can phone the company toll-free. Inquire about the company's repairmen. They should be licensed contractors, not just handymen. Ask your broker about the names of the other homebuyers who have bought the warranties, and check to see if they are satisfied with the service. Call your mortgage lending officer first to get an idea about warranty services that other homebuyers have purchased.

THE HOME OWNERS WARRANTY

The Home Owners Warranty is a national program developed by the National Association of Home Builders (NAHB) to provide reasonable assurances to home purchasers that the house they buy has been constructed with good products, using tested and accepted construction practices.

HOW, as it is known, has done the job so well that FHA and VA now automatically accept a builder's house that carries HOW protection with only a final inspection. If you want a particular HOW house, you can go after an FHA, VA, or conventional mortgage all at the same time without any move other than your lender's initial approval.

Previously, a builder had to start a new house under FHA or VA ground rules if the buyer's mortgage was to be FHA or VA. The rules required first and intermediate construction inspections by FHA or VA. But that's no longer necessary for HOW houses.

New Jersey is the first state to require homebuilders to register and provide a new-home warranty. Several other states are considering similar legislation. New Jersey accepts the HOW program as an alternative to the state warranty program.

Basically, the HOW plan provides a one-year coverage of

workmanship and materials, a two-year warranty on the mechanical systems, and ten-year protection against major structural defects. The builder pays a one-time premium and is liable for the first two years of coverage. The other eight years are underwritten by an independent insurer. The policy is transferable to future owners.

Under the HOW plan, a conciliation-arbitration apparatus provides an outlet for homebuyer complaints, thus relieving savings and loan associations of their role as mediator in some cases. Claims that exceed $1,000 are payable jointly to the lender and the borrower to ensure that necessary repairs are made and paid for.

In addition, builders are screened for competence, financial stability, and record of dealing with complaints.

The Federal Trade Commission ruled that local HOW councils could use conciliation to resolve differences between buyer and builder under the 1975 Magnuson-Moss Warranty Act. HOW is the only warrantor allowed the use of informal, third-party dispute-settlement techniques. In fact, HOW's conciliation-arbitration mechanism is the program's cornerstone.

If a buyer and builder cannot settle a dispute, they get together with a third party. The HOW council in Portland, Oregon, for example, once used volunteer conciliators; today, it works with a paid conciliator. The first conciliator in Denver's HOW program had been an appraiser, FHA-VA inspector, builder, and developer.

A case that fails to be resolved through conciliation goes to arbitration. In such instances the council sends a request to the American Arbitration Association for an arbitrator and sets a hearing date. At the hearing both parties present their arguments and documents, such as reports from a structural engineer or architect.

The decision of the arbitrator is binding upon the builder, but the consumer is free to take his case to court. If the builder does not effect the required changes within forty-five days, the council processes the insurance claim, and the insurance company may sue the builder.

Arbitration can be invoked only during the first two years of the life of a house. During the last eight years of a HOW warranty, claims go directly to the insurance company, thus reducing builder liability.

The premium for HOW coverage is a one-time fee of $2 per $1,000 of the final sale price of a house. American Bankers Insurance Company was the insurance underwriter since the program's inception, but on July 1, 1978, the HOW Corporation switched to the Insurance Company of North America.

HOW continued a steady course of growth during 1978. The number of registered HOW builders rose from 6,895 at the end of 1977 to 11,289 at the end of 1978. This represents one-third of eligible NAHB builder members.

There are now 750,000 new homes covered by the ten-year protection plan, an estimated $50 billion worth of new housing. A record 220,000 homes were added to the program during 1979.

Chapter 5

What to Look for In a Community

Sooner or later most people ask: If house values are so great (the implication so far in this book), why are there houses whose value has obviously not kept up with other houses in the community? Why is there depreciation in house values?

Clearly some houses are lemons, and the problem for you, the prospective purchaser, is how to keep from making a bad decision on the house you are thinking about, or how to ensure that the house you buy will appreciate in value.

The best way to ensure that you get value is to look at the three components of value. The first is the community itself—will it add or detract from the value of the house you buy? The second is performance of the house—will it cost too much to own, will it fulfill the functions that you expect of a house for yourself and your family? And the third component is price. How much does the house cost? Is it overpriced? Will the price continue to go up as it should over time?

The first component of value, community, is usually the most important. A bad community can diminish whatever intrinsic value a house has, as well as whatever investment you put into it.

Anyone moving to a new city will have a choice of communities, either suburban or near the city center, on the north, south, east, or west side of town. If you're selling your house, or leaving an apartment, to get another house in a community you've lived in for a few years, you probably know just about all you have to know about where you want to live and what the town and neighborhood will be like in a few years—but not necessarily.

Sometimes things change rapidly, and to the consternation of old-time residents who never suspected change of any great order in the offing. This chapter should help you learn a little bit more about what might happen to familiar turf. It also suggests how to select the right new turf for your life-style.

IF YOU ARE GOING TO A NEW TOWN

There are three sources that you might want to use in establishing relative community values before you start scouting new areas: the Chamber of Commerce, the local newspapers, and the telephone book.

The Chamber of Commerce, which you can either write or visit, can tell you a great deal about things like the city's growth, its industry and employment base, business organizations, and religious and civic activities that may be important to you. It can supply you with good maps. You should take the time to go over all Chamber of Commerce materials carefully before you visit a new location.

Be especially careful about what people *don't* tell you. Most Chambers of Commerce—and you can't really blame them because they are booster organizations—play down the less attractive elements in their city, such as rising taxes, major strikes, pollution problems, crime, a large welfare population, or corrupt local politics. No one will mislead you deliberately, but something that detracts from a community as often as not simply won't be mentioned.

The next source is the local newspaper. Get a few of the local dailies about a month before you have to come to a decision on your new dwelling unit, whether it be temporary or permanent. The papers will give you a pretty good idea of the social, cultural, and recreational life in the community, or within reach of the community. The real estate sections and the classified ads will give you a very good handle on what's available in housing.

From the telephone directories in your new location, particularly the yellow pages, you can get information on many services you will need when you move, such as banks, doctors, dry cleaners, insurance companies, and hardware stores. Medical facilities can be important, since you can't tell what the future might bring.

Are you a suburban type, or should you live in the city? If you really need all kinds of outside activities in your day-to-day living—not just your job, but shopping, leisure-time pursuits, educational possibilities, nightclubs, restaurants, museums, libraries, sports events, and the like—the chances are that the closer-in-town location is for you. If, however, you want a suburban location, highway access and/or public transportation must be a priority in choosing your location.

The city can offer older houses that have big spaces inside but small space outside, and it also offers higher-density land uses, as in apartment buildings and townhouses, condominiums, co-ops, and the like. Neighborhoods closer to the center city usually offer faster emergency aid in the event that you need it—this can be particularly important as you get older. Better police and fire protection in the city may keep insurance rates lower than they might be in the suburbs. Repair services may be prompter in the city than they are in the suburbs. Furthermore, you may prefer the anonymity of living close in to a more open or recognized existence in suburban small towns. You should be able to make that judgment well before you even take a look at the new town.

But don't forget that being closer in to the city can have major drawbacks. Pollution, traffic, noise, and parking can be problems. And there may be all kinds of laws regulating parking in the street, so the cost of garage space is a real economic consideration. Smaller towns or communities usually are more friendly places to live, and this can be important if your children are young. The suburbs can offer houses with more land, should gardening and other outdoor activities be more important to you.

PERSONAL REQUIREMENTS

By now you should know how long your first look at a community will take. It may take a couple of days to explore the location, more if it is a major metropolitan area.

One of the first things you should do is to go sightseeing without benefit of any local businessman or realtor, so that you can form your own judgments of the various areas of the city or town. If you have friends in town, they can be useful by pinpointing on a map various places that you should look at, or they can go with you simply as friends, not as salespeople. You should look at shopping centers, industrial sections, the downtown commercial and entertainment centers if there are any, and, of course, schools, churches, and residential areas.

In residential areas, without even talking to anyone you can tell exactly how the people feel about their homes. The total visual impression is a true indicator of the community's personality. Older neighborhoods that have been well maintained are likely to remain that way.

Make sure that the particular house you are interested in is in the same general price range as the surrounding houses. The biggest, most expensive house on the block does not have the same resale value in a moderately priced neighborhood as it would if it were located in a neighborhood of comparably priced or higher-priced houses. Appraisers and mortgage lenders have found that the resale value of a relatively inexpensive house in a good area is pulled up by the higher-priced houses, while the large, expensive house is pulled down by surrounding lower-priced houses.

Corner lots have a double drawback. The tax assessor hits you twice, once for each frontage. Also, corner lots have more traffic to contend with, including the two- and four-legged pedestrians who believe in taking the shortest distance between two points, right across your lawn.

Talk to as many local people as you can. When you stop for coffee or to have lunch, talk to the shopkeepers, the people who serve you and whom you may have obvious reason to meet, such as local bankers and local pastors. They can give you a very good idea of how they feel about their town and off-the-cuff views of where the town is going and where the good places are to live. If you can, talk to the local grocer, hardware-store owner, pharmacist, insurance agent, and other business people.

Take a good look at your new neighbors, or the people who may be your new neighbors. How do they keep their houses? Do the yards look neat and clean? Meet them. Are they friendly and proud of the neighborhood? Are they likely to stay? Not that you ask them that question, but a brief conversation can bring out things that you might have overlooked. You should walk around the neighborhood to get the feel of it. Visit it at night and in the daytime, morning and afternoon, in as many different types of weather and times of day as you can just to see what goes on.

If possible, try to visit the house you may buy on a weekend, when the neighbors are at home pursuing outdoor activities. Are they fixing up the yard or the house, or are they repairing an automobile in the front yard?

There is an old saying: "You're not buying a house, you're buying both a community and a neighborhood." You can change the interior or the exterior, but how often do you move a house?

HOW GOOD IS THE SCHOOL SYSTEM?

There are really only two measures that determine how good the school system is from your point of view: busing and budget.

You know all about busing, and a few inquiries will give you whatever information you may need to weigh in your decision whether or not to buy. Budgets can determine whether or not a school system suits your needs.

The quality of the schools is a major concern to anyone with children, and the issue is complicated now by tax revolts across the country. Most school revenue comes from property taxes, which are heavily under the gun in most places. One of the chief victims of property tax cuts is the school system.

Obviously, you'll take a close look at how any school system stands. How do the voters regard it in the town? Will they accept the bare bones, or would they rather have better schools?

In a great many cities in California, as a result of property tax cuts (see Chapter 23), school facilities have been cut back drastically. Sports, music, film studies—the ancillary activities, outside of reading, writing, and arithmetic—have been reduced or eliminated as teachers have been laid off. A lot of parents are not unhappy—they didn't have music and film and sports programs when *they* went to school back when times were tough—and are quite willing to pay for their children's music lessons or athletic activities, but not for more teachers or school administrators.

Don't take the word of the real estate agent that local schools are great. Look at them yourself and judge their quality. Try to find out from the local school principal how many kids go to college from the local high school. Find out the level of education among the town's citizens. This information often can be obtained from the Chamber of Commerce, which gets it from the Bureau of the Census. You can also find out from the Chamber of Commerce or from the school itself how well the school may be staffed, how tough it may be on the basics, and how many ancillary courses or "gut" courses may pad its curriculum.

On the financial level, find out how much local school districts spend per year per child for all school expenses; compare this dollar amount per pupil with other areas for the same base year. Get a reading on teachers' salaries and how these compare with neighboring school districts. Investigate the local budget and bond issues as they affect the schools.

You may want to ask local people what they think of their schools. You may also want to get permission to visit classrooms while school is in session. Incidentally, if the school administrator or the board of education stalls at answering questions or is uncooperative about letting you visit take a look, you know that something is wrong. You want to be very sure that you are not making a mistake about that community and school district.

HOW TO KNOW IF A COMMUNITY IS WORTH INVESTING IN

You can tell an awful lot about a community just by looking around. If it looks good, it probably is good; but you shouldn't stop there. Look into municipal finances. Communities that look bad didn't necessarily start out looking bad. They got that way in ninety-nine cases out of one hundred because municipal finances were not sufficient, were out of balance, or were the subject of partisan politics for maybe a few generations.

Municipal finances affect you most closely in property taxes. You may have to pay a very high property tax in a community that will do little for you in return, so make it your business to know something about how those taxes are used.

The question about property taxes is twofold: How high are they, and how are they apt to change in the future—up or down? You also want to know how those tax dollars are spent—for justifiable and worthy causes, or frivolous and irresponsible ones. Bear in mind that there may be special tax districts for sewers, hospitals, libraries, and cemeteries which do not necessarily follow the corporate boundaries of a community. School district boundaries and their tax assessments also vary.

California's famous Proposition 13 has set a nationwide standard for property taxes at about 1% per year of actual market value of a property. Are the property taxes in the community you're looking at stable, are they going up, are they less than 2% of value?

How do property taxes pay for services in a given town? In some towns property taxes are quite low, yet the town is quite attractive. Smaller towns may have no police department (simply state police), no fire department (volunteer only), no garbage collection (private hauling), a volunteer ambulance service, and so on. In some communities—like Scottsdale, Arizona, for example— the fire department is a private-enterprise operation and all the municipal employees are nonunion.

On the other hand, in an area like New York's Nassau and Suffolk counties, on Long Island, everybody pays an extra $250 or so of property taxes a year for a sewer system that nobody uses because it was never completed.

Experience around the country is that the higher the property taxes in a given area, the lower the rate of house appreciation. In this way the property tax works to create greater investment risks as it rises against the value of residential real estate.

Usually property taxes are assessed at a lower level on land

and at a higher level for improvements (the house), which means that by our tax practices we tend toward horizontal growth rather than vertical or land-intensive growth. Uniform assessment of land and building value is rare in this country. The result is an accentuation of the tax impact on capital investment in buildings and other improvements.

The tax assessor's records are public property, and you can go to the town hall or the courthouse and find out, house by house, the taxes charged currently and those that have been charged over time. Every time a house is sold or reappraised, its value is put on the tax card. But selling-price information is not always shown.

Generally the record for a property can be seen if the address is known. But not all information about the next year's bill is on the record, so be sure to ask what, if any, extra assessments are likely to be added to the bill for the coming year. There may be special levies for building schools or swimming pools or other improvements that don't show on the past record but could boost the next bill considerably.

In particular, what percentage of total school expenditures is borne by the property tax on single-family houses? It can be hazardous if too high, compared with nearby districts.

HOW MUCH DO CITIES RELY ON PROPERTY TAXES?

The answer to that question varies all over the lot. In August 1978 the Tax Foundation, Inc., a nonprofit advocacy group, published the following table, based on the latest Commerce Department figures:

PER CAPITA LOCAL PROPERTY TAXES
in RELATION to TOTAL LOCAL REVENUES
All Local Governments in Selected Standard Metropolitan Statistical Areas*
Fiscal Year 1975–1976

Area**	Per capita property tax		Property tax as a percent of local revenue	
	Amount	Rank	Percent	Rank
Total, 74 major SMSAs†	$310	—	34.8	—
Anaheim–Santa Ana–Garden Grove, California	366	8	41.8	7
Atlanta, Georgia	256	23	35.3	17
Baltimore, Maryland	196	33	21.4	39
Boston, Massachusetts	483	4	55.0	1
Buffalo, New York	307	18	28.7	30
Chicago, Illinois	319	16	42.3	6
Cincinnati, Ohio–Kentucky–Indiana	197	32	26.0	33
Cleveland, Ohio	286	19	36.5	16
Columbus, Ohio	193	34	32.0	25
Dallas–Fort Worth, Texas	247	25	38.7	11

Area**	Per capita property tax		Property tax as a percent of local revenue	
	Amount	Rank	Percent	Rank
Denver-Boulder, Colorado	284	22	33.5	21
Detroit, Michigan	352	9	39.6	9
Houston, Texas	286	19	45.7	4
Indianapolis, Indiana	253	24	38.2	13
Kansas City, Missouri–Kansas	241	27	34.7	18
Los Angeles–Long Beach, California	419	7	38.4	12
Louisville, Kentucky–Indiana	142	39	25.1	36
Memphis, Tennessee–Arkansas–Mississippi	174	36	28.3	31
Miami, Florida	245	26	28.8	29
Milwaukee, Wisconsin	331	13	33.9	19
Minneapolis-St. Paul, Minnesota–Wisconsin	316	17	33.1	23
Nassau-Suffolk, New York	609	1	50.3	3
Newark, New Jersey	493	2	53.8	2
New Orleans, Louisiana	93	40	14.7	40
New York, New York–New Jersey	438	5	25.5	34
Philadelphia, Pennsylvania–New Jersey	237	28	31.4	26
Phoenix, Arizona	218	30	29.2	28
Pittsburgh, Pennsylvania	199	31	33.2	22
Portland, Oregon–Washington	328	14	42.9	5
Riverside–San Bernardino–Ontario, California	352	9	33.8	20
Rochester, New York	328	14	32.7	24
Sacramento, California	333	12	31.0	27
St. Louis, Missouri–Illinois	228	29	37.3	15
San Antonio, Texas	148	38	27.3	32
San Diego, California	341	11	37.5	14
San Francisco–Oakland, California	493	2	39.8	8
San Jose, California	435	6	39.4	10
Seattle-Everett, Washington	193	34	24.9	37
Tampa–St. Petersburg, Florida	153	37	25.5	34
Washington, D.C.–Maryland–Virginia	285	21	23.4	38

*General revenues only; excludes revenues for insurance trust operations.
**These are the 40 most populous Standard Metropolitan Statistical Areas according to estimated population as of July 1, 1975 and contain approximately 10,000 local governments.
†An SMSA is a Standard Metropolitan Statistical Area, a device used by the Bureau of the Census to specify, usually by county, a metropolitan area that is heavily urbanized in all of its surrounding counties.
Source: Department of Commerce, Bureau of Census, and Tax Foundation computations.

The table shows where the property tax burden is heaviest. And where the property tax burden per capita gets out of line, people move away. You know that population has left those communities where the per capita property tax burden is the heaviest. You know that in California when it got too heavy, the voters voted for Proposition 13. Over time, people leave such communities, or those metropolitan areas and their suburbs, and houses can lose value.

Contrary to a popular conception, California did not have the nation's highest property taxes. The Nassau-Suffolk area in New York had the highest per capita property taxes in the nation—$609 a year for fiscal 1975–76, the last year for which figures are available. Second in the size of its property tax that year, with a figure of $493 per capita, was Newark, New Jersey. The SMSA comprising

San Francisco–Oakland, California, tied with Newark for second place.

The remaining top ten SMSAs, according to the Tax Foundation, were Boston, Massachusetts ($483); New York, New York–New Jersey ($438); San Jose, California ($435); Los Angeles–Long Beach, California ($419); Anaheim–Santa Ana–Garden Grove, California ($366); Detroit, Michigan, and Riverside–San Bernadino–Ontario, California, tied for ninth place with $353.

New Orleans, Louisiana, was the SMSA enjoying the lowest per capita local property taxes ($93) for fiscal 1975–76. Other "low" areas included Louisville, Kentucky–Indiana ($142); San Antonio, Texas ($148); Tampa–St. Petersburg, Florida ($153); Memphis, Tennessee–Arkansas–Mississippi ($174); Columbus, Ohio, and Seattle-Everett, Washington (both $193); Baltimore, Maryland ($196); Cincinnati, Ohio–Kentucky–Indiana ($197); and Pittsburgh, Pennsylvania ($199).

The Tax Foundation economists asked the question: Do areas that rely most heavily on property taxes for their general revenues have the highest property taxes?

Generally, yes. In the Boston area, for example, where property taxes provide 55% of local general revenues, the highest percentage for any of the areas studied, the per capita property tax ranks fourth overall. The Newark, New Jersey, area ranks second both in its degree of reliance on the property tax and in the per capita level of the tax. Similarly, the Nassau-Suffolk, New York, area, which derives just over 50% of its revenues from property taxes (and ranks in third place in this regard), stands at the top in per capita taxes.

At the other end of the scale, there is also evidence that per capita property tax levels are lower in areas that depend less on this tax to finance local government services. New Orleans, for example, gets less than 15% of its local revenues from the property tax, the lowest percentage of any of the forty SMSAs studied; it also has the lowest per capita property tax. Other areas with relatively low standing in both utilization of the property tax and level of the tax include Baltimore, Cincinnati, Louisville, Memphis, San Antonio, Seattle, and Tampa.

The average per capita property tax for the seventy-four major SMSAs reported by the Census Bureau was $310. This represented an average of 34.8% of all local revenues for these areas, which together contain 14,337 local government units. Federal and state grants-in-aid to the localities made up the largest single source of revenues—41.2% of the total, or $367 per capita. Other sources were nonproperty taxes (largely sales and income), 9.4% of the total and $84 per capita; and charges, fees, and other nontax revenues raised locally, 14.4% and $129 per capita.

CHECK INTO PLANNING AND ZONING
FOR FUTURE GROWTH

Planning and zoning, if agencies for those functions exist in the communities you are looking at, can be an important part of your future. Zoning ordinances are intended to promote uniformity among the general building characteristics within a community. Carefully zoned areas tend to hold their property values, which can be important when it comes time to sell.

If you have any notions of expanding or converting parts of a prospective house for business purposes, zoning laws could cut these plans short. For example, a doctor who may want to add a wing for an office may be unable to do so.

The local building department or the local planning agency is the right place to start, if you want to know about the community's plans for its future and, in particular, the plans for the neighborhood you're considering. Planning and zoning maps should exist; if they don't, the town might grow at random, and you don't know what might wind up next door to you. You don't really have to be afraid of an unwanted gas station, or an all-night drive-in, being plunked down right next door to you, but you want to be sure that contiguous-land uses are not widely at variance with the residential area, because in time they could detract from the value that you expect to accrue to that property.

The local building department can give you a pretty good idea where apartments are likely to be built and where commercial or light industrial areas are in relation to residential areas. You will want to look at parks and school districts, and find out where a sports complex, regional airport, shopping center, and so on may be. And consider the time needed to reach these places; you don't want to be right next to the airport, but you do want to know how long it will take to get there.

Find out the local government's policy on granting variances— exceptions to local zoning, which are spelled out in the master plan. In the future such exceptions could, if they are widely used, put a nonresidential complex on the fringe of the suburb you are looking at, or right next door to the house you may be interested in. Be aware that local politics often make zoning laws and planning maps meaningless and essentially ineffective.

The planning agency, the city manager's office, or the building department can tell you about major utility and street improvements the local government is contemplating. You don't want to be surprised at the sudden construction of utility lines underground, the sudden appearance of new storm drains or new sidewalks in front of your house, or construction blocking your homesite for a year or two.

One of the easiest methods of estimating the resale value of a house is to review the community's growth pattern and tax history. Growth can be checked by contacting the local zoning board and asking for building-permit statistics for the past several years and the year to date. Huge numbers of permits can be translated into rapid growth. Some communities seem to be able to handle instant growth better than others.

HOMESITE VALUES

Owning land still has a mystique for most Americans. Although your first thought may be buying a house, the land that goes with it is never far behind.

Legally, the Western world has long recognized that property ownership is not really the holding, as if in one's own hand, of a parcel of land with which one may do anything one pleases. Rather it is a bundle of rights that the owner assumes when he takes title and relinquishes to others when he sells that property. Those rights are expressed in the laws, customs, and mores of our society. We expect our municipalities to protect our property rights and to enable us to act in ways that do not run counter to those land-ownership rights. But one or another of those ownership rights is removed from time to time by various levels of government as we slowly evolve land-use policies.

There are a lot of reasons why parcels of property cannot be considered as commodities, but must be considered as permanent and, say many people, public resources. Property has value for two basic reasons: location and improvements. Anything that derives value to any degree from its fixed location cannot be defined as a commodity. Assuming that property is a resource, is it a resource solely at the disposition of the owner in fee simple of the land? Our zoning ordinances alone indicate that it is not.

Real estate appreciates in value as much from the way a particular parcel is used as it does from the uses of parcels surrounding it, whether public or private. Our property is fixed in quantity, so what others may do with contiguous parcels can profoundly affect a given property and those far beyond it. For instance, the discharges from an industrial site can affect property values downwind or downstream.

One would think that in a country like ours, where urban areas take up less than 2% of the landmass, land would not be such a critical factor in residential real estate. But land has become, over the past two decades, the most variable cost factor in the production of new housing. Prices of land for development have been increasing up to 10% per year since the late 1950's in desirable single-family residential areas. The increase in the price of raw land for multifamily use has been as high as 20% per year since the late 1960's. In 1977 the average price of residential land was climbing up to four times faster than the price of the houses that would be placed on it, and the ratio of land value to new-house price was reaching 40% in some places, as compared to a 20% ratio common twenty years ago.

Figures like these are a strong indication of the value of community to houses. Some houses have greater value than others, and as much of that value lies in the nature of the community as in the nature of the house itself. Good communities obviously have much higher assessment in property values, and the ratio of land value to new-house price is higher in good communities than it is in communities that may not be quite so desirable. The community you pick will have an awful lot to do with the appreciation rate of your home.

The risk in purchasing land for development is that it may cost a great deal to improve, especially if city regulations call for land being sewered at the cost of sewer collection and extension of water and other utilities. Eight years ago an improved building site in Cincinnati may have cost $4,000. Today it may cost $10,000, but it may be cheaper at $10,000 than the possible rural site that now still may cost a builder, before improvement, only $4,000.

But financing in rural locations is more difficult than in suburban locations. You need more cash down, and you take a chance on house appreciation, which is far less predictable than in mature, stable communities.

Building sites in rural locations are not valued by the criteria used for urban sites. The reason is lack of a broadly structured market to support resale. Since use of a rural site also depends upon installation of an access drive, a well, and a septic tank, there are also direct cost-related factors.

All this makes obtaining mortgage financing more difficult in a rural location. The only federally sponsored agency making these kinds of home loans is the Farmers Home Administration, and loan limits are lower than for FHA, VA, or conventional mortgages in urban locations. The normal source is a commercial bank, when the buyer is in position to provide additional collateral and make payments to amortize the loan in fifteen years or less. In many instances the houses you see in isolated settings have been paid for with cash.

Should you decide to build or purchase a house in a remote location, be prepared to rent it for an extended period of time at rates much lower than normal, should you have to move. Houses in rural settings deteriorate rapidly when left unoccupied.

In a typical situation in the Indianapolis area, the market value for a sixty-foot fully developed lot is $15,000, while a rural site that is twice as large would be available for $5,000. It's quite possible that unless produced for an owner, the same house on the rural site would have a market value substantially below its construction cost.

HOW WE LOOK AT OUR LAND

While land values have fluctuated up and down throughout our history, the cycles, in general, stopped and became one long rise, for most desirable land, beginning about 1926, Homesite values in most metropolitan areas, and most good agricultural areas, have continued to escalate for half a century, as we became an almost totally urban civilization from an agrarian background. The experts tell us that in the decade between 1965 and 1975 land values of all kinds increased 150%, while the consumer price index increased only 80%. Between 1971 and 1975, says the National Conference of State Legislatures, assessed property values increased 45% while personal income grew by only 39% and retail sales rose about 36%.

The courts have been filled with lawsuits over land and people's rights on that land. People have lined up on both sides of the issue: commercial interest, or ownership, versus environmental interests at every government level. The issue usually was proper management not just of public lands but of the public's interest in private land.

The federal government gradually has assumed stewardship over almost all of the 2.2 billion acres of U.S. land, of which it owns only about a third. We have seen what that means in Alaska in the recent move by the Carter administration to retain a major portion of that state as wilderness. We know through an estimate by the Conference Board that at the end of 1975 almost 15% of the national wealth—including government, individuals, and business—was bound up in landholdings.

But we really should know more about land use before we, as a nation, set down regulations on urban sprawl and controlled growth.

The United States is a nation of open land, nearly a fifth of it in crops, almost a third in pastureland and range, and another third in forest.

Between 1967 and 1975 we are told that almost 14% of non-federal land in the country was converted from one use to another, but only a little more than 3 million acres were added to the country's urban area.

The 1.3 billion acres of private land in the United States amount to less than 60% of total U.S. land. Only 2% of that 1.3 billion acres is in residential use, and that 2% is owned by some 50 million individuals or families. That averages out to about half an acre per person or family for residential use.

Since 1950 urban use of land has grown by two-thirds, yet metropolitan areas still occupy only 1.5% of the total land area, and three-fourths of our population lives on less than 2% of the land.

Yet one of the hottest political battles, at the local level, is over managed growth, controlled growth, no growth, or whatever you want to call it, versus so-called urban sprawl, even though the land involved is such a small percentage of the total. We know that hemming in a city with a strong controlled-growth policy can and usually does lead to economic decline. But the political and regulatory machinery in place keeps operating with the same old myths and faith that planners and officials can play God.

A lot of people are of the opinion that the regulators of land at every level of government are profoundly unaware of the views of the public about ownership versus regulation. The average U.S. citizen who owns some land thinks of it as *his* land, while the regulator thinks of it as a national resource that is subject to restraints of all kinds for the public benefit.

Regulators always come into conflict with our traditions of free enterprise and unfettered individualism. Some thinkers on this issue of land point out that regulators viewing land as a resource fail to realize that people regard land, as, among other things, a social weapon protecting their economic, political, and other interests. In a great many ways, ownership of land is a primitive form of power, and men kill, today and throughout history, to maintain their own land.

In the face of this, Congress still issues dozens of laws on clean air, utility sizes, pest control, all kinds of mineral reserves, all kinds of conservation, wetlands acquisition, wilderness, mineral leasing, coastal-zone management, forest management, natural-gas pipelines, endangered species, and so on. The Environmental Information Center, a private firm, reported that in the second session of the 94th Congress and the first session of the 95th, the Senate passed eighty land-use laws, of which nearly two-thirds were signed into law. And the states are not outdone by Congress. The American Society of Planning Officials reported nearly two hundred new state laws governing land use in 1976.

In 1978 one congressman counted nearly 140 separate federal programs that have a significant effect on state and local land-use decisions. Almost 500 land-use disputes were brought to state courts in 1976, and federal courts had to rule repeatedly on all kinds of management and environmental statutes. But from 1926 when the landmark case of *Euclid* v. *Ambler* established the zoning ordinance in most U.S. cities, until 1974 the Supreme Court did not rule on any zoning cases. It heard three different zoning disputes in 1976.

Chapter 6

Condominiums and Living Close Together

You should go through the same planning and thinking exercise when you consider a condominium as you would for a house. Don't regard a condominium as anything other than a home. Everything that has been said about homeownership, the community, the cost of energy, the value of good building products, and so on, is applicable to the selection of a condominium.

Why would you select a condominium in the first place? Because a condominium is usually cheaper for the same interior space, or the same-sized house, if it has been built and planned correctly, than a detached single-family house on its own lot. The condominium essentially saves the extra cost of a larger share of land—which the detached single-family house has—and the larger cost of land improvements that goes with a bigger piece of ground.

As you no doubt know, the condominium is now a very common housing type in this country. The condominium concept lets you own your own dwelling unit while you and your neighbors share the ownership of the land and the land improvements underneath your home.

Incidentally, you may be a little bit confused about the term *apartment* versus *condominium*. An apartment can be a condominium and vice versa. Condominium is a form of ownership; the condominium you buy may be an apartment. In this country apartments for sale are really condominiums The term *condominium* means nothing about the space for sale except its form of ownership.

Initially, the condominium was a way to increase land-use density, not just horizontally but vertically. It was the only device for offering a high-rise multifamily unit for sale. Like cooperatives, condominiums gave developers and owners an opportunity to build and own recreational facilities in common.

Condominiums have gotten a lot of bad publicity because of abuses by developers over the leasing of recreational facilities, over the constant increase of maintenance charges per dwelling unit for common areas and facilities (inevitable with inflation and an energy crunch), hassles over other leased facilities such as master television antennas, the complexity of the condominium declaration itself, and poor management. Owners invariably know little about property management, except for their own single-family house, and management contracts with professionals must provide for increases in uncontrollable costs such as gas and insurance—which makes for another point for dispute among condominium owners.

CONDOMINIUMS' BASIC DIFFERENCES

The main advantage of a condominium is cost. Condominiums come in all sizes and all characters: attached townhouses, garden apartments, high-rise apartments in resort areas or in big cities, or single-family houses (true usually in resort areas). (For a more detailed discussion of the vacation condominium and its implications and ramifications, see Chapter 8).

The condominium also has an advantage (for some but not for all) in that you usually don't have to maintain the grounds or the exterior of your unit; your homeowners' association (HOA) does that. And you may have a lot of recreational facilities immediately available within your condominium complex.

The trouble with this setup is that the tab may seem excessive to someone capable of doing his or her own yard work and maintenance, as most American homeowners are. What you may have to pay for recreational facilities can sometimes amount to enough to buy a dozen season tickets to watch the Dallas Cowboys. Those are expensive maintenance and recreation charges to most Americans.

What are the other disadvantages to condominiums? What disadvantages there may be lie in the difference between good management and poor or bad management. Your problem will be to determine that condition, and this chapter tells you how.

Bad management brings unpleasantly to your attention that you are dependent on a lot of other people to hold up their end of a lot of bargains. You and your neighbors must solve all kinds of problems about the use and maintenance of common elements and/or the recreational facilities. You are bound up legally, and usually socially, with your neighbors. A lot of us might find that confining. In the world of condominiums those relationships are not always smooth. Some say they are, in the main, not smooth at all. Your concern is always that your neighbors won't obey the rules you all agreed to when you bought your condominium.

There is another small disadvantage to a condominium, and it is not serious; that is the legal burden in buying a condominium, which is usually heavier than the legal burden involved in buying a house. The condominium declaration (and I will explain that in a moment) is a complex document, and all the rules and regulations that the condominium builder, or the homeowners' association, could devise can be an awful lot of fine print that only a lawyer trained in condominium dealings can interpret.

WHO BUYS CONDOMINIUMS?

With an idea of the advantages, disadvantages, and gray areas of condominium buying and living, you might guess that most condominium buyers are one- or two-person households, generally either older or younger people, and you would be right. The National Association of Home Builders, through its Home Owners Warranty program, has been able to draw a profile of condominium buyers. The HOW program requires the builder to fill out for each unit an enrollment form that lists key characteristics of the condominium buyer and the condominium structure. The only limitation of the condo data is that the HOW program coverage of high-rise condominiums is very low. The sample largely surveys townhouse and garden-type condominiums.

According to respondents to the NAHB 1978 survey, condominiums are most appealing to empty-nesters over fifty-five and single persons under thirty-five, two of the fastest-growing household groups in America today. Most condominium buyers fell into two distinct age groups. Almost half were forty-five or older; 34% of those polled were fifty-five or older. Another 38% were under thirty-five years of age. The median age for condominium buyers was forty-four—or ten years older than the typical buyer of a single-family house.

Almost 50% of condo units were bought by families consisting of a husband and wife but no children (many of whom probably could be termed empty-nesters), while 23% were single persons. Only 18% of the condo buyers had children living at home. In sharp contrast, 62% of the buyers of single-family homes had children and only 4.9% were single persons, according to another survey conducted annually by the NAHB.

Other findings of the condominium survey include the following:

1. More than half, or 52% of the condo buyers had pre-

viously owned a single-family house; 39% traded in their single-family detached house before buying their condominium unit.

2. The median income of those polled was $24,267.

3. The average size of the household for condominium buyers was only 2.1 persons, compared to 3.1 persons for single-family houses.

4. "Savings" was the main source of financing for 53% of the condominium buyers, followed by "equity from the sale of previous home" for another 33.8%.

5. About 24% of the condominium buyers were four-or-more-time homeowners, compared to 13% of those buying new single-family houses.

6. Only 22.7% of the condominium buyers moved from another state.

7. Over 50% of the condominium buyers moved fewer than ten miles from their previous place of residence.

A CONDO BUYER GIVES HIS REASONS

Larry Swenson is a United Airlines pilot, in his early forties, divorced. His home base is Los Angeles, where he owns a two-bedroom condominium in a small complex with a swimming pool set amid lush landscaping in the private "green" area around which the condo units are built. His two children by his previous marriage visit occasionally, as do various other family members from Iowa. I asked him why a condo instead of an apartment.

"If this place was an apartment," says Larry, "the rent would be at least $600 a month. That's what I learned when I first started looking into condos. But that's only the beginning. You usually take the annual rental of an apartment unit—this would be, say, $7,200 per year—and multiply by nine or ten to arrive at the price of a house that you might buy instead. So this place is worth perhaps $65,000 to maybe $72,000. You can't find a house at that price for sale in any neighborhood in Los Angeles that you might want to live in.

"Okay, I pay a bit more than $600 a month for this place, but it's a very good deal for me. No maintenance, other than cleaning up in here. Swimming pool. Lock up and take off for maybe six weeks, no problems, good security, nobody's going to break in, trespass, litter the lawn, and all that.

"I'm not around that much anyway, and I like the idea that

this is money in the bank. I build equity, there's appreciation on the condo itself, and I get all the deductions any homeowner would get. The association of the owners here is a necessary obligation. We have to get together every once in a while and come to an agreement on some item or other. The only problem people in the association are the ones who are here all the time. Every day, I mean. Most of us have jobs that take us away part of the time. But some of the owners, especially the older ones maybe on fixed incomes, worry a lot about details. But with the life I lead this is a good deal, not just financially, but it fits the way I live closer than anything else I can imagine right now."

THE HOMEOWNER PARALLEL

You are responsible, in a condominium, for your own taxes and mortgage payments, but you are not responsible for those of any of your neighbors in the same condominium project. Your taxes are just for your home, not for anyone else's. You do pay a share of taxes on the common area, and you are automatically a member of the condominium association that runs the development. In some developments your association may hire a professional manager, and that, indeed, makes for a maintenance-free and carefree life-style. But you pay for all of the work done by others.

Bear in mind that the only way to have no maintenance responsibilities, to have good recreational facilities right at hand, and to get the tax advantages of homeownership is by purchasing a condominium with a good homeowners' association (good management) and a lot of recreational facilities. For most of us, however, that is an expense we would rather handle ourselves, or we would prefer to use the money for other things.

There are many condominiums with good management and no recreational facilities, however, Maintenance costs in these condos are usually low, sometimes even negligible. But you want to be sure you know what you're paying for and whether or not you really want all the elements of that monthly expense.

Take into account when you compare a condominium with a rental apartment that the condominium becomes financially more attractive for three parties: the builder, the purchaser-owner, and the town in which the unit is built. The builder can usually make more money on a condominium because it has more value when sold to a purchaser who will have the tax advantages of homeownership. The owner has the tax advantages of homeownership, and of the maintenance-free life and recreational facilities if he has them. The town usually has a higher tax assessment on the condominium than it would have on a rental unit, so it gets more return in property taxes paid.

In this day and age, when political activism clouds the rental issue and return on investments is much too close to the break-even point, a mortgage lender who finances multifamily projects finds condominium mortgages to be much more secure loans. They are also more marketable in the secondary mortgage market than apartment house loans.

THE BIG DIFFERENCE: THE HOMEOWNERS' ASSOCIATION

The HOA is the focus of all the concerns of condo owners that everybody live up to the rules and regulations. The HOA is the government of the condominium, and, like other governments, some are good and some are bad, some are easy and some are disastrous.

How do you find out about that "government" before you buy a condo? Go to HOA meetings in different condos you're thinking about; you can find out easily from salespeople when these meetings are held. Watch and listen. In short order you'll find out where the landscaping is going to go to the dogs, where the dogs are going to go, whether or not the swimming pool is dirty and will stay that way for a while, and so forth.

Managing a condo is no easier than managing a big apartment building. If the owners could not cope with the latter, what makes anyone think they can cope with a condo project? As a consequence, many condos use professional managers, and you will have to pay for that, more every year. If the professional management is no good, you can tell that easily enough by looking at the project and talking to a few residents who have been there longer than a few weeks.

If the HOA is good, and many of them are, then you must bear in mind, if you're buying and especially if you're coming out of a rental apartment, that you will be part of that "government." You will have suddenly switched from the "tenant" side to the "landlord" side. You are now in the position of setting rules and regulations for yourself and for other owners. That's a big responsibility, and your moves must be judicious. If they aren't, the HOA and your neighbors will become a pain in the neck.

Here are the qualities of good condo management:

1. Round-the-clock service for emergencies such as furnace malfunction or waterline break

2. Landscape services that perform knowledgeably year-round

3. Responsiveness to homeowners' association board decisions

4. Accurate accounting for receipt and use of all funds and availability of records to owners

5. Carefully trained, neat, and courteous staff

6. A spirit of thoughtfulness among staff people in time of emergency

DOCUMENTS YOU AND YOUR LAWYER MUST READ

The prospectus, public offering statement, and disclosure document are essentially the same, called by one or another of those names depending on where the project is. Not all states demand that a developer provide such a document. If your state does, and the seller of an occupied condominium, or the builder of a new one, has no such document, have your lawyer find out why.

The prospectus in a state like Virginia, which has very tough condominium laws, will almost always be a truthful and good description of all the facts of the project. Some state condo laws are not as good. So check this out carefully.

Among a good many other things, a good prospectus should cover adequately these four areas:

1. Text of declaration and bylaws; developer's control of the condominium; projected budget covering at least the first year of operation with a breakdown of expenses and assessments for reserves

2. Management contract, any lease of facilities or agreement affecting your use of any part of the project

3. Evidence of compliance with state or local regulations; list of any encumbrances affecting title

4. Warranties on the units and common areas beyond what is stated in the bylaws; and cancellation clause, giving buyer ten days after receipt of the current public offering statement or contract date, which ever is later

If those matters are not covered to the satisfaction of your lawyer, you may be taking a risk if you purchase.

Next is the purchase contract. Regard this just as you would a purchase contract for a single-family detached house. Again, you'll want your lawyer to read this and be satisfied with it. The condo contract will also spell out the existence of the declaration, bylaws, and the survey and plan of the project.

A proper condo contract stipulates what happens if the developer does not sell enough units. Can you cancel? Can you move in and rent? If you move in as a renter, can you apply all or part of your rent to the purchase price of the unit? What happens to your deposit money in this event? Is it applied toward rent? Is it specifically prevented from use in construction? Is it automatically returned to you? Get an answer to each of these questions.

The third and most important document is the declaration. A condominium comes into existence, essentially, when the declaration is officially recorded: that recording changes the deed to a given piece of land into a "common estate" of a given number of dwelling units whose owners will share the common estate deed—have an undivided interest in it. Each dwelling unit must be described within the common estate, and everything not specifically described as part of a dwelling unit is then owned jointly by all the owners.

A detailed survey and plan of the project are integral parts of the declaration. Study them and be sure they match the reality of the project you see around you. If they do not, demand to know why.

The declaration shows the proportion of your unit to the total number of units in the project for voting and assessment purposes. Since that figure determines your monthly payments, taxes, and voting power, it is extremely important to you. The declaration may show how this percentage can be changed. In most declarations this proportion cannot be changed without unanimous consent of the homeowners.

Most of the big hassles that you may have heard about from friends in condominium ownership come about over what is and what is not common area, who takes care of it, and how much you or the other owners must pay in assessments for maintenance. Good state laws on condos now require the declaration to be specific about these areas. Have your lawyer check carefully.

What you can and cannot do in and to the common area, what kind of insurance is carried, how damaged property is to be repaired or disposed of, description of and control over all recreational elements—and how much you pay for all this—is carefully spelled out in the declaration. If it isn't, beware, and ask a lot more questions.

If the recreational or other facilities are to be leased to the owners, you would be well advised not to buy. But not necessarily. Consult your lawyer. The trouble with leasing is that you can't control rent increases, and this is particularly galling if you don't even use the facility.

Look out for a clause in the declaration that gives the association first refusal rights to any sale of a unit. Such a clause means that when you decide to sell and have found a buyer, you must put the deal before the association, which may review it and veto the sale. The HOA must then meet the price offered, but this may entail further negotiation on your part and may delay closing or kill your deal. This kind of clause (known as a restraint on alienation) in the declaration means that you are not free to sell your unit as you should be with any property you own in fee simple.

In a new condominium project, the developer usually administers the condominium until at least 90% of the units are sold, at which time the board of directors and officers may be elected from among the owners and take over management of the project.

HOW TO FIND OUT ABOUT A CONDO PROJECT

You want more information to consider as you approach buying a condo than an ad in the newspaper or the say-so of a realtor. Zoning authorities and the town engineer or building inspector are good places to check on the local level—to make sure local ordinances and building-code regulations have been met. A call to the local zoning board secretary or town clerk can help you find out whether there are any pending or postponed problems with the development. You may wish to visit town hall to read the zoning board minutes concerning the public hearings about the project.

The local tax assessor's office is also helpful. The assessor can tell you if the developer has built other housing in the community. In many towns the assessor not only establishes a market price for a housing unit, he also determines and grades the quality of construction, the basic materials used, and the workmanship.

The state real estate commission can help you find out if the builder has met all state requirements. Ask if there is any record of criminal or noncriminal processes or adverse orders issued to the builder.

Your mortgage loan officer can get information about the developer's company and its principal officers from any mortgage lender who has approved the project for permanent mortgage loans to qualified purchasers. The sales agent or developer should know who their lenders are; if there's reluctance to let you know, beware! There's usually a reason.

CONDOMINIUM FINANCING

Getting a condo mortgage is usually as easy as getting a single-family home mortgage. Qualifying for a loan is the same; read Section III.

However, many lenders and the Federal National Mortgage Association (FNMA) will not touch condo loans where leases and long-term management contracts are part of the deal. A bill to legislate FHA and FNMA out of that area is now in Congress.

There is no question but that we are going through a period of gestation in condominiums, for the developer, the investor, and the consumer. Learning how to live with more and new regulations controlling condominium development and sale, and accepting the fact that in many instances the only way the consumer can enjoy ownership of real estate (and the appreciation that eventually gives him), is to accept the weighty legal involvement that goes along with good condominium development.

Until the gestation period is over, condominiums will not be as popular in many places as they probably will be eventually. Nevertheless, there are numerous instances of well-planned and well-designed condominiums, from a land-use, environmental, and amenities aspect, that offer more attractive living at considerably lower prices than single-family houses in the same area.

CO-OPS—THE GOOD SIDE AND THE BAD SIDE

The advantages to buying a cooperative are like those for condominium and in homeownership. By buying instead of renting, there is no worry about arbitrary rent increases, and there are tax benefits and equity buildup. The co-op owner is free to make structural and decorative changes in his unit without concern for lease strictures or for tossing money down the drain on property he does not own.

A special selling point of the cooperative over the condominium is that one need not sign one's name to a mortgage. And there are no walloping closing costs, merely a transfer fee at the "lease" signing and, of course, a lawyer's fee for handling your purchase.

Most important: the sales price of a co-op unit you are looking at may appear deceptively low, particularly if compared to a single-family house or sometimes even to a condominium. But the asking price does not include the prorated share of the building's mortgage you will be responsible for. Add the two figures together, and the co-op no longer is inexpensive.

A co-op is still apartment living, and co-operators must love their neighbors far more than condominium owners, since they are all tied to a joint mortgage on the building. That means that if one of you defaults on your maintenance payment, the rest are responsible.

Like condos with their HOAs, co-ops have rules spelled out in their "leases." You may find that the building bans pets or does not allow sublets or does not permit co-operators to have a washing machine.

The co-op board approves applications for new residents of the building. For tenant-shareholders, having potential financial deadbeats screened out is necessary and reassuring. But when it comes time to sell, those same tenants may do a lot of waiting for the board finally to approve a would-be purchaser who meets requirements for membership.

Chapter
7
Some Bargains

REVIVING AN OLD HOUSE —A LABOR OF LOVE

A lot of people have successfully revived old houses. A great many more have done it at great cost, great frustration, too much unrewarding hard work, and essentially no return, or appreciation of their property, and sometimes an outright loss.

There are some general rules on how to remodel successfully and happily:

1. Be sure the community and the immediate neighborhood are viable: that others, too, are investing in property, commercial as well as residential; that the town is not going to raise property taxes sky high as a result of the rehabilitation because the community, financially, is headed down the drain; that the middle class and small businessmen find the neighborhood good to live and do business in.

That's a pretty big order—to determine whether or not the community is headed down the drain. Investigate the way you would if you were considering a new house in a new neighborhood. Find out, about property taxes, services, and so on. Then, find out if other people are remodeling townhouses or older houses in the area. If they are, the area is probably going to be viable, the community wants it to be viable, and the city fathers are probably making concessions, particularly on taxes, so that people like you will find the neighborhood attractive.

2. Be sure that you are capable of doing a lot of the remodeling, repair, or rehabilitation work yourself, and that you *want* to do it. This does not mean that you have to be a skilled craftsperson, but it does mean that you have to have the will. Learning how to do much of what you'll have to do

is not hard. As I explained earlier in this book, there are all kinds of do-it-yourself guides available, and your friends probably know a certain amount. For the tough stuff, such as the electrical, plumbing, and heating systems, you should use good subcontractors. They won't make mistakes, and they'll work within the building code, so you won't get in any trouble, particularly when you want to sell your house.

3. Be sure that you really love that old house, no matter what shape it's in. Love can conquer all, including beat-up old houses. Don't do this for investment purposes—it's too risky. There are better places for your money, if a good investment is what you want. Buy a good house in a good community. Not that you can't make money in fixing up an old house; you can. But don't bet on it. You're going to do this one for love. Period.

4. Be careful about taking the advice of anybody who calls himself a remodeling contractor, a kitchen specialist, or a bathroom specialist. About 90% of them, if given the opportunity, will do things that will make you angry and will usually cost you more than you thought at the outset. You've heard the horror stories. I'm not saying that remodeling contractors are dishonest. It's just that their concept of being in the building business is so alien to the usual patterns that the only business they can find to be in is remodeling. Before signing any contract, check references. If you still aren't sure, call the Better Business Bureau.

5. Use professionals, unless your skills in various areas are almost professional. Use a good architect. Talk to at least two. Use a good decorator. Talk to a good builder. He probably won't want to do any work for you, but he can give you good advice and give you the names of his good electrical, plumbing, and finished carpentry subcontractors. You can also find such people by asking your mortagage loan officer. If you don't have one, go to one or two banks or savings and loans and meet some. They can be very helpful with recommendations, and you're going to need some money on the best terms available anyway. The mortgage loan officer is the place to start.

6. Before you sign anything or give anybody any money with an intent to buy, get a professional inspection of the house (see Chapter 4). A professional can give you a ball-park estimate of what it will cost to get everything in working order, what must be totally replaced, how worn out various me-

chanical systems are, how energy efficient the house is (see
Chapter 22).

7. If you're at all unsure about your old house, approach
the whole problem as you would approach any house purchase.
In other words, follow the steps in this book.

CONSIDER THE SIZE OF THE JOB

How much you can tackle depends on four things: your energy, your persistence, your pocketbook, and your skills. You want
to be sure on all counts that you can follow through to finish a job.
A remodeling task that doesn't get finished can be a real pain in
the neck, so plan your remodeling in steps so that you can complete
one at a time.

Sooner or later every homeowner does a certain amount of
remodeling, even if it's only a new coat of paint or a few new
kitchen cabinets. If you are considering a major remodeling job,
however—one that involves many structural changes or new additions to the house—you will want to give it careful thought be-
forehand, to make sure that the remodeling will prove worthwhile.

Bear in mind that what you spend on remodeling is not always
reflected in the price you can get for the house if you should decide
to sell. Kitchen and bathroom improvements usually add substantially to the value of a house, but in most other cases you must
consider the money as spent for your family's enjoyment, not for
a possible profit later.

Consider first whether you can possibly achieve what you need
by rearranging the space you have. A lack of bedroom space can
sometimes be solved by finishing the attic or by dividing one oversized room into two smaller ones. If you need a family room or
larger living room, you may be able to convert the garage or car-
port. Or you can make a screened porch into an enclosed room to
give you extra inside living space.

In rearranging your existing floor plan, you must bear certain
factors in mind:

1. Interior nonbearing walls can be easily removed; bearing walls can be removed, too, but this is more complicated.

2. You can make doors into windows, windows into
doors, close existing openings altogether, or make new
ones.

3. You can move light fixtures and outlets fairly easily,
but heating ducts are more difficult.

4. If you can possibly avoid it, do not cut into any wall containing plumbing lines—they are costly and difficult to move. If new plumbing fixtures are being added, locate them near existing plumbing lines to save money.

If you're going to buy an old house that needs work, buy one to which you won't have to make structural additions. If that's not possible, given other more important considerations such as location, think the possibilities over carefully.

If rearranging existing space will not give you the room you need, you'll have to enlarge the house. In some cases you can do this by installing a shed dormer. Or, if there is already a one-story wing on a two-story house, you can extend your second floor out over the wing. This is usually cheaper than a ground-floor addition, because no foundation work is involved. If you plan a ground-floor addition, you'll need a plot plan, and you must find out from local building inspectors how close you can build to the front, rear, and sides of the lot, as well as other restrictions that may affect your plans. You must also consider the location of the septic tank—you can't build over it without installing a new one elsewhere.

Consider in advance whether your present heating system is large enough to heat the new addition or a new unit will have to be added.

The appearance of the new addition from the outside is also an important consideration. New roof lines must harmonize with the existing roof. Window lines and styles must match. Be sure everything about the new addition ties in architecturally with the old part of the house.

Consider also how the new addition will affect the layout of the existing house. Will you convert part of an existing room to a corridor by adding the new room? If you are adding a new living room, what will you do with the existing living room? If you need a new bedroom, it may be smarter to convert your present living room to a bedroom and add a new and larger living room.

The possibilities for remodeling are endless; only you and your family can decide how best to remodel your house. Try to create a good traffic pattern, so that children don't have to go through the kitchen when they come in from outside, so that guests don't have to go through a bedroom to get to the bathroom, and so forth.

Kitchen remodeling can run into a lot of money—thousands of dollars in some cases—especially if you install the newest and latest appliances. But a modern kitchen usually adds substantially to the value of a house and makes life much simpler for the cook.

If your house is short of bathroom facilities, or you are adding a new room that requires new plumbing, the first thing to do is decide exactly where the new bathroom is most needed and makes most sense. Since the space occupied by a bathroom is small, you can usually find the room you need by taking over a large closet, part of a hallway, or part of a good-sized bedroom. For a full bath, allow a minimum of five by seven feet. Remember that an outside window is not a necessity; ventilating fans are equally acceptable.

You will save money if your new bathroom can be located near existing plumbing lines; if possible, the new bathroom should be adjacent to, or directly above or below, the old one. You will need a plumber to advise you on this point and to tell you how much the job will cost. New plumbing work is not inexpensive by any means. Unless you are really handy and experienced, it is absolutely necessary to have a plumber install waste and water lines for you.

THE LAW AND REMODELING

Building codes are important. You have to comply with them. Remember this: you may have a house that predates a code or a new ruling. Some communities say that as long as you do not touch a building, you do not have to improve it to meet current code standards; but as soon as you start major repairs, some codes insist that you bring the total structure up to code. Generally, new codes have to be complied with when repairs are deemed by building authorities to be "major." Lawyers will tell you that many people have been caught on that rule, so inquire before you act.

If you are making electrical or wiring changes, or adding to the basic structure of your house (by adding a room, porch, or dormer), you must draw a plan of the structure and get a permit for the job from your building department.

If you put in a new electrical outlet (and the wiring that goes with it) without a permit, your fire insurance could be voided. If a fire were to start because of faulty wiring, you would be out of luck. If you put in new waste lines for a new toilet or basin without a permit, you might later be ordered to take them out and redo the work if it does not conform to local regulations. If you add a room or other basic structure, materials and workmanship must meet basic requirements for safety.

A building permit signifies that (1) the work conforms to local building codes and zoning ordinances; (2) you are competent to handle the work (if a contractor does the job, he takes out the permit); (3) the work will be inspected by the building department to see that it has been done correctly and safely.

You cannot do anything inside a house that would change its occupancy—for instance, making a one-family house into a two-family house—without first checking with the building department. In putting a new addition on a house, the work must conform not only to the zoning requirements but also to the area ratio; the lot size simply may not permit a larger dwelling unit. Many communities require that plumbing and electrical work be done by licensed journeymen.

When making substantial changes to a dwelling, do not forget the insurance policy. If you subsequently suffer a loss, you may be short-changed if the homeowner policy does not reflect a realistic current value of the property.

A COUPLE LOOK WITH PLEASURE ON A JOB THEY TACKLED

Tom and Dorothy Lingard live in Watertown, Massachusetts, a suburb of Boston. They have five children, and Tom is a lawyer with a firm that doesn't pay him a giant salary. When the Lingards started looking for a house, when Tom first got his position with the Boston law firm ten years ago, they settled on the suburb of Watertown because by car it was not far from downtown Boston, yet it did have a suburban-type climate, and it was only about two miles from Harvard Square, a cultural center in the Boston area.

They bought a Victorian house that needed a great deal of work. The house didn't have storm sash, it was uninsulated, it had three stories and an ancient heating system. But the location was ideal, in a good community. Furthermore, Boston at that time was about to encourage home improvement in its property tax bills by exempting improvements that upgraded houses. This occurred also in suburban towns, some of which listed what could or could not be done subject to increased property taxes. Among those things was replacing the heating system; if a good contractor did the job, the tax bill wouldn't automatically go up.

Says Tom, "Anybody looking into the remodeling or rehabilitation of an older house, like this Victorian beauty, would do well to go down to the building department, before he even puts a pencil to paper, and find out in what ways the property taxes may go up because of improvements.

"As a lawyer I am aware that in the past an extensive remodeling job might have doubled the property tax bill. But the city fathers no longer penalize those who want to improve the neighborhood and maybe make the tax base a lot more viable, if not a lot more uniform.

"We needed this big old house because we have five children, and they all wanted their own bedrooms. There was no way at the time we purchased that we could buy a new house that would have six bedrooms and even then not cost $120,000. We only had to pay $62,000 for this house, and since then I have put another $50,000 into it, but the house now is probably worth about $200,000.

"I am fairly handy, but I certainly was not an expert in things like carpentry, electricity, and plumbing. I found, however, like so many others that I know, that there were all kinds of pamphlets and booklets at the local lumberyard that explained how to do all kinds of things.

"Once you get into a house and start contemplating its possibilities, you find that the structure of the house and all the things that are packed into it aren't all that difficult to understand.

"Dorothy and I decided that we could do an awful lot of this work ourselves, and we were right—we could and did. When I got tied up on a particular case or was taken out of town by my work for a couple of weeks, we would sometimes call in some of the local kids, including my own, and contract with them informally to paint this room or that room or the outside of the house or start helping with the reshingling of the roof.

"Our property taxes inevitably have gone up as we knew they would, but they haven't gone up to the degree that one might suppose if one had put $50,000 into a remodeling job. In other words, they haven't really doubled in the ten years we have owned the house, and we find that well worth the effort. The community realized that there was great benefit in fixing up any house in this town.

"There is something else that we both believe, and that is that you really have to like the neighborhood and like the house or else all that sweat and inconvenience and effort can get you down in the long run. Obviously, we do like the neighborhood and we do like the house, and knocking yourself out, and smashing your thumbnail, or getting your hands cut doing this or that job is worth the effort, because you can gradually see the steps being accomplished as you work.

"And that is another important point: we only outlined for ourselves one or two steps at a time so that we could see a given step finished and not be troubled by the prospect of everything being undone for months on end. We didn't tackle the kitchen until that was the only job in front of us. After we finished that, we contemplated the next job."

I asked Tom how he had gotten the names of subcontractors who had helped.

"Well, I have a number of friends on the city council, partly because I have run a couple of times for city council and lost. But I know who the players are, and I simply asked them. They gave me the names of some good guys, and I have had qualified and licensed journeymen electricians and plumbers do all of the electrical and plumbing work. Often on weekends I would watch these guys work. What they did wasn't all that difficult, and I am sure that I could have done it. But on the other hand the head of the building department told me that I had better stick to the codes for financial reasons—against resale at some future date—more than perhaps any other thing. He would have looked the other way had I wanted to do the electrical work and plumbing myself, but he pointed out, and he was quite right, that it is really not worth it if anybody questions the quality of the work or if anything does happen to go wrong.

"There are remodeling contractors in this area and occasionally they advertise, and when we started work on the exterior (and this was simply a paint job), a number of them came around and tried to sell their services. Well, we listened and didn't commit ourselves one way or another, but after talking again to some of my friends in the local government, I realized what a mare's nest of trouble a remodeling contractor can become.

"Now on the other hand, when we realized that we had to get an expert to handle the problem of storm sash, we did go to a window outfit that was in the business of windows, garage doors, and a few other items. They contracted to do the storm sash and they did a good job, so our energy bills today are not anywhere near what they would be if we did not have storm sash.

"We did the same thing on the insulation problem about six years ago and got a good job there, too. He was a good insulation contractor who carried all of the registrations and licenses and tags on his truck to show he was a legitimate insulation contractor. I don't know what all of the tags mean, but I looked into it at the time, and this guy was bona fide.

"One of the first things we did was to replace the heating system. It was an oil burner, and the prior owner had used a local fuel supplier, a good and well-known fuel supplier in the town. He had his men come out and size up our needs and arranged to put in an entire new furnace and some extra duct work where we lacked sufficient warm air. They put in a new furnace in something like a day and a half and did the duct work at one fell swoop. They didn't waste any time. Obviously, one of the things that had them do such a fast and good clean-up job was the fact that they wanted to sell us fuel for the rest of the time we owned this house. Of course, we still buy our fuel from them.

"Most of the work that Dorothy and I and the kids did involved painting and patching some floors, removing a wall, laying some new floor tile, and in one case putting down a new hardwood floor. We got booklets on all of that and it wasn't difficult for us to do; it just took a lot of time and made us work a little harder than we thought we were going to have to.

"We got a book on structures from the lumberyard, and we could figure out by punching holes in the ceiling in a few key spots where there were critical bearing walls and where there were nonbearing walls. We removed one nonbearing wall between what had been a library and the living room to make the living room about twice as big. I did that job and it was dusty and messy for a while, but it didn't take long to remove the wall and clean up, only about two weekends. I patched with drywall and joint compound and that came out slick as a whistle.

"I'm not suggesting that it was easy. There were some electric lines to move and the electrician had to come in and do that, but it didn't take him longer than an hour. There was some floor patching to do, some of it oak parquet, but I could handle that as long as I took my time and didn't try to get it done in a big rush.

"All in all the experience has been satisfying. I believe that the $50,000—and I have the canceled checks to prove it—that we have put into this place so far since purchase has probably at least doubled, through sweat equity, so that the house really is today a $200,000 property on which I have hardly any mortgage left."

FINANCING MAJOR REMODELING

A lot of remodeling can be done piecemeal, if you plan carefully and don't need financing. But some work may require it. First, go and see your mortgage loan officer and tell him or her what you have in mind. He'll have a number of ideas, including refinancing your mortgage; taking a mortgage if you don't have one; borrowing on your life insurance policy; getting a personal loan; applying for an FHA Title I loan. Each of these options costs a slightly different amount; your mortgage loan officer can tell you exactly how much.

Most improvements are accepted by the FHA, except perhaps room air conditioning, outdoor fireplaces, swimming pools, and similar luxury projects. The FHA also says no to such extras as burglar alarms, fire alarms, and the like. You can get an FHA loan for wall-to-wall carpeting, provided the carpeting is a permanent installation. The installing dealer has to certify in writing that it is a quality carpet approved for such installations.

Be careful of second mortgages. You have to be alert to make absolutely sure that you are doing business with a reputable concern. You have to read the agreement carefully, like any contract, before signing it. Watch out for hidden charges. Use your lawyer.

Keep records. The homeowner who does not keep good financial records of all outlays in maintaining his house will very likely end up with a huge tax on any appreciation of value if he decides to sell the house. Don't neglect even the little items.

Put down all expenses beyond the usual running costs such as utilities and fuel. Landscaping can be expensive, but it adds to the value of the property. Keep a notebook with details of work done, who did it, what it cost, plus canceled checks and receipted bills.

THE "BASIC" HOUSE VERSUS THE USED HOUSE

A "basic" house is supposed to be one that doesn't have "everything." It's supposed to be cheap because it is partly "unfinished," but it isn't cheap—it's just unfinished.

There really isn't any such thing in new housing as a basic house. A basic house is almost always a house that needs a lot of work by the purchaser.

The basic house concept is to make stripped-down houses available to buyers with lower incomes who can't quite qualify to buy an entirely finished house. The buyer finishes the attic or the kitchen, or does whatever needs doing about insulation, drywall, and the like. Basic houses are essentially small houses, and wherever they can really be found is in the existing housing stock— older, smaller houses that need considerable remodeling and repair. That's why they come on the market at lower prices than anything else.

In some established communities it may be cheaper to buy a used house and fix it up, but that is not a general rule. The community has more to do with the value of a house than the house's actual condition and level of amenity—size, appliances, fireplaces, and so forth. The community dominates.

However, it is true that the owner of a used house usually has a large equity in it, gained mostly by appreciation as we have pointed out, and consequently he can knock his price down to the point where the house usually competes very handily with a new house. The builder of a new house cannot knock down the price, as it is fixed by his costs. People buy about three times as many used single-family detached houses as they do new houses built in the course of a year.

You should have the expert opinion of a good realtor as to the condition of the house and the neighborhood and the price. You may want to use an engineer who specializes in house inspection. There are plenty of professionals in this work, and a realtor, or your lender, will know of them. This person can tell you fairly accurately about the mechanical, structural, and drainage conditions in the house and what it is going to cost to repair shortcomings. If you are from out of town, especially, you need this kind of expertise so that you purchase at the fairest price possible.

MOBILE HOMES—SOME BARGAINS, SOME DISASTERS

Just about all of us have heard or read about bargains in mobile homes. It is true that some of them are inexpensive and good, but you must be very careful. Many people have been burned badly by purchasing mobile homes that are poorly built and are financed with consumer financing, which is always more expensive per month for the homeowner than real estate or mortgage financing.

New mobile homes today are supposed to comply with the Housing Act of 1974, which requires that mobile homes be built to high enough standards that they can qualify for real estate mortgages. If the purchaser of a new mobile home cannot get a mortgage, either the lender distrusts the mobile home in general as an alternative to regular housing, or the manufacturer of the mobile home has not met federal standards. In the opinion of the experts, about half of the mobile homes manufactured today do not meet the new federal standards that would make them eligible for real estate mortgages.

Even when mobile homes do meet the 1974 federal standards, they are not necessarily bargains. Buying a house usually means that you are buying the improved lot that goes with it; the price of a mobile home includes no lot. The purchasers of mobile homes must add lot rental (which is usually the case in a mobile home park) or lot purchase price. What it all adds up to is that a mobile home of a given size in a semirural area is not necessarily cheaper

per square foot of livable space than an existing house of comparable size and comparable situation that meets ordinary building codes.

It takes a little explaining to see how some of us started thinking that mobile homes were bargains. Mobile homes first made their appearance generally in this country in the 1920's. They were a cheap answer to unavailable residential real estate—that is, real estate that was unavailable to most Americans at the time because of its expense. Mobile homes were built to low standards, which meant that they depreciated to zero value in approximately eight years. As a consequence, only consumer financing was available. This meant that up until the 1970's people who purchased mobile homes were usually purchasing a pig in a poke. The Housing Act of 1974 purported to change all that, and with a great many mobile home manufacturers it did. A good many of the new ones will last the life of the mortgage. But you have to be careful, especially if you are buying a used mobile home which may in fact have depreciated drastically. In sum, the idea that you will get a housing bargain, in housing expense per month, in mobile homes is almost always a myth.

Chapter 8

A Vacation Home for Fun and Profit

Just about all of us have thought, "Wouldn't it be great if we had a place in . . ." (and you fill in the place, depending upon the time of year) "and we could . . ." (and you name your favorite activity of the moment) "and after cocktails we could go to . . ." (you name some exotic place) "or have for dinner . . ." (your favorite food of the moment) . . . and your daydream goes on.

But a vacation home has to be thought over very carefully, even if you're rich. How much are you going to use it, and for what kind of things? Reflect on what kind of vacation life-style you'll pursue for a long time, in what part of the country, for what times of the year, and for how long each time. How often might you go there each year? Will it be worth the money? The questions could go on and on.

A vacation home is, or can be, desirable from many points of view, including as an investment, although vacation homes are hardly ever regarded in that light alone. There are some very practical reasons for owning a vacation home, aside from investment potential.

What if you live in a city, or a part of the city, that is becoming uninhabitable for whatever reasons, including atmospheric (maybe Houston), dangerous (like parts of New York), generally dying (like parts of St. Louis, Detroit, Cleveland, and a whole lot of others)? What if you don't have to live in the city anyhow and can do your work as well in the mountains of eastern Tennessee, western North Carolina, New England, or Oregon, or in the sun of Arizona, Florida, or California? Why not start looking for something now and start fixing it up, so that in a few years you can move in for good—lock, stock, and barrel? Why not, indeed?

What if you are almost climbing the walls? You want to get away so badly it hurts; you need an alternative, or else you, and all those around you, are going to go crackers.

A lot of people start planning for a vacation home well before they retire, and the vacation home becomes their retirement home, or their new full-time home when they continue their careers, even though the company they've worked for for twenty years assumes they are retired. By that time they know all about the area around the vacation home. They've visited at all times of the year. They know people, stores, and services there. And they are very glad they started making the switch before any serious thought had been given to retirement.

You should make a list of the things, or the reasons, that would make a particular vacation home just what you need. Let me list some of the things to think about, not necessarily in any order of importance.

Location. Is it a way station or a real destination? For retirement? Is it for recreation for one or two seasons of the year, or for full-time living at any time?

Use. Can you work there? Earn money? Do you want to or have to? Are you going to be bombarded with would-be guests during the "season"? Can you put them up? Will they be a bore, a chore, drive you nuts?

Services. Do you need medical or educational facilities nearby? Entertainment, shopping, access to good transportation? Airports? Interstate highways? Big commercial centers?

Money. Is this home for investment? If so, is this the best investment? Have you asked your tax counselor, or your mortgage loan officer, or someone whose business instincts you trust implicitly?

Costs. Can you handle the expense of a second everything: phone, insurance, property tax levy, mortgage, grounds-keeping equipment, shop, car, pantry full of food, utensils, liquor, exterminator, periodic caretaker to see that the property hasn't been broken into?

You can add to that list just by talking to the person or people who share your life. You might go wild spending on that vacation house at the hardware store alone. You mean you don't have a grill, a claw hammer, a small power lawn mower, a medium-sized freezer, a snowmobile? There's this place just down the road that carries . . . You can imagine where a little irresponsibility could lead you.

What do you want and for how long? Sun country, snow country, lakes, woods, just country?

If you're thinking of land, with or without a house, purchased out of state from a development company, you should know about the HUD Property Report.

The Office of Interstate Land Sales Registration of the U.S. Department of Housing and Urban Development (HUD) requires full disclosure in sales of land in projects across state lines. If the developer of the land you're interested in has followed the registration procedure, you can get the HUD Property Report. It is an abbreviated treatment of the official legal statement filed with the Office of Interstate Land Sales Registration. In the Property Report the seller must disclose who owns the development company and details about the property, including information about parts under water or impossible to build upon without considerable improvement, and the kind of improvements necessary. HUD regulations require that every interstate buyer be offered such a Property Report before purchase. The sale can be voided if the buyer has not been given the Property Report.

You never can tell when you may want to sell, or have to sell, your vacation home. You should think about its market value in the years ahead, unless your desire is so strong that market value a few years away is of little consequence. Most of us have to consider the possibility of selling, but a strong desire for a particular place, come what may, is not at all uncommon.

A vacation home perched on a mountainside, five or fifty miles from any place, is a great retreat, but its resale value may be zero, and it may be unfinanceable for that reason. No prudent lender is going to put a mortgage on a property that in the marketplace has no more value than the face value of the mortgage.

Where vacation lots have been laid out in a subdivision plan and people are buying lots and building houses, you're likely to find real market values, mortgage financing, and resale possibilities that may or may not give you a good profit but will at least let you get your money out if you have to.

In special locations, where there are fancy resort facilities and people already own many vacation properties, you may find a handsome appreciation on your property, but you will also find that the purchase price is pretty handsome.

I'm sure that none of this discussion has discouraged you, once you have thought about a vacation home. And I don't want to discourage you: a vacation home is a very good idea, if you have thought long and carefully about it and planned it well. It can be the second best acquisition in your life, the first being your first good house.

HOW ONE FAMILY GOT IT ALL TOGETHER

George Rand is a senior engineer for Texas Instruments in Dallas. He and his wife, Marie, and three children (his oldest is at the University of Texas in Austin) live in a pleasant suburb of fairly big single-family ranch houses, just outside Dallas. George and Marie originally came from Ohio and have found Dallas, in the last five to ten years anyhow, to be more "big city" than anything they had seen or thought about back in Ohio. Not that they don't like Dallas—they do; but their desire for some escape, some relief, from the big city and its big suburbs has been real for some years.

"After the first few years here, back in 1967, we decided that there wasn't that much family back in Ohio to draw us back there for my vacations," says George, "and we started a period when we'd rent a place on a lake, within four hours of Dallas, and there are plenty of lakes here in Texas, contrary to what my folks back in Ohio used to think.

"Well, we tried three different lake areas in three years, and in 1969 we liked this area so much that we spent a good part of my three and a half weeks here looking at local real estate, fairly big pieces of acreage, with or without a house. This is nice country, hills, the kids like horses . . . there were a lot of things we could do. And we didn't particularly want to be right on a lake. A good lake can turn into a regular carnival here in Texas on a big summer weekend. It seems that everybody has a power boat and a big beer cooler and people like to tie up and party, and if your cottage or house is near anybody else's on the lakeshore, two o'clock in the morning on a July 4th weekend doesn't mean a hell of a lot to people in Texas.

"So here we are. We bought these six acres. It's good-looking land, has pretty good privacy on a secondary road, and it's really only two hours from our house in Dallas. By 1970 my mortgage on the Dallas house was paid way down, I was moving up in the company, and through contacts in Dallas, good friends, I had no trouble arranging the financing—I would eventually get a modest long-term mortgage—to purchase the land and have a contractor put up the basic vacation house. He did all the paper work locally, built the house, as you can see here, big living room with kitchen and dining area sort of part of it and three small bedrooms off it with one full bath. We added the garage—mostly for winter storage of the boat, its trailer, and the old jalopy the kids use in summer—and the half bath off the kitchen in 1975.

"I suppose I should be embarrassed to tell you that we all started to act like kids with a brand-new toy, almost before we got the land. What we weren't going to have and to buy for that place I can't begin to tell you. When we first began to use this house in 1971, everything we needed for the house and the place became an imperative. Someone would say, if we've gone to this effort, we might as well enjoy, enjoy.

"By 1972, I had to put my foot down. We're not Noah and the Ark, we don't need two of everything, for Pete's sake. We can bring a lot of this stuff from Dallas when we come or you kids come by yourselves.

"We finally got the whole business shaken down, but only after a bad case of the shorts in the checkbook. But no regrets, mind you. I probably use the place eight weeks a year, Marie is here from Memorial Day almost to the end of September, plus Easter time. The kids and Marie like to stay in Dallas for the holidays for all the parties, but I'm a little sick of them and would rather be here, like I was last year and will be again this year. I can have as much merriment and memories here as I can in Dallas, and I can be damn choosy about the company I want to share that with here.

"Last year my mother and her sister used the place from mid-September until Easter and went to see friends in Arizona over the holidays when I came up here with Marie and two other couples.

"I don't know whether I'd want to retire here, but I haven't much left on the mortgage, and the property has appreciated at a great rate. So has the house in Dallas. Come that day when I think I'll hang it up, which I may never do, because electronics is something you can carry in your head, so to speak, and work almost anyplace on new ideas . . . why, I'll have any number of options open to me as to where I may want to go. I may want to stay right here."

VACATION HOMES AS RENTAL PROPERTIES—MAYBE

Extrapolation of data from the 1970 Census show that about 6% of all homeowners in the United States have some kind of second home; the number is around 3 million. The home-building industry is building, according to best estimates, about 100,000 to 120,000 vacation, or second, houses a year these days. Back before the recession of 1974–75 and before Congress changed the tax law, the number of vacation homes that were coming on the market every year was considerably greater because many people were using them purely as investments.

But in 1976 the Congress passed the Tax Reform Act which changed the rules on tax deductions allowed to the owners of vacation houses who rent out their units when they are not using them. That act lets the owner of a vacation home use it personally for no more than fourteen days each taxable year if he plans to claim full tax benefits on the rental for the balance of the year. That law sharply curbed the business of buying vacations units or houses to build up tax losses to offset other income, which had been a very popular game with high-income owners for some time.

It is no longer as popular a game, even though there are important wrinkles in that 1976 tax act. If the taxpayer uses the vacation home for fifteen or more days in the taxable year, or more than 10% of the number of rental days, whichever is greater, he cannot deduct more than normal deductions, like interest and property taxes. But if he uses it for less than two weeks a year he can deduct maintenance, furniture, personal property, the expenses of traveling for business purposes between the first and second homes to inspect the rented home, and the commission paid to a rental agent.

But there are some big problems regarding a second home that you only occupy for less than two weeks each year as an investment, apart from whatever income it may shelter.

A big risk in trying to get an investment position in a second home is its location. In a bad location you can't get a good rental anyhow; the house has to be in some kind of resort area desirable to other people year round for one kind of activity or another. That means that the number of locations for this investment potential is quite limited.

Another major problem lies in the tenants. A destructive or irresponsible tenant can wipe out whatever profit you had in a fraction of the time it took you to build it up. You have to be very selective about tenants. Check their credentials, their employment, their previous living situations and landlords. Find out why they left their last residence. You will, of course, have at least a month's rent as security, but that's hardly gilt-edged protection.

You have to be able to evict easily and never let the tenant fall behind in his rent.

Don't get involved with your tenants unless you have a fairly high tolerance for aggravation. Even good tenants look to you for just about any maintenance and repair that exceeds changing a light bulb. Spell out in advance—in writing—just what you are responsible for and what you expect your tenants to fix themselves. Your best bet is to have your property managed for you by a real estate management firm, but that can use up most of your real profit.

Furthermore, you have to maintain a cash reserve equal to a few months' rent. You need that cushion for unexpected repairs, increases in property taxes and energy costs, and odd months when the house goes unrented. Don't get involved with this kind of investment if you aren't in a position to tie up your money for at least four years. A second house is not a liquid investment, and if you have to sell it within a year or two, broker's commissions and other transaction costs will eat up any profits you might have made.

A LOOK AT VACATION-HOME INCOME

A carefully picked-out vacation home can be one of the best of all possible investments for someone with a lot of money, for those who may have some money set aside and with a high income and in a high tax bracket. It is a way to generate an estate or preserve the value of savings. That is particularly true these days when municipal bonds are eroded by inflation, the stock market has been a shambles for the last five or six years, and inflation is running along at over 10%. About the only safe place for money in inflationary times is in real estate. Some fairly wealthy owners of second homes will tell you that their second home is really one of the best investments they ever made. So it is worth taking a look at their position. But bear in mind that this is a case where the vacation home is really not a vacation home; it is just money in the bank, so to speak.

For people who can have a "vacation" home for that reason, the resort-type home can be written off over the years as a tax deduction. In your declining years you could live there, and the home would have cost you nothing.

For that kind of investment, newly built second homes can be depreciated more advantageously than used homes. For example, the useful life of a typical seashore or mountain vacation home might be set at twenty-five years under IRS guidelines. Under the "straight-line" method of depreciation normally used, the house itself (not the land) can be depreciated by 4% a year multiplied by 200%; for a used home a multiplier of 125% is used. The actual allowable depreciation is 8% for a new home or 5% for a used home. Thus, a buyer in a 30% tax bracket who buys a new second home with a $50,000 house value would be able to cut his tax bill by $1,200 through first-year depreciation alone.

The rise in value of a good home in a desirable area can be rapid. At a 10% annual appreciation—about the national average—a property doubles in value in just seven years. Annual appreciation of 20% is not unusual for some resort-area real estate. At that rate, a property doubles in value in about three and a half years.

The Tax Reform Act of 1976 still leaves a lot of uncertainty concerning vacation homes and the tax breaks owners can get on them when they rent them out. Before you make any moves, consult your tax counselor to see if this can work for you.

For those who would like to make some money out of their vacation home without any particular tax break, other than deduction of mortgage interest and property taxes, it is necessary to have a vacation home in a highly desirable vacation area, for instance, the Hamptons of Long Island. If you can rent a vacation home there for $6,000 for the summer season, the rent may help you cover some of your costs. But you won't make any real money, or even enough money to cover the cost of ownership of a house in a location like that. So if you are contemplating such a purchase, you should be able to enjoy the location in some time other than "the season" and not expect to make any money from rental income generated because of the location.

THE VACATION CONDOMINIUM

You have probably heard a great deal about vacation condominiums and their popularity both in this country and around the world. Americans have found vacation spots with condominiums for sale in Europe's Alps, Mexico, Spain, and right here in the United States, in the sunny South as well as New England and Colorado. It is a small trend in this country, and it comes under the same IRS scrutiny as any other kind of rental of a vacation property. It is a murky area, and it has the same liabilities that any other owned rental property presents its owner. But it can prove to be a good investment that you can own free and clear one day, having sheltered your investment throughout the years that you rented it.

You may have been to very desirable resort areas offering that kind of investment. But think carefully about this.

The Securities and Exchange Commission (SEC) seems a peculiar agency to be involved in condominium sales regulations. It is concerned with condominiums that are promoted as investments, intended to provide a return. Typically, these are resort or vacation condominium units in which the developer arranges to rent out your unit when you are not using it and promises that you will make a profit, or at least receive income. If he sells you the unit first and then suggests that you might profit from renting it out, and also that it may increase in value over the years, the SEC probably can't do a thing.

SEC regulations on disclosure do not apply across the board to all condominium sales. They are exacting and require full disclosure of the type a corporation must give when it issues stock. This means detailed data about the organization, its officers and principals, the items being marketed (in this case the units) with full descriptions, physical and financial, the cost structure of building, marketing, and profits, as well as the projected rental scheme with full information on the rents to be charged, the management fees, the competition to be expected, and much, much more. All this is included in the prospectus required by the SEC. Until this legal document is received and registered with the SEC, the units cannot be sold in interstate trade.

So ask the developer for a copy of the SEC prospectus for the project. But don't be surprised if he tells you there is none, since so few condominiums are covered.

Take into account air fares, if your vacation house is several states away. Two or three visits during the course of a year could break your budget. Hidden expenses are often not considered in the initial wave of enthusiasm for recreation facilities at the condominium. You must pay annual membership fees to use the pool, golf courses, shuffleboard courts, and other features.

If you are going out of the country, how do the nationals where you're heading feel about Americans? What about the country's economic and political stability? Tranquil island paradises, for example, can become hotbeds of revolution at the drop of a palm leaf.

In a few projects, particularly in communities with a stable year-round population, owners' contracts often prohibit sublets to preserve the character of the community and to avoid transient traffic. (In condominiums where sublets are acceptable—and they are the majority—there is no need to secure approval of your tenants from the other residents, as you must do in subletting a cooperative apartment.) Other places may have restrictive clauses about the age of unit owners and subsequently their renters. Children may be prohibited.

The ability to lease your apartment also depends on where it is. If the area is glutted with condominiums, you are competing for tenants with many other owners, some of whom may live in projects that offer fancier recreational facilities than yours.

Seasons count, too. If you choose a ski community that becomes a ghost town in the summer, you can pretty much forget about renting after the spring thaw. In Florida and the Caribbean, however, the occupancy peaks don't seem to matter anymore. The so-called "off season" now draws nearly as many visitors as the winter months.

VACATION CONDOMINIUM TIME SHARING

You've probably read or heard about this wrinkle, too, as you looked into vacation property. Quite simply, time sharing is owning a "time" portion of a condominium unit for the purpose of letting someone else use your "time" so that you can use his. What is that all about?

It works like this: Richard Neuman bought one week a year, for twenty-five years, of a condominium unit on Florida's west coast for $8,000 cash five years ago. He's never even seen the unit, let alone stayed there. Each year, through the offices of Resort Condominiums International, Indianapolis, he lines up a week in someone else's time-shared condo. For each of the last two years he's taken a week skiing in the Rockies, at different places each time. In theory, he won't really own his Florida condo to use as he wishes for twenty-five years, unless he and his lawyer do something more, legally and financially, than they have already done.

Who would do that, anyway? Well, people are doing it all across the country. In all of North America there may be some three hundred resort projects that time-share now. And there are probably 60,000 time-share owners.

The safest way to regard time sharing is not as a vacation home that you own (which to most people implies the right to use) but as prepaid room charges on resort hotel space for a few weeks a year for a period of years. Time sharing is not money in the bank, and it often is a pig in a poke. It's for you if you have plenty of money for fancy vacations.

If you're thinking of time sharing, you should discuss it thoroughly with your lawyer. In addition to the condominium concept in which you buy one or two weeks a year, say, for twenty-five years, before you actually own the unit for full-time use, there is the "right-to-use" concept: you buy the right to use a unit at a resort hotel for one or two weeks for, say, twelve years, at which time the entire unit reverts to the resort hotel owner who sold you the "right-to-use" in the first place.

The possible legal and operational pitfalls of time sharing have not been lost on buyers or the resort industry itself. One key issue is how well the property is managed over a period of time. In that respect some authorities feel that the "right-to-use" concept is superior to the condominium since it may provide the resort owner who will eventually recover the property with the incentive to maintain it.

The lack of a long-term management plan, an unrealistic operating budget at the hotel, disreputable or high-pressure selling practices—all of these are possibilities that may victimize purchasers. Changes in management or financial circumstances over which the unit owner has little control may affect the quality of the resort years hence. And some major hotel operators have dropped out of time sharing because of troubles with the buyer-owners.

How would you feel about a condo you thought you "owned" falling into such disrepair over the years, because of bad management, that it turned into a pigsty before you ever really owned it, or before your "right to use " had run out?

Chapter 9

Worksheets for Section I

Pause now to think about the ideas you have conjured up about the house of your dreams. What does that ideal exterior look like, what about it appeals to you so much, what about that property and its landscaping? What makes it your special vision? What about the floor plan—how does it work for you? How livable is the house, how expensive is it going to be to operate? Will you be able to maintain it and repair it yourself, and, if not, are there professionals you can turn to at a reasonable cost?

If you can answer these questions and you have a firm vision of the house you want, you have prepared yourself for your search, you can home in on that one house that meets your needs and skip all the rest. But since no one can find exactly what he is looking for, you should know the compromises that you are willing to make.

THIRTY-SEVEN QUESTIONS TO ASK ABOUT A HOUSE

In general

1. How is this house going to "live"? Are living areas separated clearly and cleanly from sleeping areas?
2. If the house is a story and a half, is the upper half story worth the money, even if it needs to be refinished, or would you do better with a two-story house?
3. Do people coming through the front door have to go directly into the living room, and do they have a place to hang their coats?
4. Will most of the furniture you own or intend to get fit well in the various rooms in this house?
5. Are the bedrooms big enough for the furniture you have in mind and the number of people who will use them, and are the closets big enough?

Kitchen

6. How do you get to the kitchen with bags full of groceries or with kids with muddy boots on?

7. Is the kitchen well located with respect to both the outside and the eating areas?

8. Does the kitchen have a good view, light, and ventilation?

9. Is the work triangle (food storage to cleanup to cooking) in a good relationship and with a maximum length (sum of three sides) of twenty feet?

10. Is there adequate counter surface? Is it in the right place in relationship to the range and oven as well as the sink?

11. Do you have enough cabinet space in this kitchen? If not, is there room to build more?

12. Is there a window over the sink? Does it open easily?

Storage

13. Is there sufficient storage either in furniture to be placed or in built-ins in the living and dining rooms for all the things that you might want to store there?

14. Is there convenient storage space for the inevitable miscellaneous items, such as boxes and bicycles and skis?

15. Is there storage for out-of-season clothing?

16. If you have to add storage space, is there room to do so?

Cleanup

17. Are there enough bathrooms, big enough and conveniently located? Is one easily reached from the living room and the kitchen?

18. Is there a window over a tub, or in a shower stall, that will make cold drafts in winter, drip, and rot windowsills?

19. Can you go into a bathroom without being seen by everybody?

20. Is there space for a washer and dryer someplace handy to either bedrooms or the kitchen?

Some details

21. Are the windows in children's bedrooms too low (safety), or too high (can't see out), or too small to get out of in the event of fire?

22. Are there light switches at every door of every room?

23. When you answer the front door, can you see who's there before you open it?

24. Do picture windows let the passing public get a good look at how you live?

25. If there is a basement, does the door to its stairs open toward them so that people not knowing much about the layout could fall downstairs?

Mechanical equipment

26. Are the electrical wiring and the electrical service sufficient in this house, or will they take some updating?

27. How about termite protection? What is required in the area, and what possibility is there that termites have already attacked framing members in the house?

28. How about hot-water supply and the amount available in the house? What is the tank's capacity and its recovery rate? Is the hot-water-heater insulation adequate?

Outdoors

29. Is the outdoor living area, including terraces and patios, convenient to the living area?

30. Is storage for garden tools, lawn mowers, hoses, and other equipment in the right place for ready use?

31. Are the surfaces of driveways, terraces, and patios sound and durable, or are you going to have to go to some expense to fix them? How do you like the looks of these surfaces?

32. Is there enough topsoil for planting new grass (four to six inches), shrubs (up to eighteen inches), and trees (at least two feet)?

33. Is oncoming traffic visible to you when you back out, or drive out, of the driveway? Does the driveway slope downward from street to the house (a problem when the snow falls)?

34. Is drainage good enough to lead water away from the house even in the heaviest rains? Is the bottom of the outside wall, at the foundation near the ground, splattered with mud, or does it have a ring of dirt around it—a sure sign of bad drainage? How about the rainwater from the gutters and downspouts—does it drain away properly?

35. Are there outdoor lights, especially to light people up to the door, including the back door, in the dark?

36. If it's raining hard, will someone waiting for you to answer the front door get soaked, or is there shelter, an overhang? How about getting from the car to the kitchen—is that path protected?

37. Do meter readers—gas, electric, and water—have to come inside the house to read them? Will that be a problem, or can you have meter positions changed easily?

Rating your house candidates

Fill in one of these worksheets for each house you are seriously considering.

The house (your name for it, such as "new colonial") ——————

———————————————————————————————

Seller ——————————————————————————

Asking price ——————————   Square feet of living space ——

Lot size ————————————————————————

Number of stories ——————————————————————

Property taxes ————————————————————————

Check off each room:

      Living room ——————————————————————

      Dining room——————————————————————

      Family room ——————————————————————

      Living room closet ——————————————————

      Bathroom or half bath for living room, kitchen ——————

      Garage ——————————————————————————

      Carport ——————————————————————————

      Kitchen ——————————————————————————

      Dining room or area ————————————————————

      Pantry ——————————————————————————

      Entrance hall ——————————————————————

      Workshop——————————————————————————

      Storage ——————————————————————————

Bathrooms ————————————————————

Utility room ————————————————————

Bedrooms ————————————————————

Bedroom closets ————————————————————

Walk-in closets ————————————————————

Bedroom dimensions ————   ————   ————

————   ————

Attic storage ————————————————————

Bonus room ————————   Den/library ——————————

Heating type ——————————   Air conditioning ——————————

Electrical service, no. of circuits ——————————————

220-volt ————————————————————

Carpeting ————————————————————

Fireplace ————————————————————

Floors ————————————————————

Dishwasher ————————————————————

Garbage disposal ————————————————————

Clothes washer/dryer ——————————————————

Countertops ————————————————————

Range and oven ————————————————————

Built-in oven ————————————————————

Countertop range ————————————————————

Lighting ————————————————————

Kitchen style ——————————————————————————

    Cabinet style ——————————————————————————

Built-in mirrors ——————————————————————————

Underground utilities ——————————————————————

220-volt outlet for dryer ———— TV outlet ————————————

Telephone jacks ——————————

Water-heater type ——————— Capacity ————————————

    Recovery time ———————————

Landscaping ——————————————————————————

——————————————————————————

Fencing ——————————————————————————

Roofing type ——————————————————————————

Gutters, downspouts ——————————————————————

Driveway paving ——————————————————————————

Patio, terrace surfaces ————————————————————

Barbecue ——————————————————————————

Entry-door type ——————————————————————————

Sliding glass doors ——————————————————————

Storm sash and screens ——————————————————————

Weatherstripping ——————————————————————————

Insulation: Walls ——————— Ceiling ————————————

    Floor ——————————— Foundation ————————————

Warranty program ——————————————————————————

SPECIAL CONSIDERATIONS FOR AN OLDER HOUSE

1. Has the house been inspected by a structural expert with appropriate credentials?

2. Is the foundation on solid ground or filled ground, and do any cracks show?

3. Is the basement properly waterproofed, or is there some water in it or signs of dampness and stain on basement walls inside or outside?

4. If there is a concrete floor, either slab or basement, can the salesperson tell you if there is a vapor barrier underneath it and adequate gravel bed for drainage underneath the vapor barrier?

5. If there is a crawl space, does it have adequate ventilation?

6. Is there a vapor barrier over the crawl-space earth?

7. Is there any problem of termites, and if so, when was the last time soil poisoning was done to eliminate them?

8. Has chemically treated lumber been used for sill plates and other wood structural members that are in contact with the foundation?

9. Can you or an expert find any cracks or porous areas in the foundation walls that termites might crawl up?

10. If there is a termite problem, are termite shields placed all around the top of the foundation wall to prevent entry into the house?

11. Can your structural expert locate any wood rot in the framing members or other wooden members of the house?

12. What is the fire insurance coverage on the house now?

13. Do the driveway and walkways need any repairs?

14. What is the condition of the siding? Will the outside walls require periodic painting, or is it a permanent wall surface?

15. In what condition are patios, terraces, steps, fences?

16. How about door hardware and locks, and locksets? Are top-grade doors used? How well do they fit?

17. Is a good-quality roof cover used? What kind and how long will it last?

18. What color is the roof? Does it blend well with the house?

19. Are roof gutters installed for carrying off rainwater?

20. Inside the house, how does the carpentry look? Are there any nail pops or blemishes on interior wall surfaces?

21. What kind of floor cover is used in each room? What condition is it in?

22. Are top-grade windows used? What brand? Do they fit snugly, open and close smoothly, and feel solid? Do they leak water and air?

23. Is insulating glass used, or are there storm windows and doors?

24. How do chimneys and fireplaces draw? What about prefab fireplaces and chimney cleaning?

25. Are there adequate closets and storage, particularly attic and basement, and including cabinets and shelves, pegboard, and the like?

RATING AN OLDER HOUSE

Insulation ——————————————————————————

Exterior paint and siding ————————————————

——————————————————————————————

Roof condition and type ————————————————

Gutters and downspouts —————————————————

Rust showing outside, where —————————————

Rust showing inside, where ——————————————

Heating system and condition ————————————

Plumbing fixture conditions —————————————

——————————————————————————————

Type of plumbing pipes ——————————————————

Water pressure from faucets ————————————

Lighting condition ——————————————————————

Enough electrical outlets ——————————————

220-volt ————————————   Too many extension cords?——

Fireplace condition —————————————————————

Inside wallpaper and paint ————————————————————

Ceiling condition ————————————————————————

Storage space ——————————————————————————

Closets, size ————————————————————————————

Chimney condition —————————————————————————

Window condition ——————————————————————————

Storms and screens ————————————————————————

Kitchen cabinets and counters ————————————————————

————————————————————————————————————

Garage size ————————————————————————————

Termites ————————————   Structural condition —————————

Utility bills ——————————————————————————————

Property taxes ———————————————————————————

Hot-water-heater condition ————————————————————————

Landscaping —————————————————————————————

————————————————————————————————————

Dead trees, bushes —————————————————————————

Drainage away from house ————————————————————————

MECHANICAL EQUIPMENT WORKSHEET

1. Can you or a qualified expert determine that the heating plant in the house is the right size and in good condition, and in need of no or little maintenance and repair?

2. Is the insulation in walls, ceiling, and floors, including basement, adequate to reduce your heating bills in the winter?

3. What kinds of service contracts can the real estate salesman tell you about for your fuel supply?

4. Are the thermostats, the filters, and the noise of the fan acceptable to you and/or your expert?

5. Is there central air conditioning, or is there provision for its future installation?

6. If there is central air conditioning, does the system operate well and quietly? Is it of sufficient size for the job according to an expert in air conditioning?

7. Have you taken a close look at the reliability of any air-conditioning contractor who may be recommended to you to do that particular job?

8. Is the air-conditioning equipment a top national brand? Does it contain an approval seal of the Air Conditioning and Refrigeration Institute?

9. Is the air-conditioning equipment sufficient to maintain your house at a reasonable degree of coolness in the summer, at 50% relative humidity during the hottest summer weather?

10. Is there sufficient electrical capacity in the house, 150- to 200-amp service with 220- to 240-volt circuits for clothes dryers and water heaters?

11. Are there sufficient circuits and sufficient outlets in each room?

12. Can you determine the size of wiring in your electrical circuits, and whether your outside and base outlets in places like bathrooms or basements are grounded, so that you do not run a chance of shock in the presence of moisture in bathrooms or outside connections?

13. Are there automatic closet lights and indoor control of outside lights, including those for the garage?

14. What is the condition of the outlets and switches? Will you want to replace many of them with noiseless switches or no-shock outlets for safety for your children?

15. Is the size of your water heater adequate for your house and family (fifty gallons for a family of three, sixty-five gallons for a larger family)? Does it have a good recovery rate— making more hot water fast if everyone takes a shower within a relatively short time?

16. Can the water heater take the load of a large family plus a dishwasher and a clothes washer, all being used within the same relatively short period?

17. Can you set the thermostats on the water heater, or is it a job that must be done by the utility representative or an electrical contractor? Can he do it easily?

18. How old is the water heater, and how soon might you expect to have to replace it?

19. Is there sufficient water pressure at the highest use of water with most of the taps in the kitchen and bathrooms turned on to medium level?

20. Are there stains or chipping in basins and sinks?

21. Are there any problems in the flushing mechanism of toilets or in the operation of drains?

22. Is a special inspection necessary for some kind of septic-tank condition, or do you have city sewage collection and treatment?

23. Do the bathrooms require remodeling? Must you add a new full or half bath, and how difficult will that be given the water-supply lines, waste lines, and vent lines?

24. Is there a modern kitchen or one large enough for adequate remodeling so that the kitchen can perform all the functions you want it to?

RATING A COMMUNITY

Use this checklist to evaluate the nature of a community and access to things you expect or would like to have nearby. No house could be so located as to have everything for everybody, but the worksheet should help you determine how close the house you're considering comes to perfection for you.

Go over the list carefully, thinking about the importance of each item to your life-style. You don't want to wind up with a property that lacks access or proximity to too many things in the list. The more of this your house has within easy reach, the better off you will be in the long run, both for your own use and for any resale or estate value.

Schools

Elementary (rate them) (location) ——————————

Parochial ————————————————————

Private ——————————————————————

Secondary schools and high schools ⸺⸺⸺⸺

Parochial ⸺⸺⸺⸺⸺⸺⸺⸺⸺

Private ⸺⸺⸺⸺⸺⸺⸺⸺⸺

Number of pupils per class ⸺⸺⸺⸺⸺

Expansions and improvements planned ⸺⸺⸺

Comparison of teachers' salaries with other localities ⸺⸺

School transportation ⸺⸺⸺⸺⸺

Percentage of students who go on to college ⸺⸺⸺

Provisions in schools for:

Retarded ⸺⸺⸺⸺⸺⸺⸺⸺

Bright ⸺⸺⸺⸺⸺⸺⸺⸺⸺

Physically handicapped ⸺⸺⸺⸺⸺

Shopping facilities and location

Supermarkets ⸺⸺⸺⸺⸺⸺⸺

Department stores ⸺⸺⸺⸺⸺⸺

Drugstore ⸺⸺⸺⸺⸺⸺⸺⸺

Garage (AAA?) ⸺⸺⸺⸺⸺⸺

Package store ⸺⸺⸺⸺⸺⸺

Laundromat ⸺⸺⸺⸺⸺⸺⸺

Dry cleaner ⸺⸺⸺⸺⸺⸺⸺

Hardware/housewares ⸺⸺⸺⸺⸺

Lumberyard ⸺⸺⸺⸺⸺⸺⸺

Car wash ————————————————————————

Bookshop ————————————————————————

Barber/beautician ————————————————————

Travel bureau ————————————————————

Churches

Protestant ————————————————————————

Catholic ————————————————————————

Jewish temple ————————————————————

Other ————————————————————————

Activities for children

Library with facilities for children ——————————

Little League ————————————————————

Arts and crafts ————————————————————

"Y" and other youth centers ——————————————

Swimming pool ————————————————————

Tennis courts ————————————————————

Bowling alley ————————————————————

Skating rink ————————————————————

Transportation

Walking time to nearest bus ——————————————

Number of buses daily ————————————————

Car pools to work and return ——————————————

Driving time to nearest:

Shopping center ————————————————————————

Airport ——————————————————————————————

Commuter train ————————————————————————

Hospital ——————————————————————————————

Civic center ——————————————————————————

Church ——————————————————————————————

Other ——————————————————————————————

Adult recreation

Bowling alley ————————————————————————

Swimming (lake, ocean, pool) ——————————————

Library ——————————————————————————————

Craft shop ——————————————————————————

Civic center ——————————————————————————

Fishing ——————————————————————————————

Restaurants ——————————————————————————

Golf courses:

Public ——————————————————————————————

Private ——————————————————————————————

Tennis courts ————————————————————————

Movie theater ————————————————————————

Playhouse ——————————————————————————

Horseback riding ————————————————————————

Section II

Can you afford *not* to buy? Financing your home

Almost all homeowners in this country will tell you that you can't afford *not* to buy a house. "How could anyone pass up the opportunity to own his own home if he can possibly meet the monthly expenses?" they're likely to ask.

A homeowner with a fixed-rate mortgage on a good house has just about the best financial investment available today in the United States. In fact, in an inflationary economy like ours, where real estate appreciates in dollar value all the time, there is a gradual transfer of the saver's wealth (which is loaned to you through the mortgage) to the borrowing homeowner's real wealth.

Take a look at the following table from the *Savings and Loan News* of June 1978. The important line is the bottom line. You will see that the compound rates of return at a 10% inflation rate on this down payment go as high as 27.6%. There is no other legal way in this country to get that kind of return on your money. The homeowner has used the mortgage to leverage big gains on owning his own home. And his mortgage interest and property taxes are deductible from taxable income, which means that the effective cost of owning his home might be considered zero.

RETURN ON SINGLE-FAMILY-HOME DOWN PAYMENT

	Actual case		10% inflation case	
	Median priced home	Higher priced home	Median priced home	Higher priced home
1978 resale price	$42,900	$92,500	$52,100	$126,600
1968 purchase price	20,100	48,800	20,100	48,800
Appreciation	$22,800	$43,700	$32,000	$ 77,800
Compound rate of appreciation	7.9%	6.6%	10%	10%
1978 resale price	$42,900	$92,500	$52,100	$126,600
Balance due on loan	12,654	29,429	12,654	29,429
Cash realized	$30,246	$63,071	$39,446	$ 97,171
Down payment	$ 4,600	$ 8,500	$ 4,600	$ 8,500
Compound rate of return on down payment	20.7%	22.2%	24.0%	27.6%

The median-priced house's purchase price in 1968 was $20,-100. The down payment was just under 23%—$4,600. The mortgage amount was $15,500 at 8½%, twenty-five-year term.

The higher-priced house was priced at $48,800; $8,500 was put as a down payment, roughly 17½%, and the mortgage was for $40,300 at 8½% for twenty-one years. At the 10% inflation pace you can see that the return on the down payment at a compounded annual rate was 27.6%, figuring a rate of appreciation equal to the inflation rate of 10%. The rate of appreciation that good houses were experiencing in 1978 was as high as 13%.

The last column of the table means that $2,346 is the owner's gain in a year's time on his down payment of $8,500 (27.6% times $8,500). In eleven years the additional equity realized amounts to $88,671, money that will actually be transferred into cash when the house is sold.

Chapter 10

Homeownership versus Renting

Take a look at the next table. Let's say that in 1978 you were a family of four with an income of $24,000. You purchased a $50,000 home that year on which you have a mortgage of $40,000 for twenty five years at 9½%. Your monthly payment is $349.60, of which, at the end of the third year of ownership, $306.40 is your monthly interest charge, which is all deductible. Your yearly interest payments are $3,676.80, and your yearly property taxes are $2,100. That gives you a deductible item of ownership of $5,777 a year, or in your tax bracket of 28% a yearly tax saving of $1,618 ($135 per month).

With a monthly payment of utilities, amortization, and property taxes totaling $624.60, less the monthly tax saving of $135, your net monthly outlay for shelter is $489.60, versus rental at $480.

That is only the beginning. You have an equity buildup of $500 by the end of the third year, plus appreciation at a rate of 13% per year on a $50,000 house, which when compounded annually gives a house value of $72,150. This plus your equity buildup of about $500, and less the outstanding mortgage balance of $38,635, gives you a potential equity of $34,015. In the rental situation your equity is zero.

	Renting	Owning
Monthly payment	$400.00	$349.60
Utilities	80.00	100.00
Property taxes	—	175.00
	$480.00	$624.60

119

Yearly tax deductions

Mortgage interest	—	3,676.80
Property taxes	—	2,100.00
Deductible		5,777.00
Your tax bracket (28%) saving		1,618.00
Monthly tax saving	—	135.00
Net monthly outlay for shelter	480.00	489.60
Equity build up, third year	—	500.00
Appreciation, 13% per year	—	33,515.00
Total equity	—	$34,015.00

Of course, you could invest $10,000 at 10% per year an out with an equity position of about $14,000. But even subtracting closing costs from the potential equity of $34,000 in the house, the homeowner still comes out with twice the equity of the renter—assuming that the renter has the $10,000 in the first place. The estimate of appreciation of 13% per year is not out of phase with reality if you take the advice in this book.

If you are purchasing a house for the first time, cash flow may be a special problem. Since your federal income taxes are paid currently through withholding and payments of quarterly estimates, tax credits for interest paid when you purchase a house do not become available as cash until you receive your refund check from the U. S. Treasury. This usually happens twelve to eighteen months after purchase because of the once-a-year filing of final income tax returns. What happens is that your monthly mortgage payment check includes the money that you'll be refunded from your income tax return. With interest rates in the 10% range, this sum normally ranges between $1,500 and $3,000 before you "catch up."

HOW MUCH INTEREST WILL YOU *REALLY* PAY?

Not much, really. One way to look at it is this: in an economy inflationary at 10%, a 10% mortgage represents money borrowed at zero interest rate as measured by total payments in *constant* dollars.

Another way to look at it: the U.S. Congress has given a tax benefit to home purchasers by making the interest paid on mortgages deductible from taxable income. In today's political climate the chance that this tax policy will change is very small.

Because your mortgage interest is tax deductible, what you're really paying is considerably less than the interest rate on your loan. The following table, provided by the Mortgage Guaranty Insurance Comporation of Milwaukee, Wisconsin, shows what you really pay.

Finally, because of the rate at which houses change hands, most home mortgages in this country last no longer than seven years, which means that on your mortgage loan you'll pay only seven years of interest, not twenty-five or thirty.

WHY INFLATION MAKES HOMEOWNERSHIP YOUR BEST INVESTMENT

You have read or heard about houses appreciating in value, and you may know a number of instances of that happening to your neighbors or some other member of your family. The National Association of Realtors tells us that in 1979 all single-family houses, in homeownership, in the United States had appreciated in value at a compound interest rate of 7¼% on the average for the previous eighteen years. That is 7¼% *annually*. No other investment in this country has that kind of return, including gold.

As Will Rogers once said about land, "They aren't making any more of it." The import for the homeowner is that a good house on a desirable lot is a real asset in every sense of the word; it will not disappear or be wasted away by inflation. The land may be devalued if the community starts deteriorating badly, but that happens only rarely. So inflation has clearly made homeownership the best investment of all for the average American during the last two or three generations. The average American family has most of its equity in its residential real estate, greater than anything it has in savings, stocks and bonds, jewelry and silver, or life insurance.

The price of housing has risen rapidly since about 1965. You may have heard any number of times that the price of good housing just cannot keep going up and never slump or falter—something has got to give sometime. That idea needs some careful examination as you approach one of the major purchases of your life.

Since World War II, home buying, house prices, and the volume of mortgage lending have skyrocketed. That's a major rea-

AFTER-TAX COST OF MORTGAGE INTEREST PAID
MARRIED FILING JOINTLY*

Gross Income	Loan Interest								
	9.00%	9.50%	10.00%	10.50%	11.00%	11.50%	12.00%	12.50%	13.00%
$12,000	7.52	7.94	8.36	8.78	9.20	9.62	10.04	10.46	10.88
$15,000	7.38	7.79	8.20	8.61	9.02	9.41	9.82	10.23	10.65
$18,000	7.16	7.55	7.95	8.35	8.75	9.15	9.55	9.95	10.35
$22,000	6.93	7.32	7.70	8.09	8.47	8.65	9.03	9.41	9.79
$26,000	6.62	6.99	7.36	7.73	8.10	8.44	8.71	9.18	9.54
$30,000	6.34	6.69	7.04	7.39	7.74	8.09	8.44	8.80	9.15
$35,000	5.99	6.33	6.66	6.99	7.33	7.75	8.08	8.41	8.73
$40,000	5.57	5.88	6.19	6.50	6.81	7.11	7.41	7.72	8.02
$45,000	5.13	5.42	5.70	5.99	6.27	6.56	6.84	7.13	7.41
$50,000	5.11	5.40	5.68	5.96	6.25	6.53	6.82	7.10	7.38
$60,000	4.59	4.85	5.10	5.36	5.61	5.87	6.12	6.36	6.61

*The actual net interest rate varies with an individual's situation. The chart assumes a joint return is filed claiming two dependent children (four total exemptions); all income is from wages; $3,400 of itemized deductions other than the mortgage interest; and various amounts of interest paid. The tax rates used are effective as of January 1, 1979.

SINGLE INDIVIDUALS**

Gross Income	Loan Interest								
	9.00%	9.50%	10.00%	10.50%	11.00%	11.50%	12.00%	12.50%	13.00%
$12,000	7.08	7.48	7.87	8.26	8.66	9.05	9.44	9.84	10.23
$15,000	6.76	7.13	7.51	7.89	8.26	8.64	9.01	9.39	9.77
$18,000	6.37	6.73	7.08	7.43	7.79	8.14	8.49	8.85	9.20
$22,000	5.97	6.30	6.63	6.96	7.29	7.62	7.92	8.25	8.58
$26,000	5.72	6.03	6.35	6.67	6.99	7.31	7.63	7.95	8.17
$30,000	5.46	5.77	6.07	6.37	6.68	6.98	7.28	7.58	7.98
$35,000	5.04	5.32	5.60	5.88	6.16	6.44	6.72	7.00	7.28
$40,000	4.59	4.85	5.10	5.36	5.61	5.87	6.12	6.38	6.63
$45,000	4.55	4.80	5.05	5.30	5.56	5.81	6.06	6.32	6.57
$50,000	4.50	4.75	5.00	5.25	5.50	5.75	6.00	6.25	6.50
$60,000	4.50	4.75	5.00	5.25	5.50	5.75	6.00	6.25	6.50

**The actual net interest rate varies with an individual's situation. The chart assumes a single return is filed with no dependents (one exemption); all income is from wages; $2,300 of itemized deductions other than the mortgage interest; and various amounts of interest paid. The tax rates used are effective as of January 1, 1979.

son for some to think it can't last. Here are some of their negative arguments! The population in this country from 1890 to 1970 has increased at an annual compounded rate of 1.49%; the population per square mile, at an annual compounded rate of 1.26%; these increases have done nothing to justify the longtime rise in house prices. Another negative argument: Inflation does not justify the increase in house prices, particularly when inflation from 1890 to 1965 was less than 3% except in the years of World War I, World War II, and the Korean War.

However, almost all of the growth in homeownership and all of the major ongoing rise in price since 1890 occurred after World War II. Before then, a majority of Americans were too poor, given the financial instruments available at the time, to own their own homes. That was one reason for the stability in new one-family house prices from the Victorian era right up until after World War II. You also may recall that before World War II, politicians almost never talked about housing problems of the poor. It was only after World War II that a majority of us were able to achieve home-ownership with a long-term, fixed-rate, high-loan-to-value-ratio mortgage. Before that most mortgages ran only five to eight years with 50% down. With those terms, fewer than half of us could own our own homes.

Some have called our phenomena of home buying and price rises almost manic since World War II and have compared them to the tulip-bulb mania of the eighteenth century, when bulbs were bid up to astronomical prices and fell back disastrously—they had little real intrinsic value. But you can't compare the desire to buy houses with the desire to buy tulip bulbs. Housing is a ne-cessity; the other things are not required for the health, safety, and welfare of an individual.

It's true that our mortgage debt and house prices are rising much faster than stock prices, faster than any other segment of the economy, since World War II, and the rise has largely been in-dependent of the weakness of the stock market since 1965.

The percentage of houses mortgaged has increased from 27.7% in 1890 to 45.3% in 1940 and is somewhat less than 60% today.

Little wonder. The home-buying urge grows stronger all the time. About 6 million dwelling units were sold in 1977 and again in 1978, records both. Most single-family detached-house mort-gages are paid off in seven years, and the average life of all mort-gages is only twelve years. There is a huge rollover in that mortgage debt. It is not as though everything were being hocked for thirty years.

Take a closer look at house price rises. Compare median new-house sales prices to the median family income in this country: that ratio was 2.85 in 1949 and 2.87 in 1975 and is still around 3.0. In other words, house prices have kept pace, almost in lockstep, with median family income. The income of a typical U.S. family rose faster than inflation in 1976 for the first time since 1973, and almost 18% of all families made $25,000 or more.

Some people estimate that the number of people in poverty in this country, when you really measure everything, is fewer than 7 million. So we have an incredibly affluent population whose biggest hedge against inflation is buying and owning their own homes. About 42% of homeowners have no mortgages.

Nations with the highest homeownership are usually those nations that have the highest level of inflation. The United Nations tells us that Mexico and Australia in 1970 had a homeownership ratio of over 67% while ours then was only about 63%. Ours is now about 67%. Israel then had a homeownership ratio of 65%, and Latin American nations have higher homeownership ratios than such industrialized nations as Japan, Great Britain, Switzerland, Sweden, France, and West Germany—all because Latin American nations have had a high level of inflation for generations.

The price of housing reflects as much as anything else replacement costs, which set a ceiling on housing prices. If home building is intense, competition manages to hold prices down to realistic levels in most markets. But the housing market is not an entirely free market. Federal government actions—for example, making mortgage money less available (see Chapter 13)—can impede housing activity, which in a way artificially raises house prices by reducing the availability of dwelling units for sale; fewer new dwelling units are built to add to the housing stock that a growing population wants to live in.

The rise in house prices coincides exactly with the higher individual income tax rates that were imposed beginning right after World War II. To encourage homeownership, Congress has allowed deductibility of mortgage interest and property taxes, which has partly alleviated the bite of those higher tax rates.

In 1978 Congress passed a law that allows a homeowner selling his home a $100,000 tax-free gain, another profound incentive to homeownership. That tax-free gain is permissible after the age of fifty-five for a homeowner and once in a lifetime, if the house has been his residence for three of the previous five years. Throughout the life of the mortgage, the homeowner has been deducting mortgage interest and property taxes, so that gain has a significant impact on his future fortunes and perhaps those of his children.

Remember that these tax benefits do not accrue to people who rent. The appreciation through inflation accrues to an owner of a house, not a lender, and not a renter. It is the major incentive for people to own housing, especially as they contemplate their later years.

Something like 93% of all Americans are now living on less than 2% of our total landmass, and that makes a situation in which land values inevitably have gone up. They have risen steadily for the last seventy-five years, and there is no reason to suppose that that cycle need ever come to an end.

The average size of houses has increased substantially over the last twenty years. In southern California the average new-house square footage has increased by more than 60% since 1946, in spite of inflation, higher prices, land costs, and development costs. Yet 1977 was a record year for housing starts and so was 1978.

Since World War II, then, the majority of Americans have become affluent enough to own their own homes. Their incomes, through inflation, have kept pace with the rising cost of housing. The relationship between income and house cost promises to remain steady, so there is no reason why the home-buying trend shouldn't continue.

BEWARE THE PROPHETS OF DOOM—THEY'RE WRONG

I have given you a great many guidelines for the selection of your house, whether it be a dream house or something a lot closer to reality. As you search out that house, you will encounter people who will shake your faith in house value. In the event that any of them are convincing, perhaps you should come back and read over some of these points, especially the ones concerning how housing has made the American dream more possible than almost anything else.

What a professional investor has to say about his house gives a rare insight into the value of good residential property. Denis Kelly is an investment banker in New York City. Shortly after he bought a house for weekends and vacations a hundred miles north of the city, I asked him about his decision.

"My first notion of value in owning a house is not the house itself but rather the value of the houses and the property that surrounds whatever it is that you are buying. When we looked at this piece of property, we looked up the hill and down the hill. I took a walk up the lane to look at the other houses, and it was clear to us that the people in the immediate neighborhood had put a considerable amount of money into their houses. It was first of all a desirable neighborhood.

"Going out from the immediate neighborhood is the town. We looked at a number of towns up here. Values vary from town to town. Towns have reputations—this one has a reputation of having a lot of well-to-do people, pretty buildings, and a nice lake. It has an upper-class reputation. That connotes value.

"As far as the house is concerned, that is probably number three in my criteria for value. It is relatively unimportant, once you have established the other two, the neighborhood and the town. Those two really determine value, because you can't change them, but you can always change the structure. This house is not particularly well built. It was built inexpensively, except for the basement, which is well done, and the addition was reasonably well done. The main part is old and not well built, so the value of this house will be in how we remodel it for our own pleasure. But the other two factors will make this more valuable than what we paid for it and what we'll put into it.

"A very real element of value is in the contiguous property. Here I have only a half acre, but it is a half acre that enjoys increased value because of the land all around it."

I asked, "What about alternative investments that you might have made? You mentioned the value of the stock market."

"We took money out of the stock market, in which we had made some money, to put into this house. I am all out of the market. Before making this move I did a value analysis, you might say.

"What you have to do as a young person is to figure out first of all what kind of investor you are more than what kind of investment you want to make—whether or not you are a hot money person in the stock market. Do you want to turn things over fast, or are you the patient type? Are you the type that likes to take an investment and work with it and try to make something of it? I think we are probably in the last category. I'll take a house, do something to the house, keep it for five or six years, then get another one, maybe something more than we could afford before.

"I haven't invested in stocks in five or six years. It is very difficult to make money in the stock market. You have to be extremely lucky, and it takes an awful lot of time. Real estate investment takes time only to investigate an initial purchase. Then you either work with a house, or you sit on the house and sell it after some period of time—two, three, four years, depending upon how you financed it and what is happening to values. It is quite a different investment, because presumably it's appreciating all the time.

"Second, on a value analysis you can margin stocks 50%. The rates are quite good in margin borrowing at three-quarters to a point over the broker's rate, which is now [early 1979] 1% to 1¼% below the prime, now at 11¾%. So the broker's rate is 10¾%, plus ¾% [your borrowing rate over the broker's to buy on margin], plus 3½% to 4% commission. So in margin buying of stocks you put up half your own money, pay in effect about 15% interest on the balance you borrow, and pray that the stock will appreciate. That's a tough investment at best. You have to put up 50% of your own money.

"With an investment like this house, if you have reasonable credit, you can leverage 80% [that is, borrow 80% of the cost], and you can probably leverage more than that if you like. And the mortgage loan is at an effective rate of 10¾% only, actually less than the prime rate for the first time in history.

"Assuming a rate of inflation in the 10% category, if you leverage like that, it is literally not costing you anything to make that investment.

"There are monthly cash payments, but by the end of the year, with the inflation rate the way it is, it doesn't cost you anything to do it. If we really live in this house, whether we own it 100% or have zero equity, the appreciation is the same. So real estate is better because you can leverage it more, and to a young person that's the important thing. I am in my 'building risk' years— I can afford risk. Those are really the two alternatives we have: the stock market or buying property.

"You could look at homeownership and its alternatives in three ways. First is the homeowner's 'user' income derived from ownership, use, appreciation, and equity buildup in a house.

"Second is the potential rental income in owning residential property.

"Third is the alternative investment of dividend income and stock appreciation by investing in the stock market.

"Of the three, number one, the 'user' income, is far and away the greatest. And dividend income and stock appreciation are far and away the worst. If the Dow Jones Industrial Average had grown in real worth after 1965 as it did before then, it would now stand in excess of something like 2,600 or 2,700, instead of still being in the low 800 range.

"As we all know, rental income has been pretty much of a bust because you really can't get sufficient rents in most places, because of the political climate, to cover operating expenses, including amortization of mortgage, and still get any respectable return on your investment.

"So we come back to the 'user' income where the appreciation of real estate is running between 12% and 15% a year, where a 10% or 11% mortgage is essentially free money in the inflationary climate, and, with the tax deductibles of mortgage interest and property taxes, the effective cost of ownership is almost zero to anyone buying a house.

"But you have to remember that you don't buy a house like this just for investment. You buy this house for personal use, which costs you a percentage point a year or so, or whatever the purchase price was. If you were to keep books on this house, you would have to put a number on the use of this property. Would it cost me x dollars a month? You would add or subtract that amount, the same way you do with any other investment, to figure out what your return was.

"In other words, the prophets of gloom who compare residential values to the tulip-bulb mania in stocks a couple of hundred years ago are talking about something entirely different.

"The big difference between stocks and an asset like a house is that stocks are irrelevant to the underlying business. Obviously if a company wants to grow and it needs money, it has to sell stock. But somebody has to live somewhere. The question is what price are they going to pay to live here. So I already know that the house has value.

"There's no 'multiple' business in housing as there is in stocks. Houses don't sell in multiples. The real estate market and real estate developers work on a cash basis, a cash-flow basis—how much cash can I get out of this to do that? Stocks sell on a multiple basis. So by that very distinction the expectation of stock is what I mean by the multiple business; it is going to sell at sixteen or fifteen or twelve times next year's earnings. Real estate isn't bought and sold that way. It is sold on a basis of saying next year I can rent x units which will produce x amount of income, which is a totally different concept from an expectation over the discounted value of the future cash flows.

The value we attribute to stocks and commodity futures, for instance, are all things that don't have intrinsic value. They are very iffy because there is no use for any of them. At different times we value them differently, but there is no utilitarian purpose on the line. But if we run into a big recession, houses are still going to have value."

Chapter 11

How to Determine How Much You Can Afford to Spend on Housing

Most lenders will permit you to spend 35% of your net income per month for total housing expense, an expense that covers not just the mortgage but also your taxes, insurance, maintenance, and utilities. But that is no longer a hard-and-fast rule.

Some lenders suggest a rule of thumb of one-fourth of your gross income allowable for monthly housing expenses. But in many Western industrialized nations, middle-class families are spending over 50% of their gross income on monthly housing expense, and in this country the figure, as a percentage of gross income, has climbed from 25% to 34% for young first-time homebuyers.

The fact of the matter is that how much you can spend on monthly housing expense is flexible, depending upon you, your credit history, and your lender's experience of inflation and what it does to his mortgage portfolio.

In figuring out how much you can afford to spend, you should look at two things: the first cost of purchasing and all that that nvolves, and the ongoing monthly expense.

You are going to need professional help, you are going to need insurance, and there are a lot of other items, which are explained in this and the next two chapters. There are also some very useful worksheets in Chapter 14 that you may want to refer to now.

Part of the question of how much you can afford to spend on housing is the assurance that the mortgage loan will be there at the closing. To 99% of us the money needed for a mortgage is the largest amount of money we ever thought of getting. It is stunning the first time you contemplate the possibility that a house may cost anywhere from $60,000 to $160,000. Where on earth are you going to get that kind of money?

Well, you have a vision of the house you want, and you know that owning it is going to be a great inflation hedge; that, in effect, when you add it all up in a few years your house will have cost you nothing because of the buildup of your equity and appreciation. So to approach the problem of how you are going to afford that house, you have to think about how much per month, not how much total.

Although the rule of thumb is that a household pays 25% of its gross income for monthly housing expense, the fact of the matter is that monthly housing expense declines as a proportion of income over time. The first years of ownership always involve extra expenses for furnishings, lawn furniture, carpeting, and all the rest. Furthermore, your income rises slowly over time. The Department of Commerce tells us that the average American household spends only 15% or less of its income on monthly housing expense. The usual situation for first-time homebuyers, who may not have all the furnishings they are going to want, is that initially they spend about 30% of their net income on housing, but within five years that percentage drops to 22% or lower.

Actually, the household expense of the average American household is one of the lowest proportions of income of any nation in the world. In industrialized nations like Britain, West Germany, and Japan, a middle-class household, or family, spends from 35% to 45% of gross income on monthly housing expense and is happy to have a place to live.

Before getting too serious about looking for your house, and before you start sharpening your pencils to do a lot of arithmetic on your personal finances, the best advice is to see your own financial institution. I say "your own financial institution" because you may have an account at a local savings bank, a commercial bank, or a credit union, or you may have a good friend who is a mortgage banker. You can also talk to your insurance agent. They are all financial institutions, and every one of them, if they are in the home lending business, has a mortgage loan officer. The first thing you want to do is make an appointment to talk with your mortgage officer at your financial institution. Meet with him or her—then go house hunting.

KNOW THE BASICS

You would be well advised to know a fair amount about mortgages before meeting with your mortgage loan officer, because not all lending institutions offer a complete range of mortgage loans that are nationally available to prospective home purchasers. There are three basic types of mortgage loans: conventional (either noninsured or insured), FHA-insured, and VA-guaranteed.

Mortgage terms and the various conditions of a conventional mortgage are established by the lender. Down payments for conventional mortgages vary drastically, from 5% to 50%. Most lenders prefer to make conventional mortgages, because they are simpler to process. Many lenders make only conventional mortgages. This may mean that you will have to meet with more than one lender to get all the information you need and get the loan that fits your financial situation best.

On conventional mortgages with down payments ranging between 5% and 20% of the purchase price, lenders usually require private mortgage insurance, which adds 0.25% to the effective mortgage rate.

The second type of loan is an FHA-insured loan. The Federal Housing Administration insures mortgage lenders against default; it does not loan money. Without fear of loss through default, lenders are encouraged to make mortgage loans to applicants. FHA is a particular benefit to home purchasers who do not have large accumulations of savings or other assets and who might otherwise be refused a mortgage. FHA-insured loans can be obtained on both new and existing homes.

FHA-insured mortgages require smaller down payments and lower monthly payments than conventional loans. Currently, the FHA has set a 11½% ceiling on the mortgage interest rate and insures mortgages up to a maximum of $60,000 for a single-family house. But the borrower must also pay an additional 0.5% mortgage insurance premium. Only 3% down payment is required on any loan amount up to the first $25,000. On any amount in excess of $25,000, 5% is required for the additional down payment. Any mortgage can be determined in increments of $50.

The third type of loan is a VA-guaranteed loan. These loans, available only to veterans, carry the most favorable terms available at all times. There is no time limitation on obtaining a VA loan. Because VA guarantees the top portion—the first 20%—of the loan, private lending institutions have strong security positions in the loans and usually approve them with little hesitation. Currently VA mortgages have a limit of $100,000 and the interest rate is set at 9½%. There is no down payment requirement.

The guidelines that follow are oriented to the FHA underwriting process—what a mortgage loan officer does in getting you a mortgage. The procedure for conventional mortgages and VA-guaranteed mortgages closely follow this FHA underwriting process.

Since the FHA is not a mortgage-lending agency, application

must first be made to an FHA-approved lending institution, which then forwards the application to the FHA. After appraising the property, the FHA sets the mortgage amount it will insure.

The rule of thumb for lenders is that annual mortgage payments and property taxes shouldn't take more than 25% of gross annual income. If the down payment is a limit on what can be bought, you may have to settle for a less expensive house than you had originally thought.

There is yet another rule that you will run into when you first talk to your mortgage lending officer: although you may have sufficient down payment, and the monthly mortgage and property tax payments are less than 25% of your income, if you have a lot of recurring expenses there may still be a problem. Recurring expenses are defined as expense or installment accounts that will not be paid off in a ten-month period—such as alimony, child support, an automobile loan, a college education loan.

If the total of mortgage payment, property taxes, home insurance, and payments on long-term debt exceeds 33% of your annual income, the mortgage loan officer may not accept you for a loan. You can find all this out very readily by going to see him before you get serious about the houses you are interested in.

In that regard, if you are contemplating a long-term loan that covers something like an automobile or a college education, you should buy your house first if at all possible. The fact that you hold the deed to your house, even with a big mortgage or deed of trust (see the glossary) is far better collateral to any lender than anything else you have. You may be able to secure that long-term loan for an automobile or a college education at much lower rates than you would if you did not own a house. Truth-in-lending laws show you paying up to 21%, and perhaps even more, for department store loans. But you can borrow for cars, education, and other major big-ticket items, with your house serving as collateral, at considerably lower rates.

Another way the FHA figures how much mortgage loan you might qualify for is to use a qualification statement like the following. They compute the net effective income after federal withholding taxes and check that against the total housing expense. Total housing expense is defined as principal and interest, taxes, hazard insurance, mortgage insurance, heat and utilities, and maintenance. The housing expense should not exceed 35% of the net effective income. The total fixed payment should not be more than 50% of the net effective income to qualify for an FHA loan.

FHA Income Qualification

First qualification (35%)

Gross monthly income	$1,500.00
Less federal withholding taxes	195.40
Net income per month	1,304.60
Percent allowable for total housing expense	x35%
Maximum amount available for housing expense	$ 456.61 (1)

Housing expense

Principal and interest	$ 249.36
FHA insurance premium	12.32
Taxes	25.00
Hazard insurance	10.00
Maintenance	13.00
Heat and utilities	83.00
Total housing expense	$ 392.68 (2)

Second qualification (50%)

Net income per month	$1,304.60
Less Social Security, state, city taxes (9% of gross)	135.00
Net effective income per month	1,169.60
Percent allowable for home and other recurring charges	×50%
Maximum amount available for housing and other recurring charges	$ 584.80 (3)

FHA guidelines state that the purchaser's total housing expense plus his recurring charges (any installment debts having twelve months or more remaining; any revolving charge accounts, regardless of how few payments remain) cannot exceed 50% of his net effective income per month.

Total housing expense	$ 392.68
Plus recurring charges	100.00
	$ 492.68 (4)

To qualify: (1) must be higher than (2), and (3) must be higher than (4).

Example:

Sale price	$30,000	Married—two children
Closing cost	700	Earnings per month $1,500
Total acquisition cost	30,700	1,200 square feet/GFA furnace
Down payment	1,050	1 story—less than 30 years old
Mortgage amount	29,650	Recurring expenses $100/month

In this calculation FHA includes Social Security taxes and state and city taxes. Most FHA offices use a factor of 9% of your income to represent this total. Just ask your mortgage loan officer what the factor is for your area.

If the net remaining income, per month per person, is no lower than $200, you may qualify for an FHA loan. That is a conservative standard, and you might well want to try that arithmetic yourself to see if you qualify.

At the close of your interview with your mortgage loan officer, you may want to ask for a loan application form and have him go over it with you.

AN AMORTIZATION SCHEDULE—BIG INTEREST UP FRONT

Amortization refers to the putting aside of money at intervals for gradual repayment of a debt or a mortgage. A level of amortization schedule is one in which the total of interest and principal payments is the same every month.

The amortization schedules show interest and principal payments for three different amounts of mortgage loans for two interest rates, as well as the balance still owed. The monthly payment is the sum of the principal and interest for each of the mortgage loan amounts. You can see that in the opening years of the loan almost all of the payment is in interest; not until the loan is nearly ten years old do the principal payments really become of any great significance. Because most single-family home mortgage loans last no more than seven years, we have not continued this schedule up to its full twenty-five years.

You can see that in today's inflationary climate the increase in equity in the opening years of a mortgage at 9¾% is minimal. Most of the value increase in a house is in market appreciation, which amounts to many times what the buildup of equity (by paying off the mortgage) amounts to. Appreciation on good single-family detached housing, at the time of this writing in the late 1970's, was running between 10% and 15% per year in the United States.

Bear in mind that a 9¾% rate on a $50,000 mortgage loan for twenty-five years (a house priced at roughly $62,500 with a 25% down payment) produces a monthly payment for amortization alone of $446 a month. If that loan were at 6½%, which was the mortgage rate when our inflation rate was below 3% back in the mid-60's, your monthly payment for the same loan would be $338. The

Here's what two amortization schedules look like for twenty-five-year mortgage loans with fixed payments

9¾% Interest Rate

Amount of mtg. loan $40,000

Year	Mo.	Int.	Princ.	Bal.	Int.	Princ.	Bal.	Int.	Princ.	Bal.
						$50,000				$70,000
0	1	$325	$32	$39,968	$407	$40	$49,961	$569	$55	$69,945
3	0	314	42	38,676	393	53	48,346	550	74	67,684
5	0	306	51	37,555	382	64	46,944	535	90	65,722
8	0	288	68	35,406	361	86	44,257	505	120	61,960
10	0	274	83	33,582	342	104	41,977	479	146	58,768

11½% Interest Rate

Amount of mtg. loan $40,000

Year	Mo.	Int.	Princ.	Bal.	Int.	Princ.	Bal.	Int.	Princ.	Bal.
						$70,000				$100,000
0	1	$391	$16	$39,984	$684	$28	$69,972	$976	$40	$99,960
3	0	377	30	39,000	659	53	68,250	941	75	97,500
5	0	370	37	38,120	648	64	66,710	924	92	95,300
8	0	359	48	36,360	500	112	63,630	856	160	90,900
10	0	334	70	34,800	589	123	61,000	841	175	87,000

difference between the two monthly payments is clearly the ravages of inflation.

The following table shows what your monthly payments would be for different amounts and interest rates.

HOW BIG A DOWN PAYMENT?

Obviously, if you are conservative in your financial affairs you want to make as large a down payment as possible to reduce your monthly payments on interest and principal for any mortgage you get. The drawback with a large initial down payment is that you "lose" some of the tax advantages; you pay less interest and thus deduct less from taxable income. Another disadvantage—and this is a little bit farther out—has to do with losing some "leverage" on borrowing money at a fixed interest rate while your house appreciates: inflation makes the lowest down payment provide you with the greatest return on your investment because, after the first month of mortgage payments, you're paying back *increasingly devaluing* dollars, or less and less real money.

The $10,000 you pay back in 1988 will have only, say, $5,800 in buying power. But your income will have kept pace with inflation, so that the $10,000 will come to you more easily in 1988. That's why, most of the time, people are smart to maximize their mortgages.

There are exceptions. You shouldn't maximize when you're close to retirement and an inflation-resistant income is not certain. And you shouldn't when you face a serious disability or other severe cut in income.

But a higher down payment is the conservative policy and leads to a faster payoff of the total loan so that at some time, if major trouble should strike, you can own your home free and clear well before the twenty- to twenty-five-year term of your mortgage. Your house then will probably represent your largest equity, as it does for a majority of American families.

One of the best ways to increase a down payment; or accumulate one in the first place, is to visit your local bank or savings and loan and talk to one of its financial counselors about your problem. The institution will almost always be happy to work out a budget of monthly payments for your savings to build up that down payment, so that within only a few years you may have sufficient capital to purchase a house and secure the mortgage from the very bank at which you have been saving. The bank will look

ESTIMATING MONTHLY MORTGAGE PAYMENTS

(Figures are for interest and principal only. They *do not* include money in escrow which is put aside monthly to pay annual property taxes and insurance premiums.)

Mortgage Interest Rate	9%			10%			11%			12%		
Number of years of loan	20	25	30	20	25	30	20	25	30	20	25	30
$20,000	$180	$168	$161	$193	$182	$176	$204	$196	$191	$220	$211	$206
$25,000	225	210	201	241	227	219	255	245	238	275	263	257
$30,000	270	252	241	290	273	263	306	294	286	331	316	309
$35,000	315	294	282	338	318	307	357	343	333	386	369	360
$40,000	360	336	322	386	363	351	408	392	381	441	421	412
$45,000	405	378	362	434	408	395	459	441	429	496	474	463
$50,000	450	420	402	483	454	439	510	490	476	551	527	515
$55,000	485	462	443	531	500	483	561	539	524	606	579	566

$60,000	540	504	483	580	546	527	612	589	572	661	632	618
$65,000	585	546	523	628	591	571	662	638	619	716	685	669
$70,000	630	588	564	676	636	615	713	687	667	771	737	720
$75,000	675	630	604	724	682	659	764	736	714	826	790	772
$80,000	720	672	644	773	727	703	815	785	762	881	843	823
$85,000	764	714	684	821	773	747	866	834	810	936	895	875
$90,000	810	756	725	869	818	791	917	883	857	992	948	926
$95,000	855	798	765	918	864	834	968	932	905	1,046	1,001	978
$100,000	900	840	805	966	909	878	1,019	981	953	1,102	1,053	1,029

more kindly on someone applying for a mortgage if the savings have been built up by monthly payments in their own accounts.

These bank plans are tailored to fit your own financial ability and your particular goals. If your goals seem to be too high, the counselor at the bank will usually try to lower your sights to something easier to achieve. Then, with private mortgage insurance, you can, at a good thrift institution, buy a house with only 5% down, with a private mortgage insurance company insuring the top 15% to 20% of the mortgage loan. If a 5% or 10% down payment is your goal, you may be able to reach it within two years, sometimes even within a year if you really save in earnest.

But start with your local thrift institution's financial counselor. Your savings can be regular passbook savings, a special coupon book, a monthly reminder from the bank, a payroll deposit made by your employer, or an automatic transfer from a checking account to a savings account.

When you buy anything on an installment plan, you have to pay interest; in a savings account worked out for a down payment goal at a thrift institution, you will receive interest.

Usually, when you have accumulated your down payment, you are eligible for an early commitment on a mortgage loan from the same bank. The financial counselor may advise you sixty days prior to your reaching a down payment goal that you are approaching the time when a commitment may be made, and you can start things rolling with your builder or real estate broker for that final closing.

THE PROFESSIONALS YOU NEED

Rule number one: Do not get involved in the purchase or sale of real estate without the guidance and counsel of an attorney. Certainly it is possible to transfer real estate properly, and in sound fashion, without an attorney. It is also possible to pull one of your own teeth, but who would recommend it? While a realtor may be well versed in certain aspects of the law pertaining to real estate, he is not a lawyer and should not attempt to advise you on legal matters.

There can be many complications and complexities attending the transfer of real estate, considering all the contracts and documents involved. Your best bet is to have yourself covered from the very beginning.

If you are moving to a distant town, you can have your local legal counsel recommend someone to handle the sale in the town in which you are going to buy a house. It is always good practice to use a lawyer in the community where your purchase is being made. And a good lawyer is not confined just to seeing that contract terms are fair—he or she should also be useful to you in matters such as title search and title insurance, as well as the adjustment of any monies involved in taxes, utilities and the like. A mortgage loan officer usually insists on title insurance, but even if he doesn't, you will probably want it.

If you don't know a good real estate lawyer, don't call the local bar association for advice. They automatically lump the good with the bad and won't tell you the difference. Instead, call your mortgage loan officer. He or she should be happy to recommend several reputable attorneys who specialize in real estate. Whatever you do, don't pick one out of a hat.

The services of an attorney add to your cost. Ask him at the outset what his fee is for representing you in the sale of your present property. You may also want him to represent you, or to arrange for an out-of-town attorney to represent you, in the purchase of your new property. He should be able to give you a fairly close estimate of what legal expenses will be and what your other out-of-pocket costs might be for such things as the recording of documents.

You also need to talk to your tax consultant and insurance agent. The consultant will advise you on tax implications in the sale of property as well as in the move you are about to make. To obtain maximum tax advantages, or to avoid tax liability, provide him with accurate records and receipts of capital expenditures you have made on your house. He can help you work out the optimum program for your income tax return. He can also assist you in the orderly accumulation of evidence necessary to establish maximum deductions with regard to your moving expenses. Also, if you have been using tax consultants regularly for your income tax work, you may want him to assist you in contacting a new consultant in your new city.

Your insurance agent must be consulted on the termination of your homeowner policy. Obviously, you do not want to terminate your insurance protection while you still may have an interest in the property. The normal time for termination is at closing or actual transfer. Even if the buyer is assuming your mortgage, your insurance agent should advise you how you might be protected by having your name on the new buyer's policies "as your interest may appear." This means that if you retain secondary liability on the mortgage, you would be protected in the event fire destroys the property.

The insurance agent's role becomes more important with regard to the move itself. He should see that you are personally protected and that your property is protected during transit and relocation. Prior to the actual move itself, it's essential that you have a conference with your insurance agent to ascertain proper coverage during the limbo days when you and your property are en route. He can also assist you in locating an agent in your new city and in helping you make certain that you are immediately and properly covered upon your arrival there.

OTHER INSURANCE

All lenders require, and you should want, hazard insurance, a policy that protects the house and its contents against disasters such as fire, wind, and theft. It may also provide personal liability protection to cover injuries to other persons while on the property, insurance for other buildings, such as garages or sheds, and money for your temporary living expenses in the event that damage makes your house uninhabitable. While this coverage is broad, it is important that you understand that it is limited to certain hazards spelled out in the policy.

The basic protection, of course, is to the house itself, and the most serious hazard covered in a typical homeowner's policy is fire. The policy offers protection against other dangers, including windstorm or hail, riot or civil disturbance; damage from aircraft or other vehicles, smoke, glass breakage, or falling objects; weight of ice, snow, or sleet; building collapse; accidents in plumbing, heating, or electrical systems; and theft. In most cases this coverage is not unconditional. The exceptions are enumerated in the policy, and sometimes they can be very technical.

In addition to specific exceptions, all policies have general exclusions, the most common of which are damage caused by war or insurrection, nuclear radiation, earthquakes and mudslides, the backing up of sewers, and floods.

Perhaps second in importance only to fire insurance is protection against theft. Here again you must understand what is covered and what is not.

Basically, there are two kinds of coverage: unscheduled personal property, which is included in the overall policy, and scheduled personal property, which is optional at additional cost. Unscheduled property is that which is not listed separately.

Under the basic terms of the policy, unscheduled personal

property is covered for a percentage, generally 50%, of the coverage on the dwelling itself. If the house is insured for $60,000, the contents are automatically insured for $30,000. (The maximum payment if house and contents were totally destroyed would be $60,000.)

There are limits on this protection too, however. Payment for jewelry, for example, may be limited to $500. For this reason, expensive items such as jewelry and furs should be listed on a separate schedule. This accomplishes two purposes: it provides adequate protection for the valuables, and it releases more of the blanket coverage under the unscheduled property clause for other items. Cost for this coverage varies from area to area, depending on factors such as crime rates.

Personal property covered by a homeowner's policy is also (again with certain exceptions) protected against loss when it is off the premises. For example, a set of golf clubs or a fur coat stolen from an automobile, though not covered by automobile insurance, may be protected by the homeowner's policy if the thief had to make forcible entry into the car.

Many homeowners overlook an elementary point about insurance: you cannot file a claim if you do not know what has been taken or destroyed. One of the first things you should do after settling in a new house is take inventory. Go through the house room by room and make a list of everything of value—clothes, furniture, appliances, jewelry, and so on. Include such things as date of purchase, model number, and price. Keep a copy of all this information away from the house, at an office or in a safety deposit box. It won't do you any good if it is burned or stolen.

At the time of house purchase, your lender will probably make sure that you are not underinsured, since he wants his investment fully protected. His interest, however, is limited to the amount of the loan. He does not share in any appreciation. The lender wants to be sure that money will be available to make the loan payments or pay off the remaining balance if some disaster befalls the house.

Since the lender's interest in the house declines as the loan is paid off, it is up to you to make sure that your insurance keeps up with inflation in property values and construction costs. Review the insurance every two or three years. If in doubt about its adequacy, increase the coverage a bit. You may be overinsuring, but an extra $1,000 of coverage costs only a few dollars, a small price for a little peace of mind.

Coverage for at least 80% of replacement cost is necessary to assure full payment of losses up to the limits of the policy. If coverage drops below 80%, the company will not pay the full cost of repair or replacement. Payment will be limited to the cash value of the part of the building damaged or destroyed—replacement cost less depreciation—or a portion of the replacement cost equal to the ratio of the total amount of insurance purchased to 80% of the replacement cost. In effect, you become a co-insurer.

How about flood and crime insurance? In the past, flood insurance was virtually impossible to obtain, except at very high cost, because the only people who wanted it were those living in flood-prone areas and were thus high-risk cases. In such cases the basic principle of insurance—spreading the cost of losses over a large number of policyholders, most of whom will not have claims—does not work. To fill this gap for flood-endangered property, the federal government stepped in. The government agreed to subsidize the cost of flood insurance in those qualifying cities that adopted building codes and zoning regulations to prevent unrestricted development in flood-prone areas.

A homeowner interested in this insurance must first find out if his city has qualified for the program. His real estate agent, mortgage lender, or insurance agent may know. If the city has qualified, the homeowner must find an insurance agent who is willing to handle the special flood insurance, since the government does not sell the policies itself. A new $10 minimum commission may soften agents' resistance to the program.

The federal government also has a crime insurance program to provide protection to homeowners, as well as commercial property owners, who have been unable to buy burglary and robbery insurance because of a high incidence of crime in their neighborhoods.

Residential coverage may be purchased in amounts up to $10,000. The premium varies according to the crime rate. In the highest crime areas, the annual cost of a $10,000 robbery-burglary policy is $80. To be eligible for this insurance, a homeowner must take certain protective measures, such as the use of deadbolts or self-locking dead latches on all nonsliding exterior doors.

Chapter 12
Your Monthly Energy and Tax Bills

Property taxes used to be the major concern of homeowners after making their monthly mortgage payment. In a great many places today, in January and February, fuel or electric bills that run as high as mortgage payments, and higher, have become commonplace. Those monthly energy bills are as important to the mortgage lender as they are to you, the prospective buyer. So anybody buying a house today must be conscious of the fact that energy is going to cost a lot of money and that whoever sells him his house is going to have to deal in one way or another with the problem. Today, by law, builders must disclose in sales contracts "the type, thickness and R-value of the insulation that will be installed in each part of the house to comply with Federal Trade Commission regulations."

In Portland, Oregon, a law is in force that requires all houses to meet certain energy requirements before they can be sold. The California Energy Commission is encouraging insulation without force of legislation, but the matter has even come up before the U.S. Congress.

In the fall of 1980 the United States adopted a new Building Energy Performance Standard for new housing, a super standard on energy efficiency. And the 95th Congress in 1978 passed the National Energy Conservation Policy Act, which put utilities in a central position of advising homeowners on energy efficiency in existing housing. Utilities must offer all their customers a home energy audit. If a customer accepts the utility's audit offer, an inspector recommends improvements that will ease energy use and provides the homeowner with lists of lenders willing to finance improvements.

The problem for all of us, in new houses or old, is to keep energy costs within reasonable bounds by owning an energy-efficient house.

145

The following table was used by FHA and VA offices in Cincinnati in 1978 (you could double the figure for 1980) to figure the monthly costs of maintenance, heating, and utilities for one- and two-story houses thirty years old or older and the costs of heating and utilities for houses less than thirty years old. If a house is heated by oil, for instance, all of the costs of heating and utilities (including electricity for appliances) come under the column headed "oil." You can see that the heating and electric costs for a 2,500-square foot two-story house thirty years old or older, heated by oil, would be $169 a month. You would add $50 a month for maintenance of the house.

For houses less than thirty years old, figures for electric heating are given, and no figures for maintenance, since maintenance is not usually significant in early years.

Lenders—both those using VA-guaranteed or FHA-insured mortgages and conventional lenders using the same table—view those heating and utility costs as very real issues in underwriting or making mortgages. Obviously, the table is not for energy-efficient houses but for existing houses, most of which are not as energy efficient as they could easily be.

Perhaps the best way to approach the problem of energy costs is to examine what you and a builder might do when planning for a new house. In new construction, energy requirements can be cut up to 50% from what might have been done ten or fifteen years ago; in older houses, remodeling can at best cut energy requirements up to about 40%.

If the house you are buying is an existing house, you should ask for the utility bills for the previous twelve months. A serious seller or realtor should be able to furnish that information easily.

If you are not completely comfortable in your own diagnosis of a heating system and what it's likely to cost you next February, get some expert advice. No book on the subject can analyze the problems you may have in a particular house on a particular property.

DETERMINING YOUR ENERGY COSTS

This is a difficult and not very accurate process, because differing life-styles can make costs in one house be twice as much or more in an identical house, and many data, such as degree days, are often inaccurate, may not apply during a particularly harsh or mild season, or may be subject to sometimes misleading interpretations.

MONTHLY MAINTENANCE, HEATING, AND UTILITY COSTS

Sq. ft	Homes 30 years or older						Homes less than 30 years old					
	1-story			2-story			1-story			2-story		
	Maint.	Gas	Oil	Gas	Oil	Maint.	Gas	Oil	Elec.	Gas	Oil	Elec.
700	$15	$59	$61	$54	$67	$14	$54	$67	$54	$51	$66	$53
800	19	62	65	56	72	17	56	72	47	54	70	55
900	20	66	69	59	76	19	59	76	62	56	75	60
1,000	22	70	74	64	81	20	62	81	66	59	80	64
1,100	24	72	80	67	89	22	66	89	70	62	87	67
1,200	25	76	85	70	94	23	69	94	75	66	89	73
1,300	28	80	91	84	100	25	72	100	78	69	97	77
1,400	29	83	96	76	105	26	76	105	83	72	102	81
1,500	32	86	100	80	110	31	78	110	87	76	108	84
1,600	33	88	107	83	119	31	81	119	91	78	114	87
1,700	35	92	112	84	124	32	84	124	94	81	119	88
1,800	36	92	118	87	131	34	87	131	98	84	125	92
1,900	39	100	122	89	135	36	91	135	103	87	131	98
2,000	41	102	128	94	138	37	95	138	108	91	135	102
2,100	43	105	133	98	144	39	97	144	113	95	139	108
2,200	45	108	138	103	152	40	100	152	119	97	146	113
2,300	48	113	143	106	158	43	103	158	124	98	152	122
2,400	52	117	147	110	164	46	109	164	130	103	157	128
2,500	55	121	153	114	169	50	113	171	135	109	164	133

The British thermal units (Btu) in a given amount of fuel delivered to the house do not translate directly into a proportional amount of heat. A striking example is the heat pump. No matter how cold the outside air, there's always some heat in it. The heat pump captures it and pumps it indoors to keep you warm. It's like a conventional air conditioner in reverse. In fact, during hot weather, the heat pump changes direction and pumps heat out of your house to keep you cool. It's a heating and air-conditioning unit all in one.

Very often an electrically powered heat-pump system is cheaper to operate, year-round, than oil-fired heat and electric air conditioning. The cost of electricity "through the meter" may be two or three times the cost of fuel oil "in the tank" per Btu, but on a useful basis inside the house, electricity may be quite close to the cost of fuel oil. You may want to consider having a heat pump, which can use as little as one-third to one-half as much energy as an electric-resistance heating system.

With any electric heating system no hot flue gases are lost up the chimney as there are with fuels that must be combusted within the house to produce heat. That means that because of increased efficiency, the difference between the operating cost of electricity and that of other fuels such as gas is not as great as it might appear to be when measured through the meter.

Even the experts disagree on the precision of energy-use calculations. For instance, "useful" heat is what you actually experience inside the house when the heating system is operating. But useful heat, or heat felt in the house divided by the total Btu heat content of the energy being consumed by your heating system, varies with both fuel type and system design.

The Btu heat content of energy used in the heating system is what the engineers tell us is theoretically there when the energy comes through the meter, out of the tank or the pipe—electricity, oil, or gas. Because of such things as heat loss up the flue, a natural-gas heating system may have a useful heat of 0.6 (what you actually feel divided by Btu content of natural gas through the meter). An electric heat-pump system, collecting heat from a large mass of air, may have a useful heat of up to 1.6. The useful heat actually varies depending upon fuel type, equipment type, distribution system, time of year, geographical location, control systems, and occupant habits.

Over 30 million Btu per year consumed on site in a residence is in the form of electricity. Much of this energy serves as useful space heating. The energy required to operate things like pumps and blowers should be considered as heating system input energy.

Here, for example, is how useful heat can be used to calculate energy costs, starting with basic data.

Energy system or source	Heat unit	Btu/heat unit	Assumed useful heat
Natural gas	Therm	100,000	0.6
No. 2 fuel oil	Gallon	138,000	0.50
Electricity			
Direct resistance	Kilowatt	3,413	1.41
Electric furnace	Kilowatt	3,413	.9
Heat pump	Kilowatt	3,413	varies 1.3–1.8

Let's say that you want your house to have an inside temperature of 68 degrees in cold weather, and that it takes 10,000 Btu per hour for twenty-four hours to keep it that way. That works out to 240,000 Btu. If you were using No. 2 fuel oil with a useful heat of 0.50, you would need 480,000 Btu worth of fuel oil, or 3.47 gallons (138,000 Btu per gallon), and if the oil cost $0.50 a gallon, it would cost you $1.73 per day to heat your house.

If you were using an electric heat-pump system with a useful heat of 1.6, you would need only 150,000 Btu. If your electric rate is $0.035 per kilowatt-hour, 150,000 Btu divided by 3,413 (Btu per kilowatt) times $0.035 equals $1.53 for one day's heating electricity. In this example, it's cheaper than oil.

PROPERTY TAXES

The other big item in your monthly housing expense—besides your mortgage amortization payment—is your property taxes. Amortization is likely to stay level, or, under newer forms of mortgages, like graduated-payment mortgages, go down slightly; but property taxes are likely, almost certain, to rise over time.

An increase in taxes is least likely if the house you buy is in an established area where few or no new services and new schools are needed. It is most likely in a growing area or a new development. If new schools, new roads, new sewers, and other such facilities are needed, taxes will go up, and you must pay your share. It's as simple as that. The greater the local growth expected, the greater the future tax increase to be expected.

Generally, property taxes are now 1% of the market value in new suburban fringes, and they are not likely to increase by more than 0.5% or 0.75% per year. And that increase would not last forever, just as it did not in California; Proposition 13 cut that levy back to 1% all over the state.

An across-the-board hike in local real estate taxes is generally the way you pay for expanded services, such as more police and fire protection or new schools. In addition, there may be special assessments levied on property owners to pay for capital improvements such as new water mains, sidewalks and curbs, street paving, garbage collection, even streetlights and fire hydrants, and, usually most expensive of all, a new sewer system. Not all of these can be foreseen, but remember that they are not arbitrary decisions by government officials, rather the result of vocal public demand.

In this regard, Texas is a state with an interesting situation: it has municipal utility districts which can be funded by private bond issues paid off by consumers' paying for tapping on of sewer and water for new housing. Sometimes those tap-on fees can be very high. They usually crop up only in newly developed areas, but they can be an unexpected burden.

Being hit with a series of increases in your tax bill can make things financially difficult for you, especially if they come on top of homeownership bills that are already as high as your income will allow. Realistically, it is a good idea to allow a cushion in your budget to pay for possible tax hikes if you buy a house in a new development or a rapidly growing area. If you examine the tax records of the past twenty years at the courthouse, you can see what might be expected in your area. If there is a pattern of great increases in property taxes per year, you will want to find out why.

A visit to the local tax assessor's office can also shed light on the prospects for new taxes. Ask him how much the local real estate taxes are expected to rise in the near future and what the likelihood of special assessments in the area is. Don't be fooled if someone tells you taxes can't go up because there's a legal ceiling on the tax rate. New services cost money, and the local government can boost taxes by hiking all assessments without changing the tax base.

Inflation affects your property taxes greatly too; property is periodically reevaluated, and inflation can drive the value way up until your community reaches the point California reached just before Proposition 13.

Chapter 13

Mortgage Credit— The Essential Ingredient

To most people now, the question is not so much "What will the interest rate on a mortgage be?" but rather, "Will I be able to get a mortgage?" The answer, happily, is yes, you will be able to get mortgage money, even when the interest rate is higher than a cat's back, as long as the federal government does not radically alter the present structure of the mortgage market. While possible, it's not likely to happen.

In the years ahead there will be times when getting a mortgage of the size you need may be fairly tough, no matter how qualified you may be. You should know why cycles of mortgage availability come and go, and why mortgage rates rise and fall, so that you can adjust your purchasing moves if you have to. This also means that you must know about usury laws in some states.

Historically, money to finance home loans in the United States has come largely from commercial banks, thrift institutions, and insurance companies. Although thrift institutions, commercial banks, and life insurance companies are similar in some respects, the latter two are more diversified in their operations than thrift institutions and have more investment opportunities available to them. Thrift institutions—especially the savings and loan associations—were created as specialized lenders: they are largely regulated to serve the mortgage market, the financing of homes, apartment houses, shopping centers, and other kinds of real estate developments.

A related type of business that fulfills a key role in the home finance industry in the United States is that of the mortgage company or the mortgage banker. He brings together those who have money and those who need money. Among other things, this helps satisfy the requirements of capital-surplus areas of the country for investment opportunities and the needs of capital-deficient areas for investment funds. A mortgage banker characteristically has

151

business contacts with several different institutions in various places which have funds to invest in mortgages. He channels their investment funds into houses, apartment buildings, and other kinds of construction projects, depending upon the needs of the borrower and the investment wishes of the institution.

All of these enterprises dealing in mortgage money have one thing in common: they are subject to periodic fluctuations in the cost of money. This in turn causes distortions in money availability, which affects the number of loans that can be made.

A period of higher interest rates generally means that the diversified institutions—the commercial banks and insurance companies—can make more money by putting their funds in investments other than mortgages. For savings and loans, higher interest rates generally mean that savers put their money elsewhere. (Savings and loan associations are limited by regulation as to the rate of interest that can be paid on savings.) This means the flow into savings decreases, and this important source of funds for home loans is unable to meet the demand.

The mortgage market includes all financial institutions that make mortgage loans. The market has two main categories, primary and secondary. The primary mortgage market is the one in which actual mortgage transactions are made between borrowers and the initial, or primary, lender. This market serves to bring together those looking for mortgage money to buy a house and those wishing to invest their money. In the secondary market, mortgages are bought and sold after their origination in the primary market. Mortgages may be sold through participation with other lenders, by themselves as marketable securities, or as the backing for marketable securities.

The secondary market provides a means for holders of mortgages to sell part of their mortgage holdings to get more money to buy additional mortgages. It therefore enables investors in areas of the country having surplus funds to help finance mortgages in regions where funds are in tight supply. In most cases, the homeowner continues to make payments to the lender who made the loan in the first place. The lender passes this money on to the investor who has purchased the mortgage, and collects a fee for servicing.

In brief, the secondary mortgage market affords the opportunity to lend long (in mortgages) even with funds that are secured on a short-term basis (through savings, demand deposits, and other short-term time funds). It can then sell off in the secondary market its long-term mortgages while retaining the originating fees plus maintaining an income as servicer of the mortgages.

Essential to understanding the secondary mortgage market is understanding the investment characteristic of the home mortgage. A mortgage is an investment; it is written so that the original issuer expects a return on the advanced funds, plus a profit. A mortgage can be bought or sold.

Four types of institutions—savings and loan associations, commercial banks, insurance companies, and mutual savings banks—supply more than 70% of all mortgage credit for the primary mortgage market. The rest comes from trust companies, pension funds, mortgage investment companies, credit unions, state financing and development agencies, federal agencies, fraternal and benevolent organizations, assessment associations, trustees of union funds, individual trustees, corporate trustees, endowment funds, foundations, estates, and individuals. These same sources of primary mortgage credit also operate in the secondary mortgage market, selling the loans they originate and service to raise money to make more primary loans.

Let's look at state usury laws. These laws, which establish ceilings on the interest rates home purchasers can pay for mortgages in the name of "consumer interest," are idiotic. They prevent citizens living in states with such laws from being able to borrow the money they need for home purchases at a time that may be most opportune. All should be repealed since tax credits for interest paid reduces the effective interest rate several percentage points below the market rate for most people. Usury laws tend to constrain the orderly functioning of secondary mortgage markets.

In summary, mortgage credit in the United States is now so much a part of our national financial structure that anyone who qualifies and perseveres can secure a mortgage loan. The only meaningful barriers reside in state usury laws.

HOW MORTGAGES HAVE CHANGED

With today's *amortized* level-payment mortgage, you pay some interest and some *principal* every month. But the five-year nonamortizing mortgage was the common debt instrument for home purchases before World War II. In general, the homebuyer paid only interest each year until the fifth, when the total principal outstanding became due. At that time the mortgage holder usually refinanced the note, since he was not likely to have the money necessary to repay. During the Great Depression many homeowners lost their houses under this system because they couldn't make the payments and couldn't raise cash when the note came due.

To solve this problem, Congress created the Federal Housing Administration (FHA). The new organization began by insuring level-payment mortgages (amortizing) for periods of up to twenty years. The new mortgages were desirable to homebuyers because at the end of their term they were fully paid. Lenders readily accepted the instruments because they offered a major increase in the effective interest yielded by a given mortgage and because they were insured against loss by an agency of the federal government.

In the 1950's the default experience on the new FHA-insured mortgage loans was so low that numbers of lenders, led and encouraged by the Federal Home Loan Bank Board, decided to make · them standard forms without requiring insurance. In addition, as housing prices began to rise faster than income, Congress authorized extended terms, first for FHA and VA and then for conventional loans, so that the loans could be repaid over thirty years rather than twenty. These time extensions were beneficial to the potential buyer, since lengthening the term resulted in a reduction in the effective monthly payment and therefore increased loan amounts available to a homebuyer.

It became apparent during the late 1950's and early 1960's that a further lengthening of the repayment period beyond the thirty-year term would not be effective. Compounding interest for periods longer than thirty years results in only small reductions in monthly payments and offers little meaningful aid to the borrower.

Since World War II, home building has gone through seven short-term cycles of boom and bust in response to changes due to inflation in the availability and cost of mortgage credit. Because housing is the largest private user of credit in the nation—using even more than corporations—and is a highly durable product, retaining its values over decades, it is extremely sensitive to conditions in long-term money markets.

Housing used to serve as a balance wheel for the rest of the economy, generally booming during periods of slack activity in the industrialized sectors, when there was less competition for money, then slowing as increasing economic activity competed with home building for available funds. Consequently, for decades home building played a major role in nationwide economic stability by cooling an overheated economy or leading the way out of recession. But the price paid through increased housing costs, in restricted volume, particularly when the number of houses available has never been sufficient to fulfill the market demands of the American people, still rises.

Because the building and selling of homes is almost entirely dependent on borrowed money, the impact of inflation on interest rates—the cost of borrowing money—used to hit particularly hard on housing. The inflation of roughly the past decade and a half put an apparent premium on money, resulting in higher and higher interest rates. Mortgage rates began inching up from 6% since 1966, as inflation began accelerating. The real money problems for housing appeared when the Federal Reserve Board (see the section "What Lies Behind Our Ability to Get Mortgages?") applied monetary restraints to slow inflation.

Such restraint used to cause a net *outflow* of savings from savings banks and savings and loan institutions (collectively known as thrift institutions). An outflow of savings, called disintermediation, signals a drying up of mortgage money from thrifts. They lose savings as money is diverted into short-term government and corporate securities that return higher yields than the savings institutions. Inflation has prompted savers to be more sophisticated with their money; they watch money markets more closely and move into higher-yielding investments with greater alacrity.

During the money crunch of 1974, an inflationary psychology further aggravated disintermediation. Despite record interest rates for the dwindling supply of money, the government, corporations, and consumers kept spending and borrowing heavily to pay for inflation-bloated costs of financing established projects and to make purchases in order to avoid paying more later on. Mortgage money all but disappeared. Builders were forced to slash projects in the face of 15% to 18% interest rates on construction loans. And prospective buyers postponed acquiring a house rather than make 30% to 40% down payments and sign up for 11% mortgages.

POINTS AND WHO REALLY PAYS

If you are thinking of an FHA or VA mortgage, you will hear a fair amount about points. The subject is not as complicated as many people make it seem. Look at it this way:

Points developed through the need to make the mortgage yield match the market interest rate of a comparable investment. All money for FHA-insured and VA-guaranteed mortgages comes from lending institutions. This places lenders in a peculiar position. Because maximum interest rates are preset under these programs, usually below the rate for conventional mortgages, the investment return of these federally supported mortgages might not be at market interest rates.

To offset the lower interest rate on VA and FHA loans, as compared to conventional loans, lending institutions often assess one-time charges called "points." A point is equal to 1% of the mortgage amount.

At any given time the rate of mortgage loans is the function of money market prices. It is not a rate that can be fixed by government. When interest rates are fixed by the federal government, however, whether they be FHA, VA, or usury rates in the various states, the rate that actually prevails in the marketplace forces the discount, or the paying of points, of the mortgage. For instance, if the market price for long-term mortgage money is 10%, and a borrower wants a $50,000 mortgage, and the FHA rate is 9½%, he may have to take out a mortgage of $52,200 to maintain the same monthly payments that he qualified for with the mortgage lender. The points are represented by the higher mortgage amount.

The equation looks like this: A thirty-year mortgage for $50,000 at 10% (the real market rate) calls for a monthly payment of $438.78. Amortization tables tell us that for that same amount of money per month, $438.78, the amount of mortgage face value at 9½%, or the FHA rate, is $52,200. So the buyer signs a note for $2,200 more than the $50,000 he originally needed to maintain the same monthly payment. It is a nonproblem to both the borrower and the lender. It is simply numbers on a piece of paper to make the money yield what the marketplace demands.

ADJUSTMENTS FOR INFLATION

The federal government responded to inflation with the development of a series of innovations. During the early 1960's, programs were created that subsidized interest rates. The Omnibus Housing Act of 1968 and the Emergency Home Finance Act of 1970 reinforced the trend by establishing government subsidy programs that allowed a renter or a homebuyer to pay interest rates of 1%. The programs were enormously popular, as might have been expected, and constituted a primary force behind the housing boom that occurred in the early 1970's.

The programs obviously could not be used in the private sector, though, since builders and lenders lacked the ability to absorb the huge interest subsidy costs on the loans (history indicates that the government has had difficulty making these payments itself).

As a result, the private sector concurrently began to develop new types of mortgage documents that would both maintain effective monthly costs at a reasonable level to the borrower and offer lenders an acceptable return. The first such idea introduced was the variable-payment mortgage, whereby interest rates would be allowed to fluctuate within given ranges based on changes in market interest rates.

While the variable-rate mortgage was quite acceptable to many borrowers, it drew criticism on two major points: (1) all the financial risk of borrowing is transferred to the borrower; and (2) over time the variable-rate mortgage is more expensive, hence inflationary to the consumer. Payments by all odds add up to a bigger amount than payments on a fixed-rate loan.

New variable-rate mortgages are being used effectively for hundreds of thousands of loans in California. At the moment up to about half of all mortgage loans held by some state-chartered savings and loans in California provide for the variable rates which insulate lenders against the risk of rising money costs. Congress on two occasions, however, has taken such severe exception to variable-rate mortgages that the likelihood of their ever becoming a nationwide instrument seems minimal. Congress feared that such mortgages would drive homeowners out of their houses in periods of rapidly rising interest rates. Homebuyers were also wary of variable-rate mortgages since over the past forty years they have been conditioned to accept equal monthly mortgage payments. This belief was one of the motivations for purchasing a home during a period of high inflation.

A strong case can be made for variable-rate mortgages, graduated-payment mortgages, and the like in the future. Simply to say that consumers can't have them because they may be hurt, as Congress did in the closing sessions of 1978, is a little bit silly when so much is "indexed" against the effects of our inflation.

To compensate for the eroding effects of inflation on people and institutions, we have "indexed" Social Security, pensions, government employee wages, and labor union contracts. We increasingly use cost-plus contracts in the private sector to handle inflation, and in the financial world we really have an inflation-indexing system in interest rates for business loans, market or going-rate commitments on other kinds of loans, and the variable-rate six-month certificates of deposit, tied to Treasury bills at thrift institutions. There is no particular reason why we should not adjust the mortgage market, and most particularly mortgage rates, for inflation.

The graduated-payment mortgage (GPM), on the other hand, is a loan that Congress believed could have great merit. It incorporates concepts developed in the life insurance industry forty years ago. Basically the graduated-payment feature is based on a descending amortization schedule. For example, the standard twenty-five-year mortgage might provide for a first-year payment on a basis of a fifty-year term, second-year payments on the basis of a forty-five-year term, and so on, until the end of the fifth year, when the payment is based on a twenty-five-year term for the balance of the mortgage. In theory, a graduated-payment mortgage allows the homebuyer to pay a constant interest rate over the term of the mortgage, regardless of changes in interest rates. In the first five or ten years of the mortgage's life, however, the homeowner makes lower monthly payments than required by a conventional mortgage. At the end of this time, the monthly payment increases to repay the lender for those interest and principal payments not collected earlier. Presumably this escalating payment structure coincides with rising income, thus allowing the borrower to purchase housing corresponding to a future income level without suffering the onerous burden of fixed payments on a lower income level in the early years of the mortgage.

This mortgage appeals to lenders because interest and principal payments deferred in the initial period increase the size of debt outstanding and consequently mean additional interest charges. The net effect is that the lender receives a higher effective rate of interest over the full term of the mortgage than with a level-payment mortgage (see table). The graduated-payment mortgage may not be any more inflationary than a fixed-rate mortgage, but again the homeowner pays more for it over time than he would for a fixed-rate mortgage.

The Federal Home Loan Bank Board has okayed graduated-payment mortgages. That is good news especially to younger buyers, who often cannot qualify for a level-payment mortgage because payments are too high for their income. They can qualify very frequently under the graduated-payment mortgage.

State-chartered savings and loans in California, permitted to offer both graduated-payment and variable-rate mortgages, seem to be growing 30% faster than federally chartered savings and loans in California that cannot offer them. There is no question that more people can qualify under graduated-payment mortgages, whether conventional or FHA's GPM, and quite a few more under the variable-rate mortgage. The Alternative Mortgage Instruments Research Study (AMIRS) done by the Federal Home Loan Bank

Board estimated that approximately 19.5 million households—primarily young renters and owners with lower than median incomes—would qualify for homeownership with a GPM. This total represents 28.6% of the potential market of eligible buyers nationwide.

COMPARISON OF MONTHLY PAYMENT SCHEDULES OF LEVEL-PAYMENT MORTGAGE AND GPM

$60,000 loan, 11% interest, 30-year term

Year	Level-payment Loan Principal and Interest Only	GPM	Difference (in dollars)
1	$571	$471	−100
2	571	484	−87
3	571	499	−72
4	571	515	−56
5	571	531	−40
6	571	547	−24
7	571	562	−9
8	571	580	9
9	571	598	27
10	571	615	44
11 and on	571	633	62

THE U.S. MORTGAGE CREDIT SYSTEM

The Federal Reserve System—the Fed—is the United States' money manager. It is a quasi-governmental agency created in 1913 by the Federal Reserve Act to serve as the country's central bank. By managing the nation's money supply, it influences the availability and cost of money and credit.

The Fed is composed of twelve regional Reserve Banks. All U.S. national banks and many state-chartered banks are members of the Fed through the Reserve Bank in their region.

In the early years of the Great Depression, the federal government laid the foundations for a complete overhaul of the mortgage lending industry in the United States. These moves lay in four areas:

1. A specialized form of reserve banking system, tailored to the needs of family savings and home mortgage lending, structured so as to maintain a flow of funds in times of short credit, as well as to permit a geographic flow of funds from regions with surplus funds for home mortgage investment to those where funds are in short supply

2. A loosely integrated national system of local savings institutions primarily engaged in home mortgage lending and built around a broad base of federally chartered institutions designed to illustrate the benefits of mutual ownership and serve as models of good practice and community service

3. Federally underwritten insurance that guarantees the safety of individual savings in federal and insured member institutions

4. Overall, a Federal Home Loan Bank Board with broad regulatory, supervisory, and, within limits, disciplinary powers

More than four decades later this basic structure has developed well and is still essentially intact, although a multitude of detailed regulatory changes have been made.

The Federal Home Loan Bank System was created in 1932 by the Federal Home Loan Bank Act to set up a central credit system for mortgage lending similar to the Federal Reserve System for commercial banks. It supplements the resources of member savings institutions in order to smooth supply-demand pressures by easing the flow of funds from capital-surplus areas to capital-deficit areas. The system is composed of the Federal Home Loan Bank Board (FHLBB), the Federal Savings and Loan Insurance Corporation (FSLIC), twelve regional Federal Home Loan Banks, member savings institutions, and the Federal Home Loan Mortgage Corporation (FHLMC).

The Federal Home Loan Bank Board has three members appointed by the president of the United States and confirmed by the Senate to serve four-year terms in Washington, D.C. The board governs the entire system and is an independent executive branch agency.

The twelve regional Federal Home Loan Banks serve as central credit banks for member institutions. Their main function is to supply their members with credit to meet unexpected withdrawals and to increase the supply of mortgage money.

The Federal National Mortgage Association (FNMA, or "Fannie Mae") was created in 1938 as part of the federal government.

In 1968, in keeping with congressional intent expressed fourteen years earlier, FNMA was converted to a private corporation. It operates entirely on its own funds and pays full federal corporate income taxes.

FNMA was the first of several organizations whose active participation in the secondary mortgage market tends to smooth out the cyclic flow of funds into the mortgage market. By purchasing mortgages actively when mortgage funds of the financial institutions are drying up, these organizations assure that mortgage market funds continue to be available. Thus, a financial institution under pressure in times of tight money can turn to these governmental bodies for added funds and thereby continue to sustain normal mortgage lending activity to the consumer area it serves.

The FNMA is the largest single institutional supplier of mortgage funds in the United States. Its primary purpose is to provide supplemental liquidity for the secondary market by investing in mortgages originated by FNMA-qualified lenders (known as "approved sellers"). FNMA's net mortgage portfolio grew from less than $2 billion in 1963 to about $50 billion at the end of 1979.

Essentially what FNMA does is put money into the mortgage market when the supply of funds from other sources is limited. When there is an ample supply of mortgage investment funds from other sources, the volume of mortgages purchased by FNMA may be reduced. FNMA thus acts to supplement the mortgage market, buying more mortgages when money is in short supply, buying fewer mortgages when more money is available. At such times FNMA may sell mortgages it holds in its portfolio.

In recent years, however, purchases have outrun sales by a wide margin, making FNMA primarily a long-term investor in mortgages. Even when FNMA reduced its purchases and increased sales during the money boom of 1971-72, its purchases exceeded sales by 13 to 1. In 1974 it purchased more than $6.9 billion worth of mortgages, while selling only $4.3 million worth—a ratio of more than 1,600 to 1. Therefore, most of its income is derived from payments on the mortgages it holds and for fees it charges for committing itself to future mortgage purchases. These earnings pay for operating expenses and interest on its sizable debt, which rose above $28 billion at the end of 1974.

FNMA pays for its purchases by borrowing, which makes it, in most years, the largest single borrower of funds in the United States, with the exception of the U.S. Treasury. FNMA borrows through the sale of obligations on the open market in the form of short-term discount notes similar to commercial paper and longer-term debentures and mortgage-backed bonds. It also issues stock, which is traded on the New York, Midwest, and Pacific Coast stock exchanges and which must be purchased by those who accept FNMA commitments to buy their mortgages. FNMA can borrow funds at favorable rates because it is a government-sponsored corporation whose obligations are blue-chip federal agency securities.

The Emergency Housing Finance Act of 1970 and the Emergency Home Purchase Act of 1974 so restructured the secondary mortgage market that by 1977 one-fifth of all residential mortgage money came through that market, from investors, not depositors at thrifts. In 1978 the proportion rose to a fourth. In 1979 it was a third.

All of that secondary market activity lent great stability to mortgage rates in the face of roaring inflation: by the end of 1978 mortgage rates were actually lower than the prime lending rate at commercial banks. That had never happened before.

Since FNMA, other players have become key factors in that secondary market. The Government National Mortgage Association (GNMA), or "Ginnie Mae" as a government corporation with HUD has a basic responsibility: to support mortgage market activities that cannot be economically carried out by the private sector. It receives no federal appropriations, obtaining its funds by borrowing from the U.S. Treasury.

GNMA is responsible for servicing and liquidating old government-owned mortgages, as well as purchasing new mortgages that are needed to help meet national housing needs. GNMA issues commitments at a fair market rate to purchase mortgages from lenders who have provided homebuyers with mortgages at agreed-upon rates below private market yields. GNMA then sells these mortgages, either as whole loans or as mortgage-backed securities, through competitive bidding at discounts that permit the investor to receive reasonable yields. GNMA, and therefore the federal government, bears the losses between the purchase and eventual resale prices in order to help stimulate particular types of housing as they are most needed. At one time all GNMA purchases were limited to government-backed mortgages, but the Emergency Home Purchase Assistance Act of 1974 expanded its programs temporarily to include conventional mortgages.

GNMA also has the job of guaranteeing the timely payment of principal and interest on mortgage-backed securities issued against pools of government-backed mortgages equal in quality to government bonds. These popular pass-through securities, known as Ginnie Maes, are issued by mortgage bankers and institutions that originate government-backed mortgages for resale.

The system is this: the full faith and credit of the United States has been placed behind pass-through mortgage-backed bonds, in units of $25,000 and above. This allows investors to own freely marketable securities that have as their security FHA-insured and VA-guaranteed housing mortgages, together with the U.S. guaranty. The volume of GNMA securities exceeded $100 billion during 1979, and many investors consider them the highest-quality securities in the world. Their market acceptance has become the balloon for the secondary mortgage market and has developed the foundation for all other forms of marketable mortgage securities. GNMAs are largely responsible for home purchasers being able to borrow money in the face of high inflation.

The Federal Home Loan Mortgage Corporation (FHLMC, or "Freddie Mac") was created in response to the credit crunch of 1969. It was established under the Emergency Home Finance Act of 1970 to expand the secondary mortgage market and attract new money from large institutional investors. FHLMC is a private corporation owned by the FHLB system and receives no government funding. It is exclusively involved in the secondary market, buying single-family and multi-family home mortgages from qualified lenders. Although it does purchase FHA- and VA-secured mortgages, its primary emphasis is on conventional loans.

FHLMC gets its funds through the sale of mortgages it has purchased, many of which are pooled as backing for Participation Sale Certificates (PCs), by selling mortgage-backed securities guaranteed by the Government National Mortgage Association and by borrowing from the regional banks. In early 1975 FHLMC first issued its Government Mortgage Certificates (GMCs) to offer investors, such as pension funds, mortgage-backed securities that are more like bonds. They pay interest semi-annually, return a portion of the principal annually, and provide the holder with an option to have FHLMC purchase the remaining principal at the end of fifteen years.

Large savings and loans, banks, and mortgage bankers are also playing increasingly important roles in the secondary market, packaging and selling pools of mortgages.

It's interesting to note that the basic rate of mortgage money for long-term, fixed-payment payback is roughly 3% plus the inflation rate. That was true back when mortgages were 4¼%. Today, because of the restructuring of the mortgage market and the near-universal recognition that real estate may be better than gold, the rate is lower: in early 1979 the prime rate stood at 11½%, inflation was going up from 10% to 16% (depending on whom you believed), and the effective new-home mortgage rate across the country, according to the Federal Home Loan Bank Board, was 10.2%.

In March of 1980 the prime rate hit 20%, but by the end of June it was back to 11% and mortgages stood at 10½%.

Chapter 14

Worksheets for Section II

The following worksheets are designed to help you to determine, before you start visiting lenders, your ability to buy. There is a financial qualifications sheet, a repeat of the one used in Chapter 11; a personal finances worksheet; and one to help you figure out how to make the down payment.

INCOME QUALIFICATION

Use this sample FHA form to determine whether you would qualify for a mortgage.

First qualification (35%)

Gross monthly income	$_____
Less federal withholding taxes	_____
Net income per month	_____
Percent allowable for total housing expense	x_____%
Maximum amount available for housing expense	_____(1)

Housing Expense

Principal and interest	_____
FHA insurance premium	_____
Taxes	_____
Hazard insurance	_____
Maintenance	_____
Heat and utilities	_____
Total housing expense	_____(2)

Second qualification (50%)

Net income per month $_____
Less Social Security, state, city taxes (9% of gross)   _____
Net effective income per month   _____
Percent allowable for home and other recurring charges   x_____%
Maximum amount available for housing and
    other recurring charges   _____(3)

> FHA guidelines state that the purchaser's total housing expense plus his re-
> curring charges (any installment debts having twelve months or more remain-
> ing; any revolving charge accounts, regardless of how few payments remain)
> cannot exceed 50% of his net effective income per month.

Total housing expense $_____
Plus recurring charges   _____

                                                          _____(4)

To qualify: (1) must be higher than (2) *and* (3) must be higher than (4).

YOUR PERSONAL FINANCIAL FIGURES

By now you should have a good idea of what you would like to spend on a house. Let's get down to some more fine points.

How much house can you really afford initially? The rule of thumb for most lenders in these inflationary times for incomes at the lower end of the scale—let's say under $25,000—is that the house price should not be much more than two times annual income. At the upper end of the income scale lenders may accept house prices two and a half and sometimes three times income.

Working from the monthly expense, the total monthly payment for shelter ideally should not exceed one week's take-home pay. But with the effects of inflation on food, clothing, automobiles, gasoline, energy, and medical care, figuring that simplistically might land you in a little trouble. So first you really should take the time to go back over the past twelve months and review all your expenses, using your canceled checks, and total the amounts spent in every category you can think of. You might break them down as in the worksheet given here.

If you're really serious about buying, you would have to add estimates for property taxes, fire insurance, energy, water, telephone, maintenance, and any special fees or assessments for the proposed new house. The seller, especially if he is a real estate agent, can give you a pretty good idea about all of these things; if he can't, he is not as skilled in his profession as he should be, and you ought to talk to some other realtors. A rule of thumb for estimating monthly maintenance is 1% or 2% of the purchase price per year divided by 12.

Figure each item on the following worksheet on a prorated basis for monthly after-tax income. It would be best *not* to include your spouse's earnings, if he or she works full-time and is under forty-five. Take-home pay is your pay less withholding for federal, state, and city taxes and Social Security, and less automatic pension contributions and union dues.

The last item in the list, the amount available for shelter, has to cover mortgage amortization, property taxes, utilities, and maintenance.

Monthly after-tax income (your take-home pay)
   plus any income from other sources $_____

Food $_____

Clothing $_____

Medical and dental expenses $_____

Automobile (payment, insurance, gasoline, repairs) $_____

Installment debts (of any kind) $_____

Life insurance $_____

Health insurance $_____

Savings (what you would like to save each month) $_____

Entertainment, recreation, family vacation $_____

Children's education (current or savings
   earmarked for future) $_____

Charitable contributions $_____

Pocket money (incidentals, lunches, transportation) $_____

Special circumstances (child support, alimony,
   support of elderly parents, etc.) $_____

Total expenses $_____

AMOUNT AVAILABLE FOR SHELTER $_____

Or try it this way: use the figures from your 1979 income tax return to fill in the blanks.

Income before taxes $_____

Less itemized deductions:
  Medical and dental $_____

  Property taxes $_____

  Other taxes $_____

  Mortgage interest $_____

  Other interest $_____

  Other deductions $_____

  Total deductions $_____

Less personal exemptions $_____

Net taxable income $_____

Income tax from appropriate table $_____

Last year's tax $_____

Yearly saving with homeownership $_____

Divide yearly saving with ownership by 12 to
  get monthly saving $_____

Estimated total mortgage payment $_____

Less monthly saving $_____

NET MONTHLY SHELTER COST $_____

Now let's assume that all of this adds up to something like $600 for shelter, and you assume that your utilities, maintenance, taxes, and insurance are $300. That leaves $300 for a monthly mortgage payment for principal and interest. From the next worksheet you can see that on a 10% mortgage with a term of twenty to twenty-five years the mortgage amount can only be around $32,500. That means that with a 25% down payment, all you can afford initially is a $40,625 house.

Bear in mind that if you have two incomes in your family—if your spouse works full-time—the mortgage lender must by law account for his or her income in qualifying for a mortgage, and that might bring you much higher.

But as I indicated previously, if you have several small children it would be safer to budget your monthly expenses on just your income so that in the event of some unforeseen happenstance you aren't caught with a severe case of the shorts.

HOW MUCH DO YOU HAVE FOR A DOWN PAYMENT?

Savings on hand $_____

Equity in previous home $_____

Anticipated savings within the next new months $_____

Other sources $_____

Total on hand $_____

Borrowing sources $_____

Insurance policy $_____

Family loan $_____

Personal note $_____

Total borrowing ability $_____

Total available for down payment, closing, and
    moving expenses $_____

Section III

The Mechanics of Buying a House

At this point you know the nature of the house you want; you have chosen a community; and you know what kind of financing you can handle.

You are going to meet those who sell houses, either owners or professionals. You should now know enough to judge the value of what they are selling for yourself.

When you find the house you want, the next step is completing the purchase. This section gives you some ground rules to help you through the closing and the home purchase contract—the legal and detail work that will make the house yours.

You may also be in a position of selling your present house at the same time. That takes some careful planning on your part, but millions of people have successfully done it. This section also includes some helpful rules to follow for selling your present house.

Chapter 15

First Encounters: The Sellers

What houses are on the market? How are you going to know enough about those houses to know if they fit your needs? How can you make a careful choice? If you are ready to buy, you are ready to meet a realtor, a builder, a builder's or realtor's salesman, or an owner/seller. They're all sellers; for simplicity's sake I'll call all of them realtors.

The most important rule is to take your time. You know what you want, and now you're going to find out what you may have to settle for. Be deliberate, don't make hasty or premature decisions. The decision-making process ahead is crucial. This is especially true when you are moving into an unfamiliar community. You are starting from ground zero. Take your time, or you will make a mistake that you will have to live with a long time.

There are several steps you should follow when you are in the market for a house.

1. Think back and draw on your own experience. Whom do you know who has a feel for your new community? What immediate contacts can you draw on? Relatives, business acquaintances, and friends can help greatly in this process. Don't hesitate to question anyone who may know about life in your new community and neighborhood, prices, services, and the like. This kind of advice should be weighed carefully, though; some people you talk to may lack sufficient insight and judgment.

2. If you are moving to a new town, you are probably going there on a job transfer. Agencies that specialize in employee relocation can help you find a new house and sell your old one. Your employer may already have plans for taking care of the problems and financial arrangements you will face.

3. Local real estate boards, the local Chamber of Com-

merce, and the classified advertising pages of local newspapers
are good places to look to get acquainted with what is being
offered. Real estate ads are usually broken down by community within a major metropolitan area. Frequently, you can
tell from a paper which brokers seem to be most knowledgeable and most active in the area. You can learn a great deal
about prices in a given area simply from scanning the real
estate section. All of this helps you to home in on those communities that seem to fit your needs and to discard those
communities that don't.

4. You should have a detailed map of any area that you
are going to look at. This can usually be supplied by the local
newspaper or the local Chamber of Commerce. Write to them,
and in short order you can probably get a map that will have
on it every street in town. You also may find home finders'
directories, buyers' guides, and other periodicals that can be
most useful to house hunters from out of town. These often
are produced by independent entrepreneurs working with real
estate boards or Chambers of Commerce. They contain cap-
sulized information on property tax rates, schools, commuting
time, cost of transportation, zoning regulations, garbage collection, distances to hospitals, police and fire protection,
churches, and other services.

5. Talk with at least two mortgage loan officers of local
financial institutions. They often have a better understanding
of how a town is growing and what neighborhood values are
than anyone else.

6. You'll want to know, before contacting a realtor, if
builders' new houses are offered through most realtors. In
some places those new houses are sold only by builders. You
do not want to shut yourself out of the new-house market
unwittingly, especially given the new concerns of energy consumption, a condition that often makes the more expensive
new house cheaper per month, in the long run than the older
house. Go to the home shows and the local Home Builders
Association Parade of Homes. Get all the literature you can.

7. How do you sort fact from fiction in all this information
you have gathered? Probably the most helpful factual information comes from a good real estate broker, agent, or salesperson. These professionals are more productive and can
quickly pinpoint areas that you may be interested in.

The best route to a realtor is through a personal recom-
mendation from someone who has dealt with the broker before

and has found him conscientious and reliable. Your employer or prospective employer may have a list of brokers who have successfully found houses for others. Brokers with whom you have dealt in the community you are leaving are another good source of references.

8. Visit various communities, both by day and by night, to check the accuracy of what you have been told. Check with somebody who lives in the neighborhood and knows the people and the area well, such as a local minister.

Now you're ready to go.

REALTORS: WHO THEY ARE AND WHAT THEY DO

If you are like most of the rest of us, the key person in your house search will be a real estate broker, agent, or salesperson. That real estate man or woman is at the center of your house-hunting effort, especially if you are looking at a community you're not familiar with. The real estate broker can give you more useful information about a community, a neighborhood, a house, and the services and amenities surrounding that house than almost anybody else. The broker can also focus on your price range and other criteria that you have set better than almost anyone else, eliminating wasted time in your house hunt.

As a house hunter, your goal is to gain exposure to as many offerings as possible of the type of house you are seeking in the price range you can afford. Usually your task is simplified by putting yourself in the hands of a single broker who can show you all the available houses that are suitable.

Whether the broker is independent or is a member of a large firm is relatively unimportant. In some cities you may find that the biggest real estate company in town devotes most of its energies to commercial or industrial properties and pays very little attention to house sales. You may be able, on the other hand, to turn up a small independent broker who has an intimate knowledge of the market for houses in the particular area where you want to buy; that broker would be just the one for you.

The broker's role is frequently misunderstood. In each of the fifty states he is a licensed professional, but the educational qualifications and experience requirements vary widely from state to state. There are more than a half a million real estate brokers and salespeople in the country. They include executives of large realty companies as well as part-time housewives and students who show houses on weekends.

A good many of them are members of what is by far the largest organization in the field, the National Association of Realtors. Brokers who are members of the organization are entitled to use the copyrighted designation "Realtor" in their professional capacity. They may also belong to any of about 1,600 local boards. To qualify as a Realtor, a broker must meet certain standards set by the national association apart from state licensing requirements. He must also subscribe to a code of ethics and adhere to certain professional standards.

Realtors have a mechanism for handling complaints on alleged violations of ethical practices, giving you and the person who may sell his house to you a good means of settling any complaints. In some communities arbitration panels, made up of third parties, have been set up by these real estate groups to handle grievances.

Another well-known group of professional brokers is the National Association of Real Estate Brokers, which has as its copyrighted designation "Realtist." This association, which came into existence as a result of discrimination, also has a code of ethics, an emblem, and an international membership, although it is much smaller than that of the Realtors. Realtists are predominantly minority-group members, but anybody can be a member.

THE REALTOR'S COMMISSION

The broker usually gets a commission based only on the closing of a transaction. Commissions usually are not negotiable, and they are now running around 6% to 7% in most communities; in special circumstances, such as in resort areas they could run higher.

Does the broker's commission add to the cost of the house? Couldn't you buy for less if the seller were to receive the full price without the commission being deducted?

The real estate broker is entitled to his commission under the laws of most states. The commission comes from the seller because, in theory, the broker represents the seller. This does not mean that the broker doesn't protect your interests. In practice, that is the only way that he can make the sale. Under the law and the code of ethics of the broker groups, he must protect your interests or lose his status as a licensed professional.

You can expect the broker's commission to be included in the asking price of the house. The broker or salesperson is working as an independent professional. He or she hopes to bring buyer and seller together and makes every effort to do so. But you as a buyer have a right to demand honesty. You rely on your realtor to perform a very important function, and each of you should know exactly where the other stands at the outset.

If you didn't have to pay the commission as a part of the sale price, couldn't you get the house for a lower price? Obviously you could. But the price of a house is determined by the free market, or by supply and demand. Nothing prevents a seller of a house from trying to market his house without the assistance of a professional real estate person, but if a house has buyer appeal, it will be taken readily at a fair market price whether or not a broker is involved. A house that is priced too high for the market can be sold only if the seller accepts a lower price, whether or not a commission is included.

HOW REALTORS GET THEIR LISTINGS

A realtor is the focal point for prices that match most closely real values in the marketplace. In this regard, his most significant job is to obtain and service salable listings of both new and old housing.

You may not be concerned about how a broker gets a house to sell, but it might be useful for you to understand how brokers carry houses in their "inventory" and what arrangements they have with the sellers of those houses. The usual arrangement is for a broker to have an open listing; an owner simply informs one or more realtors that his house is up for sale. Each broker understands that the first one who finds a buyer for the house, at a price the seller is willing to accept, gets the commission. There is no time limit on an open listing, and the seller can terminate it whenever he wants simply by telling the broker that his house is no longer for sale. If, however, the seller does sell a house to a buyer who has been produced by a real estate broker, the seller is still liable for the commission.

You should also be familiar with the multiple-listing system, which operates in most metropolitan areas. In this system several brokers, usually through their board of realtors, join in a cooperative venture that gives each participating broker access to listings provided by the others. In this way, the broker to whom you as a prospective buyer go is able to offer more listings than he alone has. If you buy a house, the participating broker who shows you the house receives half the commission and the listing broker receives the other half.

Brokers have at their fingertips detailed listings of cooperating brokers. A broker can feed into a computer terminal your requirements of size, location, and price range, and within seconds a selection of addresses is printed out for you to inspect.

Another form of listing is the exclusive right to sell. This means that regardless of who produces the buyer of a house, even if the seller does it all by himself, the broker receives a commission.

Frequently two realtors are involved in a house sale—one for the seller and one for the buyer. But the purchaser must be careful of that situation; he could be shut out from a major portion of the market by the two realtors getting together.

You should know, however, that many desirable houses are sold without ever being listed by local realtors. Furthermore, some neighborhoods do not allow "for sale" signs to be placed in front of houses. You've got to be a real detective to find out about some of these.

HOW TO JUDGE A REALTOR

When you first visit a good broker's office you will be asked to fill out a questionnaire that will detail your needs in a house (see the sample in Chapter 21). Any broker who does this will be most productive; the questionnaire certainly helps narrow down your choices right off the bat. Detailed information you can give, including such things as distance to work that you would settle for (a thirty-minute commute might be okay, but one hour is out of the question), or the kind of heating system or access to shopping centers, makes the broker's job of sorting out the houses that would be acceptable to you and your family easier and faster. It saves time for both of you.

A lot of us are often wary of too much enthusiasm in salespeople. But a certain amount of boosterism—enthusiasm for the community—is to be expected of a real estate broker. After all, if his opinion of the area where he earns his living were low, he would probably work elsewhere. So he can be forgiven for a certain amount of local pride.

Yet a broker knows that painting a rosy picture of a not-so-rosy locale, or making a dilapidated house out to be a sound one, rarely clinches a sale. His strength is in being realistic in assessing the qualities of a neighborhood, a street, and a particular house and then locating the family for whom that house would be most suitable. The conscientious broker also realizes that the buyer of a house becomes a part of the community and that satisfied clients are the best means he has of acquiring new prospects.

Many brokers point out possible flaws in houses. Well established in their business, they prefer that you know about the house before you buy, rather than let a bad sale boomerang. Besides, they also make hay psychologically by telling you some of the bad as well as the good. The fact that a broker will come clean and reveal flaws to you can be impressive evidence that he is dealing fairly and squarely. This can earn him your confidence, and he knows it. And as we all know, nearly every house has flaws.

Brokers are not expected to be experts in house design and construction, so don't ask. And don't believe a broker if he says "You can easily knock out that wall, it isn't a load-bearing one." You need the opinion of an expert before you decide to knock out any walls. A really good broker keeps his mouth shut about such things. It should also be said, though, that some brokers are former builders; or through exposure to houses over the years they have developed a sixth sense about the kind of construction that stands up best in their area; or they know the houses built by the good builders. But these brokers constitute a decided minority.

Here, too, the question of energy use should be a prime concern in talking with realtors and salespeople. They should have a good idea of the condition of any house they show in this regard. A good broker always has access to heating records, particularly covering the previous full year, as well as other utility records, such as electricity and water use. Be aware that energy-saving specifications for new houses are becoming far better than those for older houses, and the difference in price (higher for the new house) may evaporate over time through reduced fuel costs.

In your house search you may encounter two distinct kinds of salespeople. By the very nature of the brokerage business, a resale salesperson negotiates prices, terms, offers, and counter-offers. The opposite is true in new-house selling. Prices are usually firmly fixed by the new-house builder. The sales specialist in that area does not have to justify the price or submit to the uncertainties of offers and counteroffers.

There is another difference that you may notice immediately: in customer control. The subdivision salesperson seldom has the same degree of control over a prospective purchaser that a resale salesperson has. Prospects at a new housing project arrive and leave in their own cars. On the other hand, the resale salesperson gets control of the buyer through counseling sessions, picking up and delivering the buyer in his own car, and determining what will be seen and in what order.

There are some things that you want to watch out for when working with realtors. Beware the realtor who immediately drags you off in his car and starts making a sales pitch before he knows anything about what you want. He's not operating like a professional, and he's wasting a lot of his time and yours. He is obviously an amateur.

Ask your realtor what "escrow" regulations govern the handling of deposits. (An escrow is simply putting away money so that neither party, or intermediary seller, buyer, or realtor, can touch the money. Chapter 17 and the Glossary explain this more fully.) Most states have regulations covering escrowed deposits to protect your money. If there are any disputes over contract terms, it is your responsibility to settle them, and your cost, should that become part of the resolution to any problem. Ask a lot of questions. If the deal falls through, does the broker withhold the deposit? If the buyer changes his mind out of fickleness, can he get his money back? The broker did his job and deserves compensation. But more often the buyer has a legitimate right to his money back. The only way, therefore, to protect your deposit is to have an escape clause in writing that assures you of its return if the deal collapses.

When troubles like these arise, you have recourse to state authorities. They can suspend or revoke the broker's license. If the broker is a realtor member of the local real estate board, you can also complain to the board and some redress may be made. But that's closing the barn door too late.

HOW TO MAKE THE MOST OF A REALTOR'S SERVICES

When you first meet your real estate broker, you should be totally open with him. Start out by letting him know the price range in which you are pretty sure you qualify to buy, or at which you want to buy. Don't give an artificial figure of what you are willing to spend, just because asking prices are usually higher than what houses are actually sold for. A good broker really knows his market, and he has a very good idea of the real market value of any house up for sale no matter what the owner's asking price may be.

Give the broker a realistic insight into your financial situation. Be sure to go over your preferences for styles of architecture and types of homes. There's no sense in looking at colonial homes if you have your heart set on a contemporary one.

Being open and candid helps a conscientious realty agent match your needs to the right house. The more you tell him, the better equipped he will be to locate the house you are looking for. His insights and evaluations are born of experience and day-to-day exposure to the market.

Most brokers work hard for their money. One may spend months showing you houses, only to see you buy through another broker. A broker who finds a house quickly may be begrudged his fee. But remember that a realtor is able to find and sell houses quickly because of his experience and the time he has invested in his business.

Be on time for appointments. After all, a broker's time is worth money too. If you have already seen a house through direct contact with the owner or through another broker and you are taken to it by a second broker, speak up at once. Do not enter it with a second broker; you leave yourself open to a lawsuit.

Builders and developers of new houses may employ real estate companies to handle their sales or have their own sales staff. Obviously a salesperson working only for a builder may not be as objective or willing to show you other properties. However, he should be thoroughly knowledgeable about the new area, the homes, options, financing, warranties, and closing costs. This can be most helpful to you in reaching a decision.

Try to schedule your inspections to make the best use of your time. If you go with a broker, tell him exactly how much time you have to spend, and make certain that you allow yourself enough time to get a full impression of each house you visit. If you deal directly with owners, try to arrange a period of time when you can inspect without committing yourself to a firm appointment. In that way you can avoid jamming up your schedule and having to rush to make an appointment, or waiting around for a considerable time between appointments.

Chapter 16
Completing the Purchase

You've made a decision to buy, you've looked at houses, and you've made up your mind about which one you want to live in. Now you're going to move forward and make that purchase.

There are those who will tell you that this whole area is the traditional American cat-and-mouse game. Wrong. This is not a game of any kind; this is serious business. Ideally, when a contract has been signed, both buyer and seller should be happy, or at least satisfied that the contract is fair. There really is no other way to do business. In buying or selling a house at its real value, nobody is stuck with a bad deal. If somebody is, there will be repercussions.

The primary function of a realtor—or your main purpose—is to negotiate a good sales contract. Everything the realtor does leads up to that. Once a contract has been negotiated and just before you sign it, your lawyer should review it thoroughly in anticipation of the closing of the sale.

GROUND RULES FOR NEGOTIATING THE CONTRACT

Now you're getting close to the nitty-gritty. Here are seven rules that will help you put your best foot forward in negotiations.

1. The first bid is likely to be turned down. Don't panic. Self-control at this time can be difficult if you really want the house, but overeagerness can destroy your bargaining position. There is nearly always ample time for additional bids.

There is always the likelihood, of course, that the house will suddenly be snapped up by a newcomer during the very time you are preparing to make another bid, but to buy a house at the lowest price you have to take that chance. If you tend toward nervousness and bargaining is distasteful to you, let the real estate broker carry the ball for you. He wants to see a sale made. If your bid is decisively rejected, you must either quit or raise it enough to make a difference.

2. Bargaining is an art that requires tact and knowledge of human nature. But you do have to learn to spar, to feint, and to allow the owner to save face. If you feel incapable of the give-and-take, deal through a broker.

3. For house prices up to about $55,000 the first bid can be at least 10% to 20% under the asking price. The higher the asking price, the more you can underbid. For houses priced over $85,000 or so, there are no general rules. Some of these houses can be bought for as much as 50% under the asking price. One factor is whether or not an owner is in a hurry to sell.

4. The brand-new house, the already finished speculatively built kind, is most likely to be overpriced, particularly if it has gone unsold for a while. It costs builders money every month to keep the houses empty, so as time goes by they are increasingly open to any reasonable offer. Naturally, a builder is tempted to overprice a new house with the hope of getting as much as possible right away. If he doesn't sell, he ordinarily has to take the best price he can get. That's why a low first bid can save you money when you buy a speculatively built house. You may be turned down, but you can come back with a higher offer. Or you may be amazed at how much you save on the house.

New houses in a new development are much more likely to be firm in price. Generally you must pay the listed price, especially for a new house that you order from the builder's model.

5. Don't be timid about negotiating. Look at property on an ugly day. Interview your future neighbors—those next door to the ones recommended by your broker. Demand a reasonable warranty on new houses. Beware of an "I-don't-know-that-to-be-a-problem" reply when you ask about, say, water stains. It's your responsibility to find out about problems.

6. The contract should assume nothing. It should stipulate everything—who pays for the new paint job, for termite extermination, for a plumbing leak, everything—in writing.

7. Don't assume that some other people make a great deal of money out of a house sale. It is often assumed that builders make huge profits, when in fact the opposite is true— many barely stay in business; or that when a homeowner sells

his house he makes a huge profit on which he takes a capital gain—the homeowner usually makes no more than the reasonable appreciation of his real estate.

NEGOTIATING THE SALE PRICE

The usual situation is that your negotiations are rapid and come to a conclusion without a lot of discussion or a lot of time. But at times negotiations can be drawn out, perhaps over a matter of days or weeks. Don't let those delays upset you.

There may be the offer and counteroffer, a duel of wits and wills that may go on for days. But much of that is really superfluous. Most experienced brokers can forecast quite accurately what a given house in their area will eventually sell for. As the hopeful buyer, you would like to obtain the house you want at the lowest possible price; the seller, naturally enough, wants the highest price. If you engage in negotiations realistically, you can probably find common ground with the seller without too much haggling.

The broker can be of considerable help here. He generally knows when an asking price is firm and when it's negotiable. And while his commission varies directly in proportion to the selling price, remember that he does not earn a cent until the house is sold and the transaction is closed.

Ninety times out of a hundred you will meet the owner through the broker who is your middleman and the owner's middleman too. Let's say that the owner has an asking price for his house and lot of $90,000. You believe that the house is worth only $60,000, and your broker says that other houses of the same size in similar locations and with the same level of amenities are priced anywhere from $75,000 to $85,000.

Presumably, before you make any commitments at all, you will ask for an inspection of the house, and you may use a professional, as discussed in Chapter 4. A professional inspector has told you what he thinks needs to be done to the house and how much he thinks it might cost you to do it.

You can probably open negotiations by telling the owner about the cost of the work that has to be done on the house, using "guestimated" figures for what a subcontractor would cost and not indicating that you can do any of the work yourself.

Your opening gambit is the offer: what you think he can lower his asking price of $90,000 to, less what you think repairs and remodeling will cost. Let's say it comes out to $68,000; that's your initial offer.

The owner's first reaction will be to say that he can't lower his price more than $3,000, or some such figure. Don't panic; simply say you are sorry and walk away. There is plenty of time, and if somebody wants to pay the full $90,000 or $87,000 for the house, you shouldn't compete anyhow if you think it is worth only $68,000. You would hate yourself for any bid much over that price that was accepted so early in negotiations.

In all dealings with the owner keep everything on a friendly basis, maintaining all the while that you can't possibly afford more, but you do like the house. He will maintain just as strongly that he thinks you would be a marvelous owner for his house, but he can't lower his price either and isn't that too bad.

He'll tell you all the things that could happen—that the market is hot, or money might get tight, or he has some interested parties ready to buy. Again, don't panic. If others are ready to buy, let them; but they are probably fictional. Take your time and don't make any move that you will regret later.

Eventually, (over a two- to eight-week period) the owner will lower his price significantly if he really wants to sell and can't find another buyer. He almost always has sufficient equity that he can lower his price as much as 20% to 30%, if he really has to sell. You can raise your price if you become, in that time span, more familiar with the value of real estate in the area.

You may come up not quite halfway, and he may come down a little bit more than halfway, so that you wind up making a deal for something like $72,500. Both parties are happy, but you are especially happy because you didn't accept the opening price. You can live with your bid without kicking yourself in years to come for having paid too much.

Let me repeat some of the things I've already said. Do not get involved in the purchase or sale of real estate without the guidance and counsel of an attorney. A realtor may be well versed in certain aspects of the law pertaining to real estate, but he is not a lawyer and should not attempt to advise you on legal matters. Certainly it is possible to transfer real estate without an attorney, but why take the risk? It is always good practice to use a local lawyer in the community where your purchase is being made.

SIGNING THE CONTRACT TO PURCHASE

When you have found the house you want and you and the seller have agreed on price, you still have to sign the contract. Remember before signing any contract that it is legally binding, your lawyer should review it carefully. After that review you will sign a conditional contract to purchase, which becomes effective at the time you and the owner/seller sign. It is conditional because it includes provisions that must be met before the contract can be closed. The most frequent provision is a contingency about getting the mortgage loan. The broker will tell you what the amount of binder, earnest money, or token deposit is, usually about 1% of the sale price.

It is often possible, but not necessary, for the conditional purchase contract to indicate the latest date at which the seller is to be out of the house so that you can move in, assuming that the closing falls within that time. If the seller cannot be out of the house, because his sale depends upon his purchase of another house, there should be a stipulation in the contract that he will pay rent to you, at so much per week, for the weeks that he remains in the house while you cannot move in.

Getting the house entirely in your hands may take three steps: (1) giving a binder or earnest money; (2) signing the conditional sales contract; and (3) closing, with you taking title and getting a mortgage, if one is needed.

Steps 1 and 2 may be concurrent. Usually they are accomplished within days of each other in a two-step process. The first step is the binder money on the day that you decide; the second step is a 5% to 10% down payment on a sales contract to show that you intend to purchase the house for the sales price you have agreed on. This can follow the binder within a week or so, even though the closing may not come about for three months. All these terms are specified in the sales contract.

Such a sales contract indicates that if the deal falls through, the money must be returned to you, the buyer; but it may also indicate that if you back out of the deal without a good reason, you lose the down payment to the present owner.

Conditional sales contracts should contain the following information:

1. The legal names of the parties involved and their relationships

2. A brief property description, the sales price, and the terms of the sale

3. Whether or not the sale is subject to an appraisal acceptable to you, and by an independent or FHA, VA appraiser

4. Whether the sale is contingent upon inspection by a construction expert

5. Specifics of any unusual easements or encumbrances to the property

6. Terms of the deposit receipt, the conditions of forfeiture, marketability of seller's title, and risk-of-loss clause

7. The date of closing and when title is to be passed to you, as well as the date when you can move in, especially if prior to closing

8. Correction of title defects

Your purchase contract should set forth what is to be done, and the time limits for such acts, if it should be discovered that there are defects in the seller's title to the property. Normal provisions give the seller a reasonable opportunity to correct defects, and if he cannot or will not, you must have the option to cancel the contract. Note that you are probably better protected by a provision giving you an option to cancel than by a provision that would automatically cancel in the event of uncured title defects. A seller might choose not to correct a minor defect just to get out of a contract if buyer would rather buy and accept the defect (and probably find a way to cure it himself) than lose the other benefits of his bargain.

9. Rent to be charged to the seller if he is still in the house after closing

10. The type of mortgage to be obtained, its terms, and whether obtaining it is a contingency

11. Designation of closing costs and title insurance costs

12. Prorations of taxes, fire insurance, fuel, and other such costs

13. The type of deed seller is to convey and whether he is to furnish an abstract of title

14. A list of any furnishings or appliances that are to go with the house

Chapter 17

Closing the Home Purchase Contract

No doubt you've heard a few dozen stories about a closing session from your friends—all those checks, all that paper, all those people. Well, it's true that there's an unholy amount of detail, but before going into all of it, let me point out a few things.

You've thought and planned about your new house at great length. If you've been careful and followed the advice in this book so far, you're probably very happy with the prospect of owning the house you're about to purchase.

The question you will probably ask immediately is: Why does it take so long between the signing of the contract to purchase and the actual closing? And the next question you will probably ask is: Why does it cost so much?

To answer both, you have to know what has to be accomplished by you, your lawyer, your lender, the seller, and his lawyer—all the requirements of a sale.

When you have signed the conditional sales contract you have made the decision to buy. It may take several weeks or even months before the actual closing to accomplish the matters that are discussed here.

Your closing takes time and careful attention, but don't let it or its prospect disturb you. All of it is done to protect your interest, and the interests of the seller, and the interests of the lender. If their interests were not protected by a proper closing, yours wouldn't be either.

In ninety-nine-plus closings out of one hundred, you need *your* lawyer, not somebody else's lawyer. Your lawyer needs to know everything about your business, your family, your financial circumstances. You can talk to him confidentially, knowing that the law protects the relationship.

Your lawyer does two basic things for you. First, and most important, he is your counselor, giving guidance and advice upon all aspects of the closing. (In most states, a lawyer can represent more than one of the participants in a real estate transaction if all consent to the arrangement. In such cases the lawyer must keep all parties fully advised of their rights. If any conflict develops between the parties, the lawyer must withdraw from further representation of any of them.)

Second, your lawyer functions as your representative as the required documentation is prepared—he looks over everything and prepares many of the documents himself. Your lawyer attends the closing, having made certain that all necessary documents are properly prepared and signed (executed). He makes certain that the transaction proceeds in an orderly legal manner.

It's possible to close without a lawyer, and you may come away suffering no legal or monetary loss, now or in the future. But only by retaining proper counsel can you know with any degree of certainty that you are obtaining all the rights in the property you are paying for.

An important detail before you close: if you are moving into a new house, it is critical that you inspect every corner of it before you accept it at closing. Any corrections that are the builder's responsibility must be identified before the closing. By compiling a written list of problems and work still to be done, you make sure that your builder knows his obligations. The lender may require that funds be left in escrow if construction of a new house is incomplete.

THE CLOSING: AN ASSEMBLAGE OF DOCUMENTS

Closing is usually four weeks to three months after the purchase contract has been signed; the time is needed to prepare all the documentation.

Every house purchase contract requires the preparation, execution, and delivery of legal documents, the making of financial adjustments between the seller and the buyer. Additional documents, and additional financial adjustments, are needed when there is an existing loan to be assumed by the buyer, or to be paid in full and the mortgage released. If you're getting a mortgage, or if the seller is taking from you a promissory note secured by a second-lien mortgage, still more documents and financial adjustments are needed.

If the closing date does not coincide with the real estate tax period, an adjustment for taxes must be made. If you purchase the unused but prepaid portion of fire and extended-coverage insurance from the seller, an adjustment must be made and instruments executed to transfer the policies.

No two closings are exactly alike. Each must be tailored to the case at hand. In order to have a smooth closing, one person must take overall responsibility for making the arrangements, preparing the documents, checking the financial adjustments, and coordinating the efforts of all parties. Sometimes the lawyer for the seller or your lawyer undertakes this function. Sometimes the lender, particularly when the lender is a large financial institution, serves as the focal point for the closing. Sometimes title companies, real estate companies, or escrow companies take charge.

No matter which party or institution takes charge of the closing, it is important that all parties cooperate and that both principals, the buyer and the seller, understand all aspects and have at hand someone to look after his interests.

The instruments used to pass title from seller to buyer is called a deed. It is the legally recognized document that shows ownership of the property. The seller is usually responsible for the satisfactory preparation of the deed. Deeds differ in three ways:

1. A general warranty deed transfers ownership of the described property to the buyer and guarantees that the title to the property is clear of any defects that might hurt the buyer's ability to resell the property.

2. A special warranty deed conveys ownership with limited warranties. This type of deed is frequently used by counties and states where municipalities sell land for development and do not wish to be involved in any subsequent claims made against the property.

3. A quitclaim deed transfers the property with all debts, liens, or other encumbrances to the buyer. Auctioned properties are often sold with this type of deed.

Usually you get a general warranty deed. With the other two deeds the seller is normally not required to come to the aid of the buyer in the case of an unclear title until the buyer has been put out of possession or at least had possession seriously threatened, and the seller may not be around when needed—he may have moved away or have died. Even if the seller can be located, he may not be in a financial position to perform his obligations. These types of deeds are of little practical value, and title examiners tend to regard them with suspicion.

Sometimes there are technical defects in titles which can most easily and economically be remedied by improving the seller's title even after the sale. The general warranty deed from the seller then operates to transfer the seller's "after acquired title" to you. Another advantage of the general warranty deed is that in the event a defect in the title is discovered after the sale and if the seller's title is covered by title insurance, the title insurance policy also covers the seller's obligations.

Before the closing there is a schedule of required documentation available to you. You and your attorney have a hand in drawing up that schedule, and you must complete the items that specifically are your responsibility. The seller completes the items that apply to him.

The documents in the preclosing statement specify the amount of cash you must have in hand or in your checking account at the closing.

BE AWARE OF DETAILS

Your mortgage loan officer, with your lawyer, arranges for a title search when the contract to purchase is signed. The title company, or the person doing the search (sometimes your lawyer), must ascertain that the seller is the true owner of the house—that legal ownership goes back as far as possible, sometimes even to the original grant—and that he has the right to sell to you.

A title search may be performed by an abstracter, a title insurance agent, an attorney, or a title insurer, depending on local law and custom. In a search, public records may be checked in the offices of recorders or registers of deeds, clerks of courts, and municipal and other county officials. These records include all recorded documents as well as judgments, other liens, general taxes, street assessments, sewer system assessments, and other special taxes and levies. Through a search, land title problems such as recorded workmen's liens against property, unsatisfied mortgages, and many others are exposed to homebuyers and mortgage lenders so that appropriate action can be taken before a transaction is completed.

Your "new" house may be a hundred years or more old, and the land, of course, has been around forever. Ownership may have changed many times, and record keeping years ago was often crude. Yet all of those transfers are still important, and an error in one can come to the surface many years later, with disastrous results. Land owned jointly by a husband and wife, for example, may have been sold by the husband without his spouse's approval or signature. Even if the property has changed hands several times since then, the wife and her heirs may still have a claim on it. If one of them pops up forty years later, the family with a house on that land may be in for a costly legal battle.

Another problem might be the existence of an overlooked easement, a strip of land on your property that a utility company has the right to use for the placement and maintenance of its lines. If your house has inadvertently been built on this easement, it may be subject to demolition. A surveying error may have resulted in faulty determination of lot lines; your house may be sitting on your neighbor's land. Other possible title problems can result from old liens, forgeries of deeds, violations of restrictive covenants, and zoning complications.

The search for judgments is so important that the representative of the title company present at the closing may check the courthouse just before papers are signed to make sure a last-minute judgment has not been filed against the property. This is why the actual time of the title closing is indicated on the closing statement.

Easements (lawyers call them encumbrances) are generally the rights of other people to certain privileges. For example, a driveway that is between two houses and is used by both owners to enter their respective garages is an easement. Drainage across another's property is also a form of easement. The right of a utility company to erect poles and to enter upon the grounds to make repairs is regarded as an easement and is so indicated on the deed.

The title search indicates whether the property has any riparian rights, that is, water rights on property bordering a river, lake, ocean, or bay. If riparian rights are part of the deed, they may include the use of the water for bathing, building a boathouse or pier, or fishing. If the water is navigable, however, any construction that juts into the water may require a permit issued by the Army Corps of Engineers. An owner may sell his property and exclude the riparian rights (he may want to keep the boathouse for his own use). This is perfectly legal. The new owner should ascertain at the time of the contract—and at title closing—just what control, if any, he will have over the water rights.

Your lawyer should review with you just what restrictions and convenants are part of the deed to the house and land. For example, there may be a restriction on, say, removing trees. In some suburbs cutting down a tree, unless it is dead, must be approved by the community.

Another important item in the closing documentation is the survey. If property has changed hands recently, the title company may accept the previous survey. It may be desirable to have a new survey made, however, especially if an extension to the house or a driveway has been built. The buyer, of course, pays for the survey, which must be made by a civil engineer or a licensed surveyor, preferably one known to the title company.

Here's a list of papers the buyer and the seller are normally required to have at the closing (some may not be necessary at yours):

1. Seller's copy of the real estate sales contract
2. The latest tax, water, assessment, gas, and electric bills and proof that they have been paid
3. The latest possible meter readings for water, gas, and electricity
4. All homeowner's insurance policies for fire and liability
5. Assignment of leases (if any)
6. Affidavit of title
7. Seller's last deed
8. Deed for purchaser
9. All documents that the seller has agreed to deliver or prepare
10. Any unrecorded instruments that might affect the title
11. Receipt for the last payment of interest on the mortgage
12. Receipts or statements showing that the following have been paid or satisfied: mechanic's liens, judgments, chattel mortgages (personal property mortgage), or mortgages that must be paid prior to closing
13. Any agreements that have been called for in the contract
14. A certificate from the lending institution showing the amount due on the mortgage and the date to which interest is paid
15. A bill of sale for all personal property covered in the real estate sales contract

The method of computing prorations and the date used for the prorations vary with the locality. In many areas the adjustments are made as of the day preceding the closing. Two other dates that might be used in the computation of the prorations, depending on the locality, are the actual day of closing or the day the buyer takes possession of the house.

THE BUYER'S DOWN PAYMENT AND CLOSING COSTS— CASH ITEMS

Closing costs for a $75,000 house may run around $4,000 or $5,000 in addition to your down payment—awful, but unavoidable, and well worth it. All those costs have already been scheduled, and you will know all about them some days before the closing.

The cash needed to buy a house that costs $75,000 is listed in the following table. Note that closing costs vary with down payment in the example given.

CASH REQUIREMENTS TO PURCHASE A $75,000 HOUSE

	Down payments	
	10%	20%
Down payment	$7,500	$15,000
Lender's originating fee	675	600
Mortgage insurance	338	0
Escrow for real estate taxes	100	100
One year's premium for homeowner's fire, hazard, theft, and liability insurance	625	625
Credit report	25	25
Appraisal fee	225	225
Title insurance	675	600
Legal and other closing costs	1,013	900
Property survey	250	250
Recording fees and transfer taxes	800	700
TOTALS	$12,226	$19,025

Remember that interest rates are calculated at market yields. The face amount of interest on the note, if below current market yield, requires discounting to gain access to the money. The rule of thumb is that a one-point discount is the equivalent of a ⅛% interest rate. For example, if a loan amount is established at $60,000 and the mortgage lender wants to write the note at 9½% when the market yield requires 10%, the loan payout would be discounted by four points. Instead of receiving $60,000 in loan proceeds, the borrower would receive $57,600. In this situation the discount is paid by the seller. To actually get $60,000, the borrower must borrow $62,400.

The contract indicates who bears the various expenses of closing the transaction or completing the sale. Local customs vary. In some areas it is customary for the seller to pay the cost of owner's title insurance for the buyer, or to give the buyer an abstract of title that has been certified up to the time of the contract of purchase. In these areas, if the seller elects to furnish the abstract, the buyer pays to have the abstract recertified after the closing and also pays for a title examination and opinion by his own lawyer. In other areas the custom is for the seller to provide nothing at all by way of title evidence, and all costs thereof are borne by the buyer.

You should consider the question of whether who pays settlement costs is negotiable. Typically, the buyer absorbs most of them, but circumstances alter cases. Negotiations depend upon such factors as how eager the seller is to sell and how eager you are to buy, the quality of the house, how long it has been on the market, whether other potential buyers are interested.

All costs and charges relating to the transaction should be reflected in one or more closing statements. In some cases all charges are shown on a single statement, and the various parties (seller, buyer, lender) can determine the effect of each item upon their situation. (See the sample closing statement form in Chapter 21). Often separate closing statements are prepared for the seller, the buyer, and the lender. This practice makes it somewhat easier for each party to follow the transaction from his own point of view.

The preclosing settlement statement is furnished well before the closing date, so that the buyer, the seller, and their lawyers can review it and resolve any problems prior to the actual closing. The preclosing settlement statement usually designates who pays exactly what amounts.

Usually the buyer pays for all the items on this list:

1. Title examination and/or title insurance
2. Property survey fee
3. Attorney's fees

4. Fee for preparation of documents (unless included in attorney's fees)

5. Closing fee (may be included in attorney's fees)

6. Escrow fee (may be included in closing fee or in attorney's fees)

7. Credit report

8. Initial service fee or origination fee, charged by lender

9. Discount, if any

10. Mortgage assumption fee, if applicable

11. Appraisal fee

12. Termite or other property inspection fee

13. Recording fee

14. Real estate sales commissions

15. Prepaid expenses:

a. Amount to mortgagee at time of closing for payment of real estate taxes

b. Deposit for payment of initial FHA mortgage insurance premium

c. Amount collected at time of closing for prepayment of hazard insurance premiums (fire and extended coverage)

d. Special assessments; for example, fees paid for improvements to municipal facilities such as roads, sidewalks, and sewers

e. Other prepaid items, such as interest on the loan accrued between the closing date and the date interest for the first mortgage payment is effective, and costs of any special services purchased by the borrower, such as premiums on life insurance policies

THE ESCROW ACCOUNT

No doubt you've heard the word *escrow*. It means an account held by the lending institution. The primary escrow account is one into which you prepay your real estate taxes, some mortgage interest and principal, and some portion of the property insurance premium with your monthly payment. At the closing you will be required to make your first contribution to the escrow account.

You can see why the lender would want to be sure that the mortgagor (the buyer) pays taxes. Otherwise, the city could confiscate the property, including the bank's share, for nonpayment of taxes before the bank could act to protect its investment. If the seller has prepaid any taxes or insurance premiums accumulated in his own escrow account, the buyer is required to reimburse him for these amounts at closing.

Lending institutions provide a service to the owner by handling all the paper work, transferring funds each month from the payment to the escrow account, and paying the taxes and insurance on time. Lenders also provide a community service by paying taxes in bulk instead of sending hundreds of checks in smaller amounts which would burden the clerical staffs of governmental offices. Because of this service, usually no interest is paid on escrow accounts. This is one of the most frequently heard complaints from homeowners. Today, while some lenders are paying interest, perhaps 1% annually, others are requesting that the owner handle his own taxes and insurance. When you are shopping for mortgages, this is another factor that may differ from lender to lender.

There are other uses for the escrow account. Earnest money and down payments before closing are often put into them. And if there is any question as to the title to the property, a sale may be closed in escrow.

Escrows usually operate somewhat as follows: Both the deed and the purchase price are delivered to some disinterested third party, often a title insurance company, with written instructions to record the deed, to order an examination of title, and, if the title shows clear, to pay the purchase price to the seller. The escrow agreement also provides that if it appears that the seller's title is defective and the defects are not cured within a certain specified time, the buyer shall be entitled to the return of his money upon reconveying the title to the seller.

Escrow practices differ quite a bit from state to state. In many communities escrows are virtually unknown; this is particularly true of small communities where seller and buyer know and trust each other. The danger that the seller will make a deed or mortgage to some third person in order to get out of the deal is not so great in these circumstances as in larger communities, where relationships are apt to be more impersonal. When a deal is closed without benefit of escrow, the buyer often requires the seller, at the time the deal is closed, to give an affidavit that he has not signed any deeds, mortgages, or contracts since the date of the contract of sale, and that since that date no judgments have been rendered against him.

Another benefit of the escrow account is that if objections to the title that can be removed by use of the purchase money appear, such as judgments against the seller or unpaid taxes, the buyer may with absolute safety, after title is recorded in his name, allow the escrow holder to use part of the purchase money to remove such objections. An escrow also assures the buyer that the seller will not change his mind and convey the property to some third person in order to escape performance of the contract. On the other hand, it assures the seller that the purchase price will be paid to him if the title is clear, and it enables a seller who has liens against his title to use the buyer's money to pay off such liens.

Chapter
18
Getting and Closing
the Mortgage Loan

The most likely contingency in your sales contract will be securing a mortgage. Successfully arranging to get that mortgage depends a great deal on the appraisal, which you must have if you are planning to use an FHA or a VA mortgage. The local FHA office can order an appraisal, and your mortgage loan officer can make that arrangement. The VA office issues a certificate of reasonable value (CRV), which your mortgage loan officer also gets. Most conventional financing lenders require their own appraisal. The mortgage amount depends on what the appraiser tells the mortgage lender about the property.

A note about the FHA appraisal: minimum property standards have been established by the U.S. Department of Housing and Urban Development, and any property that fails to meet them will not be insured. It is illegal for any seller or real estate agent to advertise a house as FHA-approved prior to this appraisal procedure.

If the lender finds the appraisal satisfactory, the applicant's credit history is sent to the FHA. Next, the FHA determines if the applicant can reasonably afford the mortgage, and if so, the lending institution arranges the closing with the purchaser applicant after processing and assurance by FHA of a "firm commitment."

Some sellers prefer buyers who can qualify for conventional mortgages because FHA can present a small problem: often a seller must take his house off the market for a period of time until he knows whether or not the FHA has approved the loan. If it does not, the deal falls through, and the seller has lost valuable time.

Although you may fully qualify for an FHA-insured mortgage, it's wise to recognize that it may take a little perseverance to find a seller and lender willing to go along with you. One word of caution: if you ever default on an FHA-insured loan, your chances of getting another one are virtually nonexistent.

Any veteran who furnishes a certificate of eligibility issued by the VA can obtain the mortgage loan guarantee. The VA does not require a down payment if the purchase price does not exceed the appraised value of the house. However, the lending institution can still require a down payment (remember, it's their money); lending institutions frequently follow the FHA formula for down payments. Neither FHA-insured nor conventional loans offer this desirable no-down-payment feature.

Obtaining an FHA-insured or VA-guaranteed mortgage is not always as easy as official guidelines indicate. Some lenders are hesitant to grant these mortgages because they require additional paper work.

Farmers Home Administration (FmHA) also makes attractive loans for houses in relatively rural areas. Rates vary and depend on family size and income. In some cases, thirty-three year terms are available. Check your local office of the Farmer's Home Administration for details.

A loan made directly to the owner for the purpose of construction and long-term financing may be made on a conventional, FHA, or VA basis. The disbursements during construction are made to the owner or, upon authorization by the owner, directly to the builder. When the papers are drawn, regular amortization of the loan generally is set to begin one month after the estimated completion date of the construction. During the construction period, interest is paid on the funds that have been paid from the building loan commitment account at the same rate as shown on the long-term note. The title to the property should be vested in the owner.

How does the appraiser arrive at his figure for the property? Most of the appraiser's judgments are done on a basis of comparison, or "comparables." An appraisal form authorized by the Society of Real Estate Appraisers includes a detailed physical description of the building with dimensions and photos; remarks on paving, curbs, walks, utilities, assessments; the price trend of the neighborhood—up, down, or stable; the condition of the house and recommended repairs; and remarks about comparable sales in the area. There is also an analysis of the value based on the reproduction cost of the building.

Another report used by appraisers, called the "green sheet," gives the proximity of the property to the downtown area, shopping, schools, and expressways; the trends of income, population, and property values; and the economic composition of the neighborhood. There is a detailed rating—good, average, or poor—of the foundation, wall construction, windows, floors, furnace and boiler, bath, kitchen, and so on.

A good appraiser checks thoroughly into the condition of everything, much as you would following the checklist questions in Chapter 9, and makes a thorough report on the market trend and the economic trend of the neighborhood. An appraisal generally costs from $100 to $400, but it is impossible to make precise estimates. The money is scheduled with your closing costs. You may be required to put up a deposit for the appraisal that will not be returned to you should the sale fall through. But don't let that be a surprise to you; it is common practice.

DON'T LET WEIGHTY DOCUMENTATION SCARE YOU

Consumer protection regulations over the past decade or so have made mortgage lending to the consumer a mountain of official details for everybody. The U.S. League of Savings Associations in 1978 compiled a list of the documentation necessary for a mortgage with no insurance, no guarantees, no complexities such as qualifying for sale to FHLMC or FNMA (see Chapter 13). A summary of the findings follows.

The file for the conventional home loan contained seventeen documents. Eight, or almost half, were mandated directly by Congress at some time during the past ten years, all to protect you (you pay for it, too). Another three documents have grown longer, more complex, and more detailed under the influence of the ten-year rash of legislation. A count of printed lines in the loan papers shows they have doubled in ten years.

MORTGAGE CLOSING REPORTS

Report	Pages	Lines or items	Copies	Mandated by law	Influenced by law
1. Notice to applicants	1	27	3	x	
2. Underwriting standards	8	320	3	x	

3. Loan application	2	216	2		x
4. Insurance information	1	3	1		
5. Good-faith estimate of closing costs	1	27	3	x	
6. Buyer's disclosure of real party in interest	1	9	3	x	
7. RESPA docket	1	28	3	x	
8. Notice of right of rescission	1	32	3	x	
9. Credit report	1	54	3		x
10. Appraisal form	1	398	2		x
11. Information on lawyers	1	46	2		
12. Loan disburse-ment record	1	80	2		
13. Regulation Z, truth in lending	1	58	3	x	
14. HUD settlement statement	1	24	3	x	
15. Loan check requisition	1	14	2		

16.	Note	1	41	3	
17.	Mortgage	4	118	3	
18.	"HUD Guide for Home Buyers"	31	1,953	2	x

In trying to protect you, the consumer, the legislative and regulatory process itself causes ambiguities. The laws and regulations keep piling up, often in a confusing manner. The laws affecting mortgage lending alone are as follows:

LOAN CLOSING LAWS

1968	Truth in Lending Act Fair Housing Act
1970	Fair Credit Reporting Act
1973	Flood Disaster Protection Act Real Estate Settlement Procedures Act (RESPA)
1974	Equal Credit Opportunity Act Significant Amendments to the Truth in Lending Act Fair Credit Billing Act
1975	Home Mortgage Disclosure Act
1976	Amendments to the Real Estate Settlement Procedures Act Significant amendments to the Equal Credit Opportunity Act Significant amendments to the Flood Disaster Protection Act Consumer Leasing Act
1977	Community Reinvestment Act

How about the ability of the borrower to understand the information contained in congressionally mandated documents? (If you lay out all the facts in writing, the homebuyer will not be misled by unscrupulous lenders, right?) Here's the way the U.S. League of Savings Associations noted the reading skills necessary to comprehend some of the documents designed to protect you:

READABILITY OF LOAN DOCUMENTS

Mandated document	Fog Index*	Reading level
Notice to applicants		
First half	12	High school senior
Second half	18	College graduate
Notice of right of rescission	16	College senior
"HUD Guide for Home Buyers"		
Page 1	16	College senior
Page 7	18	College graduate
Page 8	17	College graduate
Good-faith estimate	11	High school junior

*Measure of reading difficulty from Robert Gunning, *The Technique of Clear Writing*, rev. ed. (New York: McGraw-Hill, 1968).

The "HUD Guide for Home Buyers" proved to be a distressing case study in difficulty and obscurity. The pamphlet that associations must give every borrower requires a reading level beyond four years of college. It purports to inform all, but because of the complexity of the language and sentence structure the guide can be understood by less than 2% of the population!

Don't panic. Your lender and your lawyer can guide you through all this federal overkill.

RESPA: BUREAUCRATIC OVERKILL

You have probably heard something about RESPA. To protect the buyer from unreasonable charges, the federal Real Estate Settlement Procedures Act (RESPA, Public Law 93-533) requires mortgage lending institutions to identify clearly final costs and individual financial responsibility—in short, who pays what and how much. According to this law, the lender is required to complete the standard RESPA form on settlement expenses and to make it available for inspection one day in advance of the actual closing.

The RESPA statute also requires bankers to supply potential

borrowers with a highly detailed information booklet and an estimate of closing costs within three business days of getting a written loan application. It is basically a disclosure statute. Reading that booklet requires a singularly high level of motivation and at least a college education, says the U.S. League of Savings Associations.

Some consumer groups maintain that RESPA doesn't have enough clout to deal with what Congress saw as one of the biggest potential abuses in the real estate settlement business: kickbacks and "referral fees" on clients who might be steered by a lender or broker to a particular title insurance company or law firm, for example. Many lenders, on the other hand, think they are being needlessly strangled in red tape. Oddly enough, some consumer activists agree that RESPA puts a heavy burden on business and doesn't do much good for the consumer.

RESPA, in essence, shows you, the buyer, what you would pay in total over the twenty-five or thirty-year life of your mortgage. Since everything above the face amount of the mortgage note is interest, the initial impact on the home purchaser/borrower is misleading. Interest paid annually is a direct credit against income for income tax purposes; and besides, nearly everyone either sells his home or reworks his financing within a seven- to ten-year period.

Congress should have known better than to make lenders "policemen" at closings. Such items as prepaid taxes, insurance policies, and deed registrations carry fixed costs. Others, such as points or real estate broker's commissions, have already been incurred and are not negotiable.

When you look at all the costs itemized on the original RESPA form, the only ones the consumer realistically might reduce by shopping around are the title insurance premium, if he wants title insurance, and the attorney's fees. But in many areas the title company and the attorney are dictated by the lender, so the consumer is a captive customer.

The best advice is to look briefly at the RESPA document, let your attorney check it, and then forget it. It's necessary under law, it costs you more money, and it does almost nothing for you. But don't lie awake at night worrying about it. Ownership of your home is the only important thing.

A MARKETABLE TITLE TO THE DEED

You and the lender want to be sure that a marketable title is delivered at the closing. To make sure the title is good, a title search must be made by a title company or an attorney (see Chapter

17). After a comprehensive search, title insurance normally is purchased to protect the insured against title hazards, including those even the most thorough search cannot reveal.

There are two types of title insurance, one for the lender and one for the owner. The lending institution requires protection for its interests only—that is, for the amount of the mortgage. The buyer, for peace of mind, should purchase similar protection of his equity in the property. Payment is made once, at the closing.

The business of lender's and owner's title insurance can be a matter of great importance. For instance, let's assume that the lender gets a policy on a house that slides downhill into a ravine in a mudslide during a torrential rainstorm. The lender makes a claim for his loss, on the title company if he has a lender's policy. The title company pays the lender his claim and immediately institutes foreclosure on the house. That means that the lender gets his money and the title company gets whatever results from a foreclosure sale. But the owner may be out of luck because he did not have owner's title insurance.

That means that you want an owner's policy to protect yourself in two distinct ways: first, you want to protect your equity against any claims that can be made against it; and second, you want to protect yourself against the title company, which will surely foreclose against you in the event of a lender's claim, if you do not have an owner's title policy.

Title insurance protects property against attacks on the title based on flaws in the records; that is, it pays losses sustained because of such errors as forgeries, liens, and improper transfers of title. It also usually guarantees that the title is marketable, or generally acceptable to everyone in the area, including the courts.

Title insurance does not, however, give blanket protection against every conceivable difficulty that can arise; such insurance is virtually unheard of. The areas *not* covered are spelled out in a standard coverage policy and usually include exceptions to the title that appear on the record, such as easements; matters of survey, such as lot line violations; disputes over physical possession of the property; zoning violations.

You have no option in the purchase of mortgagee (lender) title insurance. The lender makes that decision, though the borrower must pay the premium. In the case of FHA-insured and VA-guaranteed loans, where the ultimate purchaser of the mortgage may be located in another state, title insurance becomes a part of the mortgage loan package. Savings and loan associations, which normally do not require title insurance on local mortgages, may demand insurance on out-of-town loans for the same reason.

Chapter 19

Buying and Selling at the Same Time

The complex process of buying and selling at the same time can be narrowed down to two basic actions: maintaining your present property, and getting a financing arrangement to buy a new house, whether or not your old house is sold in time for that purchase. See the section on financing in Chapter 13.

You may have to get used to some other things in the process, however. One of the most difficult may be having your family separated for a time, part occupying your new house and part staying as caretaker in the old one. If somebody does not stay in your old house after you have moved into your new one, a prospective customer will not see it in its best light—the way it looks when it is being lived in and the furniture is still in place. But leaving the house in the hands of a realtor is often necessary when you have to leave for a distant town and take everyone in your family with you.

As explained in Chapter 15, there are things that a realtor can do for you, and do well, to find prospective buyers. If you have any question about your ability to sell your own house when you are contemplating a move, you should immediately get in contact with a good realtor.

The services of a good realtor are particularly important if a moving deadline is drawing near. A realtor with a multiple-listing service not only may find you a good house in your new town, but also may handle the sale of your old house, as well as help your new buyer find financing for the purchase. He can do for the prospective buyer of your house the same things he can do for you.

You should think carefully about a good realtor when you're thinking of buying and selling at the same time. Buyers and sellers are often in adversary relationships and a skilled third party can do wonders to keep the waters smooth and cases of nerves to an absolute minimum.

A good realtor has as good an idea as anybody of what your old house will bring in the current market. He can screen prospective customers so that you won't be put on display for people who aren't serious purchasers. And he can make all inspection appointments at *your* convenience. In sum, a real estate broker can save you a lot of headaches.

ONE MAN'S EXPERIENCE

Fred Kufer's experience is a good case in point. He was a data-processing expert at Kodak in Princeton, New Jersey. He was recruited by a headhunter and now works at McDonnell-Douglas in St. Louis. He knew he was nearing the point where he could go little further at Kodak, so he jumped at the chance to move on; he and his wife made up their minds in just two days. They knew they had sixty-five days to sell their present house and find, buy, and move into the next one in St. Louis. Here's how Fred describes it:

"We'd lived in Princeton for four years, knew more than a few people, including some realtors, enough to know that there are good ones and not-so-good ones. We invited three over to the house on different evenings, giving each one of them the time frame we were operating in and where we were moving. I didn't tell them much more than that—I wanted to find out if they knew how to ask the right questions of me, a guy transferring to another city hundreds of miles away.

"Our first realtor was a disappointment. All he seemed to want to know was how much we wanted for the house, just, I guess, to get the listing. He said, almost too easily, that houses like ours were selling for $65,000 to $75,000 in the area, but he hadn't really looked carefully at the house. We told him only that we had to make the sale and that we'd get back to him. He pulled a calling card out of his wallet—you know, all curved and a little discolored. Sort of a no-class guy, really.

"Our second realtor, the next night, looked and acted like the one we wanted. He sat down, began taking notes: why we were moving, how much time we needed. He knew that we had little time to play games. He hauled a big notebook out of his briefcase and right there showed us half a dozen houses, roughly our size and in comparable neighborhoods, being offered for from $67,500 to $78,000. He made the point that we were in a strong market, and that if we listed realistically at $75,000 we'd probably get a quick response. He also said he was part of Century 21, had correspondent relationships with good realtors in St. Louis, and could help us out there. We could start 'looking' there now, while we were still tied up in New Jersey.

"Our third realtor was also good. He immediately had a good feel for the house, suggested, after looking things over carefully, that we list at $77,000 and that we'd probably sell at from $73,000 to $75,000. He was a good guy but didn't offer the St. Louis connection. He probably would have if we had talked longer with him, but he didn't make the connection right off the bat, like number two did.

"So we picked the second one, listed at $77,000, and told him we'd take anything over $73,000 as long as there were no contingencies on our part, like a second mortgage or any of that. We specified what we wanted in St. Louis, in the suburb of West Park, near work and the airport—I travel a lot—on or near the freeway, not downtown (I know St. Louis has a lot of problems there). He asked our permission to turn all the data over to a broker in St. Louis. Two weeks later Mary and I went out and looked at six houses thoroughly and their neighborhoods in a day and a half.

"The St. Louis broker showed us the first three houses just to get us oriented to the market there. The last three were much closer in concept to what we wanted. They all ran from $75,000 to $82,000, and the monthly carrying costs were well within range, with room to spare if we made a complete transfer of our equity from Princeton to St. Louis, which we did.

"The whole thing went so smoothly that we were a little uptight about it. We felt somehow we might be had, if everything could go along like this. Well, we checked with a few people, and everything was legitimate. Our house in Princeton sold fast, at $74,000, and we made the deal in St. Louis without a hitch.

"Our best advice to anyone in the same boat: screen your local realtor carefully, almost test him. If you get the right one at home, everything will be all right."

THE CORPORATE TRANSFER

Many employers provide a transfer service which can be a godsend to you. These corporate transfer services usually provide help through participating realtors and multiple-listing services that you might otherwise contact yourself. But if your company already has such a service, you should use it.

One middle-level executive, Ed Norton, of New Canaan, Connecticut, was one man who used a corporate service. Ed was an everyday commuter to New York City, where he worked for the Mobil Corporation. Not unexpectedly, one day he was told that he was being transferred to Dallas. It was a move up the ladder, and the company would put him in touch with a relocation outfit if he wanted so that he could make the move to Dallas. Ed and his wife, Peg, decided immediately that they probably would use the relocation outfit because they had two kids in school and they therefore had a lot of details other than just selling the house and buying a new one—all to be done in seventy-five days.

The relocation service, which was not part of the Mobil Corporation, had two appraisals of the house made immediately and split the difference, offering the Nortons $130,000. The Nortons could take that price, or within the next thirty days try to sell their house for more. At least they knew that they had a floor of $130,000. If the relocation company had to take the house for $130,000, they would take title and handle the sale, being paid for their trouble by Mobil's fee.

The Nortons knew exactly what they could spend in Dallas because of the $130,000 floor, so they immediately began looking, through two brokers in Dallas recommended by the relocation agency, at houses in the $160,000 price range. The Dallas brokers operated in two different suburban sections of Dallas and didn't really cross each other's paths. Says Ed Norton:

"The real estate brokers in New Canaan were willing to list our house for $160,000, in the event that we could get more than $130,000, but they wanted ninety-day exclusives and we had to get out in seventy-five days. We knew the relocation company would give us $130,000 in thirty days. So we couldn't use the brokers, but we did put an ad in the local newspaper. We started to get some traffic looking at the house, but that soon became a real hassle. People kept coming around to see the house, and Peg had all these details to take care of while I was off in the city or traveling to Dallas. We stopped advertising in two weeks and then took the $130,000 offer from the relocation company simply to get out. We had been put in touch with the brokers in Dallas, and as I said they specialized in different parts of town. In three afternoons we looked at five houses in the $150,000 to $180,000 range. We narrowed the three we liked best down to one, but financing was a problem.

"It was difficult to get the kind of mortgage we wanted so that we could use some of our equity from New Canaan for education. We took all our data to the personnel department of my corporation. They put me in touch with a customer service man at the

Republic National Bank in Dallas. The bank was only too happy to do things for me, not because I was such a great guy but because I work for Mobil, which is one of their major accounts. There was no problem in the financing with the commercial bank. They immediately provided a bridge loan [a temporary loan to handle the costs of moving and down payment until the deal on a new house can be closed with the equity from the house just sold] so that we could get a good down payment on the Dallas house and a conditional commitment for the mortgage. The whole thing was as smooth as silk simply because the bank and the relocation outfit wanted to work for Mobil, and Mobil was going to make it worth everybody's while to do a good job for Peg and me."

OPENING ACTIONS: LISTING, PRICING, AND ORIENTATION

Any realtor wants an exclusive; you would too. An exclusive means that for the period stated in a contract, only that realtor is entitled to represent you in the sale of your house, and he is entitled to a full commission even if you sell the house on your own. The exclusive is for as long as the realtor can get.

Read the realtor's agreement in detail, and have your attorney review it before you sign it. It is unlikely that the agreement requires him to spend any stated amount on advertising or to spend specific amounts of time holding open house.

If the property is in the FHA price range (roughly less than $80,000), you should contact your mortgage lending officer to order and pay for an FHA appraisal through him. This appraisal is not a market price, but it facilitates financing: an FHA appraisal is essentially a conditional commitment to put a mortgage on the house. The appraisal and its commitment represent the highest insurable mortgage loan for a qualified purchaser that FHA will give.

If you plan to give a broker an exclusive listing for your house, you probably want to limit the time to as short a period as possible. The reason for this is that if the broker does not turn up a prospect in the initial surge of selling effort, he may lose interest in your property, drop it to the bottom of his list, and not pay attention to it for a long time. A realtor can complain that you haven't given him enough time to sell your house if you put a time limit on the exclusive. You must trust him to some extent, but you must not lose sight of the fact that if he doesn't sell your house pretty quickly, he is going to stop trying very hard.

To find a good realtor, invite a few from firms whose reputations you have checked to come to your house to give you an estimate on its worth and to discuss terms of exclusive agreements, or any other agreements, that they might make with you. Schedule different times for each one, and have private but open discussions with each of them. Be careful of the realtor who agrees with everything you say and gives you an overinflated figure for the price of your house.

When you have found a good realtor, make available to him all available records of monthly expenses on your house. Assemble the records of mortgage payments, utility bills, and property taxes for the preceding twelve months if at all possible. Any buyer would want to know what these figures are.

Tell your realtor all that must be told about your house. No good purpose is served by having a prospective buyer discover a loose cellar step or a leaky kitchen faucet unknown to the realtor. The more your realtor knows about the house, the better he can deal with the potential buyer. A realtor can suggest many ways to remedy problems before public showings begin.

Be alert to his degree of enthusiasm as he learns about the house. If he seems to be getting down in the dumps about the prospects of selling the property, you might be licked before you start. If he doesn't believe in the product, he won't do an effective job of selling it.

During the early stages, you should expect the salesperson to size you up too. He expects to bring offers to you that may disappoint you, and he wants to know how you might react so that he can plan accordingly.

Brokers like to set a market price accurate enough to make a sale within a reasonable time period without a lot of extra effort or advertising expense. If you set the price too high, you may discourage a lot of pretty good prospects, and those prospects will not come back if you lower your price in the future. Before you commit yourself to a price, however, try to find out the prices of similar houses in similar neighborhoods. Most realtors should be able to give you a list of comparable sales in recent months. The change of seasons, a change in interest rates, an announcement of an unattractive or attractive building project nearby, a sudden deterioration of a neighboring property—all these factors and many others can affect your property's value.

There has never been an owner who has not sought to obtain the highest possible price for his house. What is most important for the broker to know, however, is the highest price that can be regarded within the realm of possibility.

His job is to bring you a buyer at the best price with the best terms. If he can't do this after sincere efforts, he will try to persuade you to accept a lesser offer.

You may wonder about financing for the new buyers. In the real estate market, many buyers of new and old houses are shopping for financing almost as much as for the house itself. Therefore, if the seller can arrange financing that is attractive, the house is more likely to be sold quickly and at a higher price. This is the purpose of the FHA appraisal.

SHOWING YOUR HOUSE

When you sell your house, you are trying to get top dollar. You want it to be shipshape whenever it is shown. You may, and perhaps you should, want to repaint, perhaps redecorate a good portion of the interior. Just remember that the redecorating job is not to please you or your wife, but to please a large group of prospective customers.

If your tastes run to the bizarre, be considerably more conservative when you redecorate or fix up for resale. You should tighten everything that is loose, fix everything that is broken, and adjust doors and windows that stick and faucets that drip, replace light bulbs that don't work, and clean switch box covers that are dirty.

Fix your floors and do a thorough cleaning of just about anything you can see. This includes getting all the junk out of the attic and basement. Be sure that the closets don't look overloaded, or you will give the impression that there isn't enough storage space in the house.

When a prospect sees a storage area cluttered with your junk, he may simply smile and realize he's in the same boat. But if a prospect sees a storage area that's clean, well lit, and wide open, he can envision putting all his junk into it. It's all a matter of psychology.

The female prospect will take a good look at all the closets. And she will evaluate every bedroom by the size of the closet. Get there first. It may be too early for you to empty your closets, but there are two things you can do to show them off to the best advantage: arrange everything as neatly as possible, and remove all nonseasonal clothes—store them separately in a wardrobe in the basement or with the moving company you'll be using.

Outside the house you want things spick-and-span: if there are any signs that indicate you aren't keeping the outside of the house in tip-top shape, a prospect may well suspect that there are problems lurking inside as well. The roof may have to be repaired, driveways patched up, garage doors fixed. Do more than a lick and a promise. An experienced prospective buyer can tell a haphazard job from a real repair or paint job in nothing flat.

Invest in landscaping where it can be seen immediately. A well-manicured lawn, neatly clipped shrubbery, and cleanly swept walks create a good first impression. An extra shot of fertilizer in season will make your grass look lush and green. Cut back over-grown shrubbery that looks scraggly or keeps light out of the house. Consider putting flowers outside your front door.

Paint your house if necessary. This probably does more for sales appeal than any other factor. If you decide against a complete paint job, at least consider painting the mailbox, front shutters, window frames, and the front door. Inspect the roof and gutters; replace any missing shingles, and repair or paint gutters and down-spouts. Repair broken outdoor steps.

We often neglect to notice some of the signs of wear and tear on our own house because we become accustomed to them. Ask some friends to give you their honest opinion as to what might need sprucing up to improve sales potential. Get rid of all debris or unsightly matter around the house.

Winter in northern climates creates a visual problem for any house. Be certain that snow is shoveled off the drives and walkways and that icicles are removed from overhangs. If winter days tend to be gray and dull in your area, talk to an electrician about exterior lighting. For a small amount of money, you can improve the visual qualities of the house, particularly in the late afternoon hours when many prospects are likely to call.

A visitor upon entering your home should get the impression that the house is bright and cheery, light and airy. The opposite—dark, glum, crowded—is not appealing. To give a bright, cheerful impression during daylight hours, your best bet would be to raise all the shades and open the blinds and curtains. If there is a room such as a den or study that you want to appear particularly cozy, the reverse might be true. Try various combinations of natural and artificial light to achieve the best effect for each room.

If you are expecting prospects in the evening, be certain that the house is well and brightly lit inside and out before they arrive. The house looks better, and the realtor can conduct the tour without groping around in the dark for switches. Replace burned-out light bulbs with brighter ones, and be sure that every light switch works. From the minute the prospect leaves his car and heads toward the house, lighting should give an impression of welcome warmth.

To the ladies, the kitchen is probably the single most important room. Make your kitchen gleam as brightly as you can. If your family is big on onions and garlic, there may be a lingering and possibly displeasing aroma; freshen the air as well as the physical aspects of the room. Clean the ventilating hood. If the kitchen floor is badly worn, put down new flooring. If a single tile is loose, apply heat to the tile with an iron covered with a soft cloth.

If you are using a realtor you should establish some visiting hours and "open house" hours on Saturday and/or Sunday, which usually run from noon to dusk in most places. If you are trying to sell the house yourself and you are going to use a sign on the front lawn announcing that fact, be prepared to receive prospective customers, whether or not they are able to buy anything, at just about any time of day.

A realtor can't always keep your showing hours. Be prepared for violations of this agreement. If the realtor has a hot prospect, and that prospect wants to see the house immediately, you don't really want to scare him off by not seeing him. You might have to scramble out of bed so that the broker can bring in an early morning prospect.

You're going to rankle when prospective buyers turn up their noses, saying, "The dining room is too small," or "I don't like the kitchen," or "We'd have to do so much work to make it really livable." Prospects aren't being critical of your house. They are looking at it right now simply as a building, a physical structure they may want to turn into their home. It's natural for some prospects to toss off critical remarks to indicate that they are interested in the property but want to pay less than the asking price.

To avoid being upset by critical remarks, try to be absent when the agent is showing prospects through the house. If you must be present, make believe you don't hear any remarks. Let the realtor carry the bulk of the conversation with the prospect. He's trained to parry little thrusts and to turn the buyer's attention to the attractive aspects of your property.

Most veteran brokers insist that the seller be away from the house during an "open" session and stay clear of the prospect who is brought to the house during the week. The reasoning is that the seller may tend to overstate the advantages of his house or pursue some line of nonsensical sentimentality, whereas the agent is all business and also has, or can get, all the pertinent facts.

An open house on Saturday and Sunday afternoons usually brings a stream of visitors on the first weekend of the new offering, so be prepared. Some owner-sellers prepare a one-page résumé of the features of the house and have it duplicated for distribution to lookers. A sample of such a description is in Chapter 21. Your house profile should include your name, address, and directions to major streets. Give the name of the builder of the house, the year it was finished, and the name of the subdivision or neighborhood.

The house list should also give the dimensions of the lot and can include a copy of the plat plan. You may be asked about the total square feet of living area, so you might have it in mind or list it. Some housing professionals consider room size and number more relevant. Be sure to list not only number and kinds of rooms but also dimensions and fireplace locations.

Describe the basic construction, foundation, type of roof, siding, interior walls, and any improvements on attic, basement, patio and balcony, garage, terrace, or pool fencing. Be assured that the prospective buyer does not care that you personally selected the wood for the den and put up the paneling yourself. Forget personal pride and be factual; let the prospect decide what he likes.

Water supply, disposal facilities, and details about heating, air conditioning, and the water heater are musts for the house list, as is the year each was installed. Describe the plumbing system and kitchen appliances and anything, such as the washer-dryer, that would be sold with the house. Give honest operating costs for utilities and the tax bills for the past few years. And be prepared to tell when the house was last painted, by whom, and at what cost.

Also provide mortgage information—the amount of principal unpaid, the rate of interest, name of the lending institution, and the contact there. You will probably think of a few more items to add.

Chapter
20
Handling Your Own Sale

When you assume the job of selling your house yourself, you must do all the things a realtor normally does. But first you must judge whether or not you are competent to handle the sale. To enable you to make that judgment I urge you to read this chapter in its entirety.

Your answer may be yes, and doing it yourself may be the way to sell if you are quite sure that you have a very good property, that you have a lot of time and faith in your own selling ability, and that your house is in a hot selling market—that there is an acute shortage of good houses in the area.

If you have enough time to show a whole legion of people through your house, not too many of whom indicate much interest, you can do what realtors do. And if the realtors in your town are not very good, perhaps you *should* tackle the sales job yourself.

One man who did is John Jolly, a vice-president of the Nutone Corporation in Cincinnati. In his career he has sold four of his own houses himself. The first one he sold was for $13,500, and the last, in 1970, was sold for $75,000. Says Jolly:

"If you have time and guts and enjoy meeting people, you can sell your own house and enjoy doing so. You have to work at it and you have to like people. But it is not that difficult.

"I borrowed from local realtors a number of the forms that you might need to list the elements of your house for prospective purchasers and that kind of thing. I had been through enough purchases of my own houses so that who does what and who pays for what in closing is not difficult to explain to other people.

"Give yourself three months to sell. I had always bought my next house before I sold the old house. I used classified advertising in the local newspaper exclusively, and in the ads I always put down the area first, then the number of bedrooms, and then I

216

listed all the other features, closing the ad with 'principals only' to scare off the realtors who might want to get the listing for themselves. Even so, about 25% of the people who responded to my ads over time have been realtors hoping to get a listing. They usually start off by saying, 'What do you mean by "principals only"?' And I would tell them.

"When I started to sell my first two houses, I entered the three-month period with some trepidation. I showed each house only on Sundays, because we had time to get it cleaned up and we wouldn't have traffic all the time. Because we had three months to sell, limiting traffic to Sundays was easy. You don't want people running through your house every day of the week, especially when a lot of those people are only casual lookers and not real prospects for buying.

"I didn't really have to prequalify people so much. You can almost always tell if you are used to meeting people if they are serious about buying a house and whether or not they can qualify for a mortgage. You can find out where they work and what their employment record is fairly easily with a few phone calls. Clearly, you have to be a good judge of people and know something about them to determine who are the prospects and who are only the lookers.

"The biggest problem is determining the value of the house. In inflationary times like this you may charge 10% too much and therefore not sell at all, or 5% too little and therefore not get what the marketplace will give you. If you are not really sure of the market you are in, it would be good to use an appraiser. If you are not in a big city, you can usually get a good appraisal for $400 or less. If you have little idea of what the market value of your house is, that appraisal will give you a pretty good reading.

"I have never had any problem in the financing area and nobody ever asked me for help. If anyone did, I would simply direct him to a mortgage loan officer at my local savings and loan.

"When you show your house, everything should be spick-and-span, newly painted if necessary, the lawn clipped, and so on. You should fix it up inside and out as though you were going to throw the best party of your entire life."

You can advertise, put up a "for sale by owner" sign in front of your house, or do both. Whatever you do, brokers will ring your doorbell to see if they can't change your mind and get your business. You must be prepared to put them off if your mind is set on selling your house yourself. At the same time you should recognize that good brokers can be very persuasive as well as very helpful, and they may point out to you in short order that their services would be well worth your while.

An interested broker, when he finds out that your house is for sale, will ask you how much you are asking, whether you have had any good offers, whether you have advertised, when you are moving, where you are going, if you have a sales contract or an earnest money binder order, whether you have had an appraisal, when you will have an open house. All those things can remind you that this is what brokers do as a matter of course, and you had better be prepared to handle them. The details are covered in this chapter; read it all carefully.

"FOR SALE" SIGNS ARE NOT ALWAYS LEGAL

When Bob and Ann Mayer decided to sell their house in Valley Stream, Long Island, they felt that the best way to attract a buyer was to put a "for sale" sign on their lawn.

"Two weeks later," Mrs. Mayer recalled, "we came home from shopping and found that the police had been by, threatening to give us a summons if the kids didn't take the sign down right then. We've taught them to obey the law, so of course they'd taken it down."

Angry and bewildered, the Mayers went to the police station and demanded to see a copy of the ordinance. No one had a copy. "So we went right back home and put our sign back up," Mrs. Mayer said.

The police returned, and this time, as the owner of record, Mrs. Mayer received a summons.

Ann Mayer v. *The Town of Valley Stream* is now one of two Long Island cases the Nassau County chapter of the American Civil Liberties Union has taken up. And the Mayers are not the only Long Island homeowners who have found themselves at variance with ordinances prohibiting signs. Recently David Marshall, a resident of Baldwin, Long Island, for twenty-seven years, spent a day in jail because he had refused to move a two-foot-by-twenty-inch sign in his window that said, "House for Sale, by Appointment Only."

Sign ordinances, which have been routinely passed after public hearings by several Long Island communities in recent months, have begun to stir debate as residents realize they are anything but routine.

HOW TO ADVERTISE

You have to let people know that your house is for sale and what you have to offer. Generally, it is necessary for you to invest up to 1% of the market value of the house in advertising. If your house is overpriced, you'll have to spend appreciably more to attract a buyer, if you are able to get one at all; the higher the cost, the more limited your potential market.

You've got a lot to say for that 1% budget. What's obvious is part of advertising copy: location, life-style, environment, design, money and a rental comparison, what's special, different, or unique, the neighborhood, exclusiveness, recreation, little maintenance, access to facilities.

What's not so obvious is important, too. Real estate people have always used these "hot buttons" in their copy (if the budget allows this much copy): the desire of the consumer for privacy, security, identity, and romance.

In general, too much real estate advertising is written in haste or to offset competitive advertising. It is not planned. Luckily for you, this is your competitors' approach to advertising. It is odd how many realtors are distracted by a pencil. They jot down facts as they occur to them and not at all as they would tell those same facts to a prospect. Words and phrases flow naturally as long as you realize that in advertising you are talking to a prospect.

When you address the sort of person who could and would benefit by owning your property, you must stop him, get his attention, interest him. And obviously, since you do not know who or where he is, only good advertising can find him.

Here are some elements of good advertising:

1. Every ad should have a sales approach. Perhaps it doesn't deserve to be called an advertisement if it does not. You can see in daily newspaper ads how failure to recognize the reader as a buyer has led thousands into a dull recital of commonplace facts.

2. Address the potential buyer; to gain a response the ad must be personal. The barker in a circus appeals to all within reach of his voice, for he is selling a general line of entertainment. If he talked to one man in the crowd, he'd never fill the show. But you are offering one house to one family.

3. Advertising must not recite statistics. No one, at least no one on whom you would spend your time, scans the clas-

sified pages because he has nothing better to do. He wants something, more or less urgently.

4. Boil down what you want to say. After you have planned your advertising, write out a clear, concise, but compelling sales talk, then slash out every unnecessary word. You will be surprised how good and how short the resulting ad will be.

5. Be clear. Misunderstanding a statement leaves the prospect with the impression that you have deceived him. "Near shops"—by that do you mean three blocks, which is near for any good walker? But three blocks is a long way for anyone with arthritis, or whose small daughter regularly runs errands. "Good transportation" is bad transportation for the worker who stands unsheltered for twenty minutes in a storm; "20-minute bus service two blocks" tells the same story, and no chance for the prospect to raise an objection.

6. Be simple. Because I read, it does not follow that I understand, or that I put the same meaning in a phrase that you do. If I always use short, commonplace words, I may grow hazy about the exact force of unusual words—and such words are generally long ones.

7. Be convincing. This is perhaps the most important thing to watch for in writing real estate copy. You may use only five words, but they should carry conviction.

8. With your logical buyer in mind, list on a scratch pad the features of your house, not in any logical order yet, but merely in groups. Reread and number them by their importance, not in your eyes but in those of the buyer.

9. Never take out a useful word just because it adds to the cost. The few cents you would save are less than nothing compared to the loss of a sale through failure to make the proper impression at the start. (But remember that editing usually improves the product.)

10. Take out moth-eaten words and phrases: "must be seen to be appreciated," "best buy in town," "dandy," "bargain." Do not take out commonplace words such as "homey" or "quiet" if they fit; familiarity does not detract from the offer. Never forget that adjectives are your opinion of the point, not the point itself.

Following are a few examples of good and bad ads.

Bear in mind that home is where the children are, to paraphrase an old saying. Parents, and especially grandparents, tell you there can be no home without them. Perhaps that's an over-

NOW . . . in Poco Valley

Sand Hills Ranch PHASE II

The new prestige community of luxury homes

* Design award winning homes
* Ten minutes from the Arroyo Valley
  in the picturesque foothills of Anderson County
* Proposed golf course, wilderness park, and
  acres of natural open space
* Wide pool-size lots with B/T access
* November through February occupancy
* Special second trust deed financing
  available only for Phase II buyers!
  Seven year term—No payments for two years

* Step-down living room
* Formal dining room
* Morning room
* Spacious master suites
* Air conditioning
* Tile roofs
* Slumpstone walls
* French doors
* Bay windows
* Wet bars
* Microwave ovens
* Energy saving appliances

from $130,600 to $165,000

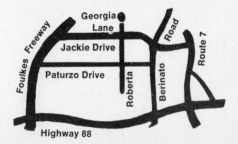

Good

Bad

SUNRISE

The Dawning of Affordable Housing.

$53,660
VA/FHA

Single-Family Homes
3 & 4 Bedrooms / 2 Baths

MODELS OPEN

Route 7

Morrissey Lane

Jackie | Drive

George | Road

Highway 59

statement, but it is amazing how seldom features for children are mentioned in real estate advertising.

What has the house got inside? Has it a playroom, family room? Baths and half baths are important to mention. Is there a specially designed and decorated nursery? Is there a large yard (not a garden)? A pool? Is there easy access to playgrounds? What about the neighborhood? Is the street quiet? Where is the school and what grade levels does it have? Is a public park nearby (how near)? A public swimming pool for after-school hours and summers? These are important considerations for families with children.

Where do you place your ads?

Newspaper classified ads. Advantages: They are read by people who want to buy now. Because virtually all real estate brokers advertise there, everyone knows that a vast real estate market is displayed there. It costs less, per reader, than any other kind of advertising. You can change your offer daily, or repeat the same message endlessly. Classified real estate advertising appears in the want-ad section among offers of jobs, rentals, and used cars.

Their availability is another advantage. Some classified medium is always found in a "home paper" as well as in most suburban communities, and often in many districts within larger cities. Classifieds are often an important part of neighborhood papers. Their continuous use proves their worth. Advertising orders can commonly be inserted by telephone at the last minute and can be canceled with equal ease.

Disadvantages: The ads appear at the back of the paper, where few "chance" readers will stumble upon them. They are printed in the smallest type, usually deprived of the selling power of pictures and diagrams. The messages are brief and crowded. We are too prone to undervalue them because they cost so little.

Newspaper display. Advantages: It creates new buyers. It permits type and borders of any size. It allows for pictures, photos, drawings, maps, and floor plans and even color. An advertiser can place copy in special news sections; for example, in the society section for high-class residential property.

Disadvantages: The reader is more interested in the news on that page. The advertiser must arouse interest in houses as a whole. An offer can be made but once. There is strong competition—automobile advertisers, merchants, and other large real estate offers. The copy does not reach potential prospects when they are in a buying mood.

Direct mail. Advantages: A selection of prospects, or one

known prospect, can be addressed. Persons whose needs are known to the sender can be given special treatment. Direct mail allows for repetition as often as necessary. Color, any size of type, and pictures can be used. There is space for great detail and long descriptions. It permits presenting one point at a time, for greater emphasis and attention.

Disadvantages: The receiver may not open the mail; overcoming this demands ingenuity. There is much high-class competition from merchants. The piece may be damaged before delivery. Fine production costs more.

HOW TO "DEAL" WITH A POTENTIAL BUYER

You should rely on professional real estate advice in setting a price on your own house. Usually, good brokers have specialists or appraisers who can, on inspection, set a maximum price for your property that would be reasonable in the current market. Like all owners, you want to get true market value for your house, and you must be realistic rather than live with the ownership of two houses.

If you're selling your house without the aid of a broker, you don't have a middleman to "cushion" the bargaining process when the time comes; you yourself must negotiate with the buyer.

Always avoid discussing price unless the buyer brings it up first. Often it won't even be an issue, and you can go ahead and write the contract at the full price suggested by your appraiser. If the buyer won't pay it, you'll find out soon enough. If you discuss price too soon, that becomes the biggest decision in the sale of your home. Concentrate on selling the benefits of owning your home, not the price.

When you and the buyer are negotiating the final price, it's good to remember that most houses sell for less than the seller would like to accept but more than the buyer would like to pay. A fair price is reached when both parties are satisfied.

You should be prepared to bargain with anyone showing serious interest. You may hear, "Well, we do like the house, but we were thinking more about paying $63,000." If you have clearly stated your price at $70,000, you can look the prospect straight in the eye and respond, "Well, we decided to sell the house ourselves in order to make certain that we would get a certain amount."

The prospects may respond positively or negatively. If they agree immediately to meet your figure and forget theirs, you have made a sale. If they hedge, be prepared to say, after some pondering, "Well, if you are really interested and want the house very much, there's no sense in being stubborn. We'll be flexible and bring the price down to $68,000," or $65,000, or whatever figure you had planned to retreat to. In eight cases out of ten, this strategy works, assuming that both parties are fairly reasonable.

Have available a binder receipt prepared by your attorney and be certain to get a check for at least $100, with the stipulation, in writing, that the prospect will sign a conditional sales contract within a few days in your attorney's office. At that time the buyer should have additional money to make up a full deposit of $500 or $1,000, depending on what your attorney tells you is standard in your area.

Fortunate is the seller who finds a buyer in a sound financial position who is willing to obtain his own financing. If he seeks help, offer to introduce him to your mortgage loan officer.

Beyond this point, there will be discussions of items such as settlement day, moving days, furniture you may want to include (the draperies or wall-to-wall carpet), which you may want to sell cheaply because they are often of little value in another house. Refer to Chapter 17 on contracts.

HOW TO BE A GOOD REAL ESTATE SALESPERSON

If you're going to sell your house yourself, you already have a good deal of confidence, but you need more than that. Here are some reminders and ideas that can help you.

Who will be your prospective customers, and what will be their recent experience in looking for a house to buy? Except for the transferee, the average homebuyer who lives in the same market area begins his search three to six months and looks over perhaps ten to twelve houses before he buys. The prospect usually narrows his interest to three or four and then to one or two. Whenever he is limited to four or fewer, he is ripe for closing. The buyer, unless heavily conditioned by factors of urgency or exposure, returns three to four times or more to the house he finally selects before he closes. The average buyer who has owned a previous residence buys a new house that is approximately 20% higher in value than the last one he owned.

The transferee, who is usually under greater pressure to make an early decision, may short-circuit this process, depending upon his prior education about the market.

Although shoppers do call resale brokers, the majority of prospects who take the aggressive action of picking up the phone to call you in response to an ad are genuinely in the market. They have already decided, in most cases, to buy something, usually in a relatively short period of time, one or two months on the outside.

That is why the average sale is made within the first week of initial contact and often within the first three homes shown.

How you get yourself ready for prospects is a vital concern. An absolute must: you should know everything about the area: when the mail comes, where the bus stops, where the schools are, what the distance to the major shopping center is.

Bear in mind that people want to be sold. Be positive, cheerful, modestly outgoing. Start the process by showing an interest in the prospect's life-style. Listen more, talk less, don't overdo; people are serious about houses. The objective is simply to get people involved in the house to such an extent that either they buy today or they want to return before making a decision on anything else. If you cannot get a decision to buy, try at least to get a decision to return.

When a prospect sees the house for the first time, he makes mental comparisons with other houses he has already seen. For that reason the salesperson has to create sufficient interest. If your prospect only sees and hears the story about living concepts and community design and does not identify with your house, you may lose him to another house where greater identity is achieved by a smarter salesperson. When your prospect leaves, he should mentally take your house with him.

You should find out as soon as possible whether or not a prospect is really a buyer so that you can devote your time to those prospects whose needs and wants can be converted into sales. This has to be done in a relaxed and sincere manner and without pressure. You cannot jump to the conclusion that the prospect knows what he wants until he has been questioned and has explored all the possibilities.

There are five basic areas in which you should judge prospects quickly: experience, urgency, ability, status and motivation.

1. Experience: How long has the prospective buyer been in the market? Has he seen many houses?

2. Urgency: How soon would the buyer like to be in his new home? How soon does he plan to make a change?

3. Ability—to purchase—is a more delicate area, yet not determining the ability of the prospect to purchase his house and qualify for financing is one of the greatest barriers to any sale.

4. Status: Is the buyer free to make a decision to purchase? Are there other factors involved? Does he have a house he must sell before he can finalize the purchase of this one?

5. Motivation is probably the most difficult of all areas to uncover. You must determine the buyer's "hot button"— what will make him buy.

One of the surest ways to find out what a prospect thinks or feels is to get him to talk. The right questions usually produce the responses you want. Learning how to ask incisive questions is a matter of practice.

One of the best ways to draw out a prospect is to reflect on what he has said: "Is this what you had in mind?" "How do you feel about this?" Always use the question as the conversational fishhook.

The name of the game is to make it easy for the buyer to say yes. Your role, above all else, is to eliminate or dilute any negatives that might prevent a buyer from making a favorable decision while you gently lead him to a greater identification with the house. From the beginning you are trying to build a bridge to agreement, starting with the prospect's own desires or interests, then pyramiding them, step by step, toward a decision.

Prospective buyers have motivational hot spots: hobbies or avocations, such as gardening, collecting, woodworking, golf or painting. They might also have attitudes about furnishings, children, neighborhoods, or special causes. It is vital to remember that people always buy houses on the strength of emotion and justify the purchase with facts. Homebuyers do not buy houses because of what they are but because of what a house does for them.

Some key points to remember: defending a property to a buyer is a sure way to destroy a climate in which to close a sale. You soon learn that you can oversell, and you can set a pace that the prospect cannot match.

Help the buyer picture living in the house, and accent the pleasures. Before he buys, he must identify with it and imagine living there. The images of enjoyment, pride, satisfaction, and security are the necessary prelude to his decision. A few well-timed comments can reinforce these mental images.

An important element of closing is creating urgency. You should emphasize the importance of making a decision before the property is gone.

You should recognize buying signals. When a buyer asks whether or not personal property is being included in the sale of the house, assume he's about to buy. If he asks, "Do the drapes stay?" you answer, "Do you want the house if the drapes are included?" If he asks, "Are the washer and dryer included?" you answer, "Do you want the house if we include the washer and dryer?"

Another signal is the conference between husband and wife as they whisper, "Well, what do you think?" or, "I think we'll be able to swing it, don't you?"

Ask "closing questions": "Would you like to move in on the first or fifteenth of June?" "Would you like me to include the refrigerator in the offer?" "Should I write a contingency in the contract that it is valid only if your lawyer approves its legal content?"

HELPING THE BUYER GET FINANCING

Most house purchases are conditional upon financing, so your deal will ride on success in getting it. Your first step is to reread Chapter 13 of this book; then talk to the bank that holds your mortgage about both your financing and your prospective buyer's financing (even though you don't yet know who he may be). In ordinary lending times (no credit crunch or very high interest rates) most commercial banks can provide a blanket mortgage on two houses to tide you over until all the dust has settled.

The down payment is, of course, the buyer's problem. But it would be useful in your selling effort to talk to the bank that now holds your mortgage, assuming you have one. If you don't, talk to your banker to get some idea on terms and loan-to-value ratios of mortgages being made on properties in your neighborhood, so that you can inform prospective buyers. This will help you get rid of those who can't in any way qualify to buy your house.

When you have a hot prospect, it is often wise to obtain a credit report on him to get some indication of how he meets his obligations. Your banker can assist you with that. If the buyer is from out of town, you should seek information from the credit bureau in his community. Again, your banker can assist you.

A word or two of caution is appropriate here. Usually the mortgage is a combination of two documents: the note and the mortgage. In some states the document is referred to as a trust deed. The note is an IOU—a promise to pay, with the terms and conditions of the obligation—and usually remains in the possession of the lender, the mortgagee. The mortgage itself is the instrument by which you give the mortgagee a security interest in the property. It is, in effect, collateral for the note. The mortgage is recorded in the appropriate county or state office so that the world is on notice that such-and-such lender has a security interest in your property. The act of recording protects the lender. A photostat of the mortgage appears in the record books, and the original document is held by the bank. Ask the bank now to give you copies of the form of documents it uses.

Read the documents carefully, and have your lawyer read them too. If you find anything in the documents that would limit or restrict your ability to sell the property, resolve the problem immediately. Such limitations or restrictions could be (1) a clause giving the bank the right to call the full balance due on the mortgage if you should sell the property; (2) a clause prohibiting you from selling the property without the bank's permission; or (3) a clause requiring the payment of a stipulated penalty should you pay off the mortgage in advance of its due date. Almost certainly your mortgage contains a clause restricting the assumption by another person without the bank's consent. Obviously, the bank doesn't want you to sell the property to a deadbeat.

During periods of rising interest rates and tight money, one of the more common and frequently practiced restrictions is for the mortgage lender to "call" the mortgage upon a sale so that it can impose a higher interest rate on the buyer. The restrictive clause itself might say, "In the event the property is sold, the entire balance shall be due and payable." The mortgage lender may not really intend for you to come up with a lump sum in cash. The clause allows the mortgage lender to say to you, "Yes, we'll let Mr. X buy the house from you and assume your mortgage, but what we're really doing is wiping out your mortgage and writing a new one for him at a higher rate of interest."

An alternative is to sell the property on a land contract. For this, too, the assistance of your attorney is essential. Technically, the transfer of property occurs when the seller gives a deed to the buyer. Under a land contract, the date of giving the deed is delayed, usually until sometime in the future. Until then you are still the title owner of the property and still fully liable for the mortgage. The buyer has an obligation to make payments to you, and you have an obligation to deliver a deed to him at some time in the future, usually when all or a substantial portion of the payments have been made. Under a land contract you do not convey the property, so there is a possibility that restrictive clauses in your mortgage would not apply. In a land contract all terms of payment, interest rate, and so on are worked out by negotiation between the parties. Do not, under any circumstances, attempt to enter into a land contract without the advice of legal counsel.

In some markets today you may have to help your prospective buyer make application for the most appropriate mortgage loan.

In an extreme case you might take a purchase-money mortgage for a maximum of five years. This would be a second mortgage held by you. It is usually risky to help your prospective buyer make up sufficient down payment for the closing.

There are some important tax angles for you to consider after the sale of your house. Our new tax law (the Tax Reform Act of 1978) lets you take up to $100,000 of profit on a house sale without capital gains tax, if you're fifty-five or over, *once in a lifetime*. If you're not yet ready to use that provision, you must invest your real estate profit in another house within one year to avoid paying tax on it. In any event, check with both your lawyer and your tax consultant right away.

YOUR BUYER MIGHT ASSUME YOUR MORTGAGE

To make it easy for your buyer you may want to arrange for him to assume the existing mortgage on your house unless there is a specific clause in the mortgage that prohibits this transaction. Under this arrangement the buyer assumes the primary responsibility for meeting the terms and conditions of the mortgage. Therefore, you want to make sure he is an excellent credit risk.

Should you have an FHA-insured mortgage on your house, the loan can be assumed by your prospective buyer by making application to your mortgage loan officer for credit approval of the new buyer. If this application is approved, you are relieved of future liability under the terms of both the note and the mortgage.

The same procedure works for assumption of a VA-guaranteed loan. In this instance, however, your VA eligibility for another loan must remain with the mortgage unless the new purchaser is also an eligible veteran. That means that if you are both veterans, you can get another VA mortgage, but if the buyer is not a veteran, you cannot get another VA mortgage.

An FHA loan may be assumed, with or without release of your existing liability. To obtain release of liability, the new purchaser must apply for a loan underwriting and qualify as an acceptable credit risk with the servicing mortgagee through his mortgage loan officer. Most mortgage lenders have "assumption packages" prepared in advance for such requests.

The procedure is the same for VA loans, with the additional provision that if another qualified veteran assumes the loan, the seller becomes eligible for his VA guarantee entitlement all over again. The transaction must leave the VA guarantee intact for the owner of the mortgage since this is the guarantee for the top portion of the loan.

Chapter 21

Worksheets and Checklists For Section III

BROKER'S QUESTIONNAIRE

This is an example of the questionnaire a real estate broker might ask you to fill in. The information you supply will help the broker find the right houses to show you.

1. Name, address, and phone number

_____

_____

2. Including yourself, what is the number of people presently living in your home? _____

3. Please check all the age brackets in which you have children living at home.

(1)_under 5 years   (4)_16 to 20 years
(2)_5 to 10 years   (5)_Over 20 years
(3)_11 to 15 years   (6)_None

4. Occupation of head of household (check one only):

(1)_Military   (8)_Professional
(2)_Jr. executive   (9)_Technical
(3)_Middle management   (10)_Educational
(4)_Sr. executive   (11)_Foreman
(5)_Sales   (12)_Industrial worker
(6)_Manager (sales or super-   (13)_Service worker
      vising)   (14)_Retired
(7)_Proprietor of a business

5. Before acquiring your present home, what were your former living arrangements?

(1)_Owned house   (5)_Lived with family
(2)_Rented house   (6)_Mobile home
(3)_Rented apartment (high-rise)   (7)_Newlyweds
(4)_Rented apartment (garden)   (8)_Military housing

6. How many homes have you owned prior to your present home?

7. What is the approximate annual income of the family?

(1)_Less than $5,000	(7)_$17,501–$20,000
(2)_$5,000–$7,500	(8)_$20,001–$25,000
(3)_$7,501–$10,000	(9)_$25,001–$30,000
(4)_$10,001–$12,500	(10)_$30,001–$40,000
(5)_$12,501–$15,000	(11)_$40,001–$50,000
(6)_$15,001–$17,500	(12)_Over $50,000

8. What was the approximate cost of your present home at time of purchase?

(1)_Under $5,000	(7)_$17,501–$20,000
(2)_$5,000–$7,500	(8)_$20,001–$25,000
(3)_$7,501–$10,000	(9)_$25,001–$30,000
(4)_$10,001–$12,500	(10)_$30,001–$40,000
(5)_$12,501–$15,000	(11)_$40,001–$50,000
(6)_$15,001–$17,500	(12)_Over $50,000

9. Comments about new homes or communities you wish to make

_____

_____

_____

10. Where will each working member of your family's job be?

_____

11. How far will each person consider traveling to work? _____

_____

12. Is convenience to the commercial airport a factor? How frequently will it be used? _____

_____

THE CLOSING STATEMENT

Here is a typical closing statement form from the American Bankers Association. Review it with your lawyer.

FIRST BANK OF ANYTOWN

CLOSING STATEMENT _____ Date _____

Branch _____

Buyer and/or borrower _____ Address _____

Seller _____ Property _____

Terms _____ Address _____

MONTHLY PAYMENT:
Principal and interest _____
Property taxes _____ First monthly payment
Hazard Insurance _____ due on the 1st day of _____, 19____
Mortgage insurance _____ and on the 1st day of
each month thereafter

Total $ _____

	BORROWER'S		SELLER'S	
	Charges	Credits	Charges	Credits
PURCHASE OR CONTRACT PRICE				
LOAN AMOUNT				
Earnest money				
Other funds deposited				
Equity credit				
Other credit				
ADJUSTMENTS:				
Prorates: (Prorate date ____)				
Taxes ____ to ____				
Fire insurance ____ to ____				
Rent ____ to ____				
Loan reserves:				
Taxes ____ Mo. @ $				
Insurance ____ Mo. @				
MIP* ____ Mo. @				
Interest:				
From ____ to ____				
Loan discount @ ____ %				
Total ◆				

INSURANCE
  Fire insurance
  Flood insurance
  Loan insurer's initial premium
LOAN COSTS:
  Credit Report $
  Appraisal fee
  Loan fee
  Photos
  Mortgagee title policy
  Recording fees
  Plot survey
  Inspections

  Total ◆

Liens
Assessments
Unpaid taxes
Mortgage or contract payoff
  Balance
  Interest from ___ to ___
Broker's commission to ___
Title insurance costs
Recording and reconveyance fees

  TOTALS ◆

BALANCE DUE TO SELLER
BALANCE DUE FROM BORROWER

FIRST BANK OF ANYTOWN

By: ___

Seller's new address: ___

The undersigned approves disbursement of funds in accordance with this statement:

ORIGINAL—BANK COPY

*Mortgage insurance premium

HOUSE PROFILE

This is a sample of a "résumé" of your house. Having duplicates made for prospective buyers will be helpful to them and to you when you are selling your own house.

Address _____ Phone _____

_____

Owner _____

Price _____ Rooms _____ BRs _____ Baths _____

Type, design, or style _____

Construction _____

Square feet living area _____

Lot size _____

Electricity _____ 100-amp _____ 200-amp _____

Most recent year's energy bills, heating, total $ _____

Gas _____   Oil _____

Taxes, most recent year _____

Roof type and condition _____

Siding type and condition _____

Sewer _____   Septic _____

Water bills, most recent year _____ Well _____

Central air conditioning ————————————————————

Carpeting, rooms ——————————————————————

Dishwasher ————————— Disposal ———————————

Fireplace ————————— Patio ———————————

Porch ————————— Garage(s) ———————————

Oven/range/make/built in? ——————————————————

Storms/screens ——————————————————————

Water softener ——————————————————————

Dining room ————————— Family room ———————

Den/library ——————————————————————

Utility room ——————————————————————

Dimensions: LR ————————— MBR ———————————

2nd BR ————————— 3rd BR ———————————

Basement————————— Slab————————— Crawl————

Other inclusions ——————————————————————

————————————————————————————————

Other exclusions ——————————————————————

————————————————————————————————

Mortgagee ——————————————————————

Mortgage balance $————————— Rate —————% Term ————

Principal, interest, taxes, insurance, total: $ ———————————

Reason for selling: ————————————————————————

Inspection procedure—make appointment ————————————

————————————————————————————————

————————————————————————————————

Remarks ————————————————————————————

————————————————————————————————

————————————————————————————————

WHAT YOU'LL NEED TO GET FROM HERE TO THERE

You've bought a house, but you're still in your old house or apartment, or perhaps you still live with your parents. How much money do you need to move? You need the biggest chunk for the down payment; next, for settlement or closing costs (see Chapter 17); then for moving expenses, utility connections, appliances, carpeting, furniture, and possibly repairs and redecorating.

You might start by filling in this worksheet:

Purchase price ————————————————————————

Down payment ————————————————————————

Settlement costs
  (estimate from bankers) ————————————————————

Moving ————————————————————————————

Utility connections plus deposits ——————————————

Appliances ——————————————————————————

Carpeting and flooring ——————————————————

Redecorating exterior ————————————————————

Redecorating interior _____

Repairs _____

Additions and/or major remodeling _____

Landscaping _____

Draperies, curtain rods, shelves, window
    shades, new locks, pegboards, etc. _____

Lighting (new fixtures or change position) _____

Recreational equipment, patio _____

Cleanup expenses and preventive maintenance
    (termites?) _____

TOTAL _____

And here are some checklists for the move itself.

Before the Move

1. Be sure to contact the following:
Gas company: get refund of deposit
Electric company: get refund of deposit
Water department: get refund of deposit
Newspaper boy: if prepaid, get refund
Milk: stop delivery
Laundry: stop service
Bank: transfer funds and arrange for checking account
in new location
Schools: request transfer of your children's records
Doctor: ask for referral and transfer of records
Dentist: ask for referral and transfer of records
Optometrist: ask for referral and transfer of records
Post office: give forwarding address
Creditors: give forwarding address
Credit-card companies: give forwarding address

Magazines: give new address at least two months before you move

2. Arrange for a moving company; get two or three bids.
3. Get packing and unpacking help.
4. Check insurance coverage for furnishings in transit.
5. Empty freezer ahead of time and defrost.
6. Have appliances ready to be moved.
7. Get clothes back from cleaner.
8. Plan for the needs of children and pets.

On Moving Day

1. Double-check closets, shelves, and drawers to be sure they're empty.
2. Carry valuables and important documents yourself.
3. Bring traveler's checks.
4. Be sure a friend or relative knows your route and schedule, including when and where you will stop overnight.

Upon Arrival at the New House

1. Have cash ready to pay movers.
2. Have telephone installed.
3. Contact gas company.
4. Contact water department.
5. Check stove at a distance; check hot-water heater and furnace.
6. Register your car within five days after arrival in a different state to avoid fine.
7. Enroll your children in school.

Section IV

Making the Most of Your Investment— Enhancing Property Value

Making your house the most valuable thing you own is really done on two levels: the physical and the political. The physical level implies a well-maintained house and lot, a pleasing, well-kept landscape, a house that looks good inside and out and clearly needs no major repairs. The political effort involves you, as a voter in a democratic society, making sure that your community is a good place for people to live and work.

The business of maintaining a house is not an arduous task. We take great pleasure in fixing up our houses and enjoying the results. Most of us can do yard work, small repairs, and redecorating. That is generally the easy part. Doing something about the way your house performs, particularly about its consumption of energy, is a bit more difficult. I have already described some of the ways to make your house more energy efficient. In the future there will be a premium on energy efficiency in all houses; you will want to know all you can on the subject, both to make your present house attractive to future buyers and to recognize the energy efficiency of your future houses. The next chapter tells you more about energy efficiency.

Chapter 22
Energy and Your Home

The energy problem is a whole series of problems. We know it's an economic problem. And from all the lengthy legislative debates in Washington we know it is a political problem, serious enough that the income tax legislation of 1978 provides up to a $300 deduction from taxable income for insulation. Energy is also a resource problem. The battle still rages on as to whether we have enough natural gas left for ten years or five thousand years. All we really know for sure is that the amounts of natural gas and oil in the earth are finite. How long our resources will last is something no one really knows. There are some "infinite" sources of energy, but developing them is expensive and in many ways unsatisfactory.

Of one thing we're sure: energy costs will continue to go up. We believe that there will be new sources of energy available to us, in time, but we can reasonably expect that they will not significantly reduce the cost of energy use in the immediate future.

In view of the grim picture often painted about the energy problem, it might be useful to indicate the sources of energy we in the United States might consider in future years. The following list is not all-inclusive, but it should suggest that we do have some alternatives; some are achievable within practical economic limits, and others remain impractical.

SOURCES of ENERGY

Finite	Infinite
Natural gas	Wind
Oil	Waves
Oil shale	Tides

Tar sands	Sun
Coal	Methanol (distillates of wood)
Uranium	Ethanol (distillates of grain)
Geopressurized methane	Methane (from animal wastes)
	Plutonium
	Wood
	Animal muscle (manpower)
	Hydroelectric
	Geothermal water

SOME BACKGROUND ON ENERGY EFFICIENCY

The subject of energy use can become so complicated and technical that even qualified scientists disagree about it. But it is important that as a homeowner you understand some of the key ideas and terms to protect yourself against misinformation in considering an energy-efficient house. The basic principles are not all that difficult to grasp.

Heat flows by *conduction, convection,* or *radiation,* or by a combination of them. Heat always flows from areas of higher temperature to areas of lower temperature, inside or out.

Here are definitions of those terms and a few others:

Conduction. Transmission of heat through an object. A common example is a metal handle on a frying pan: as the pan is heated, the handle gets hot.

Convection. Transmission of heat through air. Air heated by a heat source and flowing into a room heats that room by convection. A residential warm-air heating system, such as electrical baseboard heating, is a convection heating system.

Radiation. Transmission of heat through radiant energy. An old-fashioned hot-water "radiator" transfers heat by radiation, conduction, and convection simultaneously. The radiator conducts heat through the surfaces of the radiator. Air flowing around the radiator transfers heat by convection. The warm or hot surfaces of the radiator transfer heat by radiation to any surface at a lower temperature: people, furnishings, and the walls of the room.

Btu (British thermal unit). One Btu is the amount of heat needed to raise the temperature of one pound of water (one pint) one degree Fahrenheit. It's also roughly the amount of heat produced by the burning of one wooden kitchen match from end to end.

Heat gain. This is the heat that flows into a house in the summer months to raise the temperature above usual summer comfort levels. Heat gain is by conduction, convection, and radiation.

Heat loss. This is the loss of heat in the cool months through the house shell by conduction, convection, and some radiation. To maintain wintertime comfort levels indoors the loss must be replaced by the operation of energy-consuming heating systems.

You should give careful consideration to the amount of energy required to operate water heaters, for example, and make certain your mechanical systems are the proper size for your specific energy needs. Oversized equipment not only wastes dollars in the initial purchase but also wastes expensive energy.

In declining order of energy consumption, for both heating and cooling, these are your major areas of consideration: infiltration through the structure; ceiling heat losses and heat gains; the losses and gains through walls, windows, doors, and floors; internal loads from such things as water heaters; and mechanical-system design and equipment (for example, heating and cooling devices).

The accompanying table indicates the energy savings, ranging from 30% to 50%, that could result from improvements in the items listed. The figures are from the National Association of Home Builders.

Energy Savings

Windows and doors	30–60%
Floors	40–60%
Ceilings	30–40%
Walls	35–40%
Infiltration through the structure	35–60%
Internal loads	15–25%
System design	10–30%

Garages and carports can help reduce the energy load simply by providing dead-air space. Grading the ground surface around the house for an adequate slope so that surface water drains away from the dwelling helps keep the earth next to the foundation wall drier, and thus warmer.

Individual dwellings in condominium buildings, townhouses, semidetached dwellings, and units in apartment buildings all have less heat loss per square foot of floor area than single-family detached dwellings, because there is less exterior surface. If you assume that energy use in a single-family detached house is 100 units per year, the estimated average for a townhouse would be about 80 units, for an apartment in a low-rise or garden apartment building about 60 units, and for an apartment in a high-rise building about 50 units.

WINDOWS, DOORS, AND FLOORS

A house without windows might be very energy efficient, but you probably wouldn't want to live there, and neither would I. Windows are a prime area of heat loss in the winter and heat gain in the summer, by both conduction and convection (infiltration). The best way to handle this problem is to use the best windows you can get, carefully installed, weatherstripped, and, in the North and Midwest where heat loss can be critical, double-glazed. In double-glazed windows use a thermal break in both the window sash and its frame. A thermal break (usually made of plastic) is a relatively non-heat-conducting material used to prevent heat from being conducted from indoors to outdoors through some material that conducts heat rapidly, such as metal. For instance, an aluminum window frame should not be all aluminum straight through the wall, but should have a plastic connector all the way around between the outer frame to the inner frame to break the thermal flow of heat from inside to outside.

Exterior doors should be the insulated type. Many of them these days are steel clad and include a thermal break in their edges so that heat cannot be conducted from the inside surface of the door to the outside. All exterior doors should be weatherstripped to seal the edges of the door to its casing when it is closed.

The upper part of basement walls should be insulated. In cold climates perimeter slab insulation is used to prevent heat loss from a slab in a house—heat that gets into the slab from the heating system within the house.

Individual household energy consumption is a function of the number of occupants, their life-styles, and the construction of the house. But most variations in energy use (up to 100%)—differences between two otherwise identical houses—are attributable to variations in air infiltration.

THE INDOOR CLIMATE

The largest portion of your monthly utility bill results from your efforts to heat or cool your house. In most regions, heating during the winter months and/or cooling in summer constitutes about 80% of the typical energy charges.

If you're like most of us, it's hard to resist setting the thermostat just a little higher when it's very cold outside, or dropping the air-conditioning temperature lower to combat hot summer weather. It's fine for the utility company to suggest a 68-degree comfort zone in winter and 72 degrees in summer for economic and conservation reasons, but it's a wholly different story when you're actually faced with keeping your house just slightly colder or warmer than what you are used to.

It is tempting on a cold winter day to let the heat level surge above 68 degrees, but keeping the setting at 68 can make quite a difference in your energy bill. Energy consumption falls off sharply in the winter when you allow the temperature to settle just a few degrees cooler than normal. If, for instance, you could maintain a comfort level of 64 degrees instead of 74 degrees, you may actually reduce your energy consumption about 14%. Many homeowners install clock thermostats so that temperatures are automatically reduced at night during sleeping hours and returned to normal levels in the morning.

A good builder takes special care in selecting heating and air-conditioning equipment according to recommended engineering practices and avoids oversized systems. Oversized equipment not only costs more but results in shorter periods of operation, poor comfort conditions, lower seasonal efficiency, and more energy consumption.

If you have lived for quite some time in an older house that used an oversized furnace or boiler, it takes a while to adjust to modern, technologically sound systems for heating and cooling. In earlier days, without the benefit of precise engineering calculations and technological data, it just wasn't possible to know precisely what system would have the capability of heating or cooling a specific house, so builders made sure the house would be warm, or air-conditioned properly, by installing oversized energy systems.

Those wasteful days of total disregard for energy conservation are undoubtedly gone forever. Today we can determine the exact requirements of a particular house plan in a specific geographic region and install a heating-cooling system that meets those requirements.

In designing systems, engineers use two important design concepts you have probably heard much about. *Degree days* are used to determine sizes and system designs of *heating* installations. One degree day is one day in which the average temperature over a twenty-four-hour period is 1 degree cooler than 65 degrees Fahrenheit, or an average temperature on that day of 64 degrees. In Long Island and New Jersey the average number of degree days per year runs around 4,500; in the Chicago area, 6,500; in the Los Angeles area, 2,000; and in southern Florida around 500.

Design temperature is used to determine the conditions of outdoor heat for which engineers must design air-conditioning systems. The design temperature for a particular city is the average daytime temperature at midsummer.

Of course, there are some trade-offs to energy conservation. In your old house, if you were away for the weekend and allowed the temperature to drop significantly, a turn of the thermostat when you got back resulted in an almost instant rush of hot air into the room. In a modern house that rush has been replaced by an efficient, steady stream of warm air that heats the room over a somewhat longer period of time. You may have to keep your sweater on for just a few minutes longer as your heating system takes effect, but this slight inconvenience saves energy and reduces actual costs to you.

THE FUTURE FOR SOLAR ENERGY

Solar heating, theoretically free, is not yet economically competitive in the United States. Literally thousands of experiments are being conducted to determine its future use. It may be that in the not-too-distant future the use of solar systems for room heating and water heating will be both commonplace and economically feasible.

Today, however, we have to be realistic. The availability of solar equipment is still questionable, and the skill of mechanics is still in the formative stages. The potential for adequate maintenance is uncertain, and the payback for solar systems, on a five-year limit or term, is far from cost-competitive with more traditional systems.

Furthermore, solar systems in vogue today require costly

STATES WITH LAWS ENCOURAGING SOLAR USE

State	Solar Incentives	Solar Laws	Codes
Arizona	A state income tax credit until 1984; exemption from property tax	No	No
Arkansas	Deduction of solar cost from gross income for state tax	No	No
California	State income tax credit until 1981; for disaster-stricken homes, an interest-free loan to add solar equipment	No	Yes
Colorado	Solar systems assessed at 5% of value for property taxes	Yes	No
Connecticut	Sales, use tax exemptions; authorizes zero assessment by local tax unit	No	Standards
Florida	No incentives at present	Yes	Yes, and standards
Georgia	Refund of sales, use taxes; authorizes exemption from property tax	Yes	No
Hawaii	10% state income tax credit; exemption from property tax increase	No	No
Idaho	Cost deduction from taxable income for state	Yes	No
Illinois	Reduced valuation of solar equipment for assessment	No	No
Indiana	Annual deduction from assessed valuation of solar costs (mobile-homes included)	No	No
Iowa	Exemption of entire solar system from property tax assessment until 1986	No	No
Kansas	A 25% deduction from state income tax; reimbursement on property tax, and five-year amortization of solar on business tax returns	Yes	No
Maine	Five-year exemption from property tax; refund of sales, use tax; $400 subsidy for solar domestic hot water installation	No	No
Maryland	Authorization of property tax credits by local units; assessment reduction	Yes	No

State			Description
Massachusetts	No	No	Authorization of liberal bank, credit union loans; real estate tax exemption, and corporate tax deduction for year of solar installation
Michigan	No	No	Use tax exemption; authorization for property tax exemption; business tax break
Minnesota	Standards	Yes	Exclusion of solar equipment from assessment
Montana	No	No	State income tax credit for solar installation; property tax exemption
Nevada	No	No	Allowance for reduction of assessed valuation of solar equipment
New Hampshire	No	No	Property tax exemptions
New Jersey	No	No	Allowance for a deduction from property taxes
New Mexico	No	Yes	State income tax credit of 25% of solar cost up to $1,000
New York	No	No	Provision for a property tax exemption
North Carolina	No	No	Allowance for personal, corporate income tax credits; assessment break
North Dakota	No	Yes	Provision for state income tax credit; five-year property tax exemption
Oklahoma	No	No	Income tax credit for residence—25% up to $2,000
Oregon	No	Yes	State income tax credit of 25% up to $1,000; allows liberal veterans' loans for solar installation; allows property tax reduction
South Dakota	No	No	Allowance for residential owner's annual deduction from assessed valuation; property tax credit for new or retrofit solar on residential or commercial
Tennessee	No	No	Property tax exemption
Texas	No	No	Exemption from sales tax; business tax credit
Vermont	No	No	Personal property tax exemptions; personal, business tax credits
Virginia	No	Yes	Allowance for personal property tax exemptions
Washington	No	No	Property tax exemption

From *Housing*, August 1978.

backup systems. Even in warm-weather regions like Arizona and southern California, where solar energy is becoming increasingly popular, the need for a backup system still keeps its cost prohibitive.

There are positive developments in solar energy. California now has legislation that offers a state income tax credit of 55% of the cost of installing a solar system, up to $3,000. Other states are certain to follow suit, and the resultant economic push for solar energy is sure to be positive. The following table may be useful in this regard.

Department of Energy surveys indicate that in 1974–1978 the growth rate of solar installations was more than 150%. The rate of growth should continue, since the ever-increasing costs of traditional sources of energy are likely to spur further solar experimentation.

With present technology any active solar system providing 100% of the heating load cannot be justified, because such a system would have to include a collector and a heat-storage chamber large enough to counter the worst possible weather conditions, even though the total capacity of the collector and storage chamber would be used only on rare occasions. Such a collector and storage system would be very expensive and would probably not operate very efficiently in normal weather conditions. Conventional gas, oil, and electric systems, with all their drawbacks, are far more flexible, and collection and storage are done by the utility, not by the homeowner's system.

Any solar system saves other kinds of energy in households, however, and over time such systems will save monthly expenses by lowering utility bills. There is no doubt that, in time, lowered monthly expense will justify a solar system's payback and make solar energy systems economically competitive with more traditional systems.

THOSE OTHER ENERGY USERS

Appliances, hot-water heaters, lights, fireplaces—yes, fireplaces—can account for well over 20% of your energy bills. Lifestyles can influence energy consumption as much as thermostat settings. The degree of chill we want in refrigerators, the temperature of water in the hot-water tank, the level of electric light, and the amount of warm air a fire in the fireplace can pull out of a house on a cold winter day—all these variables can be controlled to cut down on energy use and cost. Just a slight reduction in your requirements can save you dollars on your utility bill without your making any real sacrifice. Consider how electricity is consumed in a typical house:

Item	Kwh/yr.	Percent of electricity usage
Lighting	2,000	22.7%
Refrigerator-freezer	1,830	20.8%
Range-oven (electric)	1,175	13.3%
Clothes dryer (electric)	993	11.3%
Furnace fan motor (electric for gas furnace)	394	4.5%
Color television	500	5.7%
Dishwasher	363	4.1%
Iron	144	1.6%
Coffeemaker	106	1.2%
Clothes washer	103	1.2%
Miscellaneous appliances	1,200	13.6%
	8,808	100.0%

(Kilowatt-hours and percentages are based upon a study conducted by the National Association of Home Builders of a 1,500-square-foot, two-story home in Baltimore, Maryland.)

The appliances you use have a direct bearing on your energy bills. A side-by-side refrigerator-freezer is likely to use 45% more energy than a stacked unit. Many frost-free refrigerators use up to 50% more energy than the regular type.

Water heaters are also critical. A drop in temperature of just a few degrees creates a substantial saving. Many utility companies now recommend that you set your water heater at about 130 degrees; the usual setting used to be 150 degrees, but that is not high enough to disinfect dishes or clothes anyway. In the interest of saving energy, I recommend 120 degrees. Many people choose to experiment with the hot-water setting, varying the temperature until they find the lowest acceptable level for their needs. An insulating blanket for the water heater also conserves energy.

You can cut down on hot-water use by having a low-water-consumption shower head installed. Studies show that bathing accounts for about 40% of the hot water used in the typical household, so taking showers instead of baths makes great sense. You should use water-reduction sprays on sink and basin taps too.

In the average home, lighting is the fourth-largest energy user, consuming about 5% of the total energy required in an energy-efficient house. During the winter months, in fact, heat resulting from electric lights also helps to warm the room, resulting in an extra benefit.

Of course, in the hot summer, lighting does add to the heat load within your home and places a slight added burden on your air conditioner. Wherever sensible, use fluorescent lighting, since it produces nearly four times as much illumination per watt as the typical incandescent light bulb.

One way to save energy costs is to reduce the wattage in a lamp in areas where optimum lighting for reading and other precise work is not required. Also, fixtures that use one large bulb instead of several smaller ones are much more efficient, because the amount of illumination from a single bulb with the same wattage as the sum of several bulbs is much greater.

It's a good idea to give your appliances some time off, too. Using a fireplace for warmth is usually *not* effective in the coldest winter months, but in fall and spring when only small amounts of heat are needed to keep a room at a comfortable temperature, it is effective. If you have a fireplace, you should investigate the new glass enclosures that help control heat loss.

Here are some other suggestions for energy conservation:

Doors and Windows

1. Keep doors and windows firmly closed to cut down heat loss in winter and heat gain in summer.
2. Use heavy or insulated drapes; keep them closed at night and make sure they fit tightly at the top.
3. In the summer and in warm climates, light-colored opaque curtains partially reflect the sun and help keep your house cool.

4. The best storm door obtainable does not work when it is open. Try to reduce the number of times you go in and out.

Heating and Cooling

5. Turn down thermostats in rooms not in use and at night when you are sleeping.
6. In cold weather, try to reduce room temperature at night about 5 to 10 degrees.
7. Wear a sweater when sitting around the house. An air temperature about 4 degrees higher than normal is necessary to produce equal comfort when sitting quietly compared to engaging in active housework.
8. In summer, set air-conditioning temperature as high as you can live with, perhaps 10 to 12 degrees above winter setting.
9. Change air filters regularly to help maintain cooling efficiency.
10. Use major appliances such as dishwashers and washing machines during the cooler parts of the day. Appliances and lights generate unwanted heat that adds to the air-conditioning load.

Water

11. Set the water heater at 120 degrees rather than the usual 140 to 150 degrees.
12. Take showers instead of baths.
13. Use cold water whenever possible, especially for clothes washing.
14. Turn the water heater down or off when you are out of the house on vacation or for weekends.
15. Use the washing machine and dishwasher only with full loads and with low water levels.

Lights

16. Turn the lights out when not in a room.
17. Use task lighting rather than general lighting.
18. Use fluorescent lamps whenever possible.

THE COST OF ENERGY EFFICIENCY

Energy-efficient technology doesn't make any sense if it costs too much. It must have a reasonable return or "payback"—it must save you enough within a reasonable period to cover any extra cost it may entail. Put another way, if the construction cost of an energy system is more than an alternative system, that extra cost must be absorbed by lowered operating expenses within the payback period.

Selection of a product or a technique to save energy can be made on a "life-cycle" cost basis. If a product has a usable life of saving energy of twenty-five years, will its initial cost plus the cost of twenty-five years of operation and maintenance be less than any alternative? Life-cycle criteria are useful, but looking ahead twenty-five years involves a lot more assumptions and guesswork than looking ahead safely to, say, five years for a payback. So any energy-conserving measure should return whatever extra costs it might represent—and not all of them do represent extra costs—in savings on your heating and cooling costs in, say, seven years' time.

Some obvious extra-cost items, such as more insulation and double glazing, have almost immediate operating-cost-reducing benefits which offset their added first cost. And those cost benefits result not just from reduced energy bills but sometimes from the practicality of using smaller air conditioners and furnaces, less ductwork, smaller flues, and the like.

Whether a system will pay off can be a very complex subject. The reasonable return to you in a particular design feature, construction technique, or product has these obvious variables, among others: climate; current energy prices; lessened heat loss and heat gain for each feature, technique, or product; resulting annual operating savings; estimated rate of increase in the price of energy; added real estate taxes; income tax bracket of the homeowner; the price of money (interest rate); the period of years during which the investment value is being considered; the salvage value of the technique or product.

All of these factors can add up to some fairly complex calculations, but that's how the present value of energy cost savings can be determined.

One of the key features of this method is the selection of the period of years for analysis. Many energy-saving techniques might well last for twenty, fifty, or a hundred years in the case of, for example, fiberglass insulation. For example, at a mortgage interest rate of 9% and an annual percentage rate of increase in the price of fuel or energy of 12%, the present value of $100 of energy savings in the first year is $317 when the period of analysis is three years. When the period of analysis is five years, $100 saved the first year is worth $543. It's worth $1,165 when the analysis period is ten years, and $2,692 when it is twenty years.

Thus, depending on the selection of the period of analysis, one would be justified in spending anywhere from $300 to $2,700 per $100 of savings in the first year.

The consensus is that seven years is a reasonable period of analysis. This jibes approximately with the average actual mortgage term on most houses and allows a substantial sum of money to be used for the added cost of energy-saving techniques.

Chapter
23

Local Government
and Your Costs

You've noted, and perhaps often wondered at, the fact that house prices vary widely, even for nearly identical houses in different towns. Many of these price variations seem to have little to do with prime or poor location. A house in a good neighborhood has a better market value than the same house in a bad neighborhood; that's understandable. But two towns fifty miles apart may have entirely different conditions affecting the cost of doing business. It's the cost of local government that usually makes the difference; local taxes, regulation, special assessments, and the like are real and often major cost factors.

The regulations that cover the use and development of land for housing, and the regulations that cover the building of the house itself, can make up one-sixth of the first cost of a new house: red tape and delay, costs for all the approvals and permits, compliance with environmental and building regulations, inspections, and more. Ultimately you, not the builder, pay; he passes the costs on to you. That initial cost of regulation is usually small, however, compared to the ongoing cost of property taxes, which run between 1% and 5% of the value of your property. You pay those taxes every year, as long as you live in that house.

Property taxes generally cover the municipal services that voters have asked for over time, and they are levied by people voted into office. The clear implication is that you can do something about them and that's just what happened starting in 1975, when voters across the country voted down new bond issues in record amounts and numbers.

THE PROPERTY TAX IN PERSPECTIVE

Around the turn of the century, property taxes in this country were under 4% of the gross national product. Today they are still about the same percentage, for a total of $65 billion, according to the Tax Foundation, Inc., a nonprofit organization that advocates tax cutting.

But at the turn of the century there was no income tax, no sales tax, and no payroll tax, just a few small levies and tariffs. Property taxes in general have kept pace with incomes over the years while other taxes have soared. The result is a huge difference between gross earnings and after-tax income. This has made the average taxpayer see taxation, including property taxation, as an increasing and unwelcome burden. In many cities, for some families, property tax increases have become confiscatory.

In 1976 California had an average property tax of $64 per $1,000 of personal income versus a national average of $45. Assessments outpaced inflation, and the state had a graduated income tax and a high sales tax—all of which built up surpluses for the state government that no state had ever accumulated. California officials didn't cut taxes in order to return some of this inflation bonanza to the taxpayer. So California got Proposition 13.

Proposition 13, was not a startling event. It had its roots about thirteen years earlier when taxpayers in California began complaining mightily about increases in assessments, especially on single-family property, which raised the property taxes drastically.

As the increase in house values accelerated with inflation, tax bills went up fast. Several proposals, from 1970 on, were submitted to referendum or proposed in the state legislature, and a lot of them failed. Eventually, however, Proposition 13 passed in 1978; it was primarily a property tax cut for homeowners. The politicians did what politicians can be predicted to do every time around: most of them exaggerated the dire consequences that would result. It was said that city and county budgets would have to be slashed by over half and that perhaps as many as half a million public employees in California would be laid off.

Those things didn't happen. Proposition 13's effect on tax reduction amounted to only about 8%, and the job reduction amounted to only about 100,000 people, almost all of whom simply retired or sought work elsewhere and were not replaced. Proposition 13 did transfer the burden of education and welfare costs from the local level, where they had been heavily funded by property taxes, back to the state.

Shifting the burden of local government to the state is not necessarily a good thing; it substitutes the devil you don't know for the devil you do know in your own city council. But the perception that people could rise up against government and get something done in their own interest was a healthy one. Proposition 13 did cut taxes, which increased personal spending, which increased sales tax revenues, whic more than balanced property tax cuts. Even more important, because taxes were reduced slightly, job opportunities increased in California.

Government in California, like government elsewhere always does, found another way to skin the cat. Property assessments climbed almost 14% in 1978 and 1979 in California as a result of Proposition 13. So the voters were still angry, because they felt that government was trying to get around them. By a wide margin, in November of 1979, California voters passed Proposition 4, devised by Paul Gann, co-author of Proposition 13, which stipulated state, county, and local appropriations in California must be limited solely to adjustments for population growth and inflation. It put much tougher spending limitations on government in that state than restrictions now on the books in Arizona, Hawaii, Michigan, Tennessee, and Texas.

With the drastic reduction in property taxes, the voters in California have voted themselves a windfall: a reduction in property taxes tends to raise real estate prices and values. California homeowners in effect have enlarged their equity in their own real estate. When they sell, the one-time capital gain will absorb much of the future benefits of the tax cut from the next buyer, who will have to pay higher prices.

LOCAL FISCAL STRESS AND TAX REVOLTS

In recent years municipal revenues have failed to keep pace with the inflationary growth of expenditures. The gap between the two is most notable in new and expanding communities that must shoulder the expenses attendant upon municipal growth. Older residents with fixed incomes find themselves taxed out of their homes, and newcomers are staggered by the inordinate burden imposed by municipal charges on their dream house. Small wonder, then, that the imbalance between increases in local operating costs and revenues has precipitated taxpayers' revolts in many communities.

Since the root causes of these fiscal stresses remain unclear, the public response has tended to be erratic; but this combination of stress and insecurity certainly militates against reasoned policy making. The result has been a mounting trend toward no-growth zoning. Certainly much of its vigor is based upon such considerations as race and class exclusivity, style of life, and environmental amenity, in addition to fiscal considerations.

Voters sooner or later take the position that property taxes no longer can go up more than a certain percentage of the market value of a house. The movement which is now strong in California and a few other places, will raise havoc with city councils across this nation in the next ten years.

To raise revenue to replace what is lost through property tax reductions, every jurisdiction that can is also trying to impose user fees on everything from tennis courts to garbage collection. The Los Angeles County Fire District, for example, has proposed a state law for a fire service fee based on a building's fire risk classification. Thanks to such unconventional revenues, about a dozen smaller cities are doing without the property tax altogether.

California's Proposition 13 and Proposition 4 threaten the ability of local governments to float traditional types of bonds. Debt service for future issues will have to be paid from the tightly constricted local revenues, meaning that taxpayers will have to choose directly between current expenses, such as police salaries, and capital improvements, such as a new police station. This restriction was partly an oversight and partly a reaction against lease-purchase arrangements and other devices that governments used to create debt without voter approval. The ironic result may be the rapid growth of the use of such gimmicks.

If you want to dig into it, you might take a look at the ratio of capital and debt service to total expenditures for schools and for the entire community you are considering, including principal and interest on bond issues outstanding. If debt service runs over 25% of total expenses, either for schools or for the entire municipality, you want to be wary about that community. Such debt service can put heavy pressure on the overall school budget when times are bad, and we now seem to be moving into such times. The result can be pinched expenditures for schools and all municipal services.

PROPERTY TAXES WON'T GO AWAY

In its ideal form, the property tax is more progressive than the income tax for one simple reason: property is less equally shared in this country than income. This is easily forgotten, especially after staring at income distribution charts that show half the population making much less than $18,000 a year and a handful making millions. Almost half the adults in America own no taxable property at all, but most of them pay income taxes. While a tenth of the adult population receives about 30% of the total income in this country, the top tenth of the property owners hold between 50% and 60% of the real estate.

Besides being even more progressive than the income tax—if correctly administered—the property tax has several attractive features uniquely its own:

1. It is the only major tax that is levied on wealth as well as income. In many ways wealth is even more important than income in determining who in our society has the greatest ability to pay. Wealth implies the ability to liquidate and, even more important, the ability to borrow.

2. It is a tax that differentiates between the ease with which a speculator can make $10,000 in the real estate market and the sweat it takes a coal miner to earn the same amount, working long hours in unsafe mines.

3. It is a way of compensating the public for such government projects as roads, which tend to raise real estate values. The property tax is also a way of reimbursing those who were excluded when this continent was transformed from virgin land into private property.

4. It helps plug loopholes in the income tax, which is turning increasingly into a regressive payroll tax.

5. It can be administered more equitably than the income tax, if given the same level of professional attention. Income is an imprecise concept, and cash lends itself to concealment. Property stands for the world to see, wearing a price tag provided by the marketplace.

THE BURDEN OF SCHOOL COSTS

In the 1971 *Serrano* v. *Priest* decision, the California Supreme Court held that California's system for financing public schools, through substantial dependence upon local property taxes, "invidiously discriminates against the poor" and thus violated the equal protection clause of the U.S. Constitution. The California decision rested heavily on evidence of disparities between various California school districts in what taxpayers paid and what they got in "per pupil" expenditures for schools. Rich Beverly Hills residents paid $2.38 per $100 of assessed valuation and got $1,232 per pupil in spending; poor folks in the Baldwin Park section of Los Angeles paid $5.48 but got only $577.

Studies have shown that this sort of disadvantage by no means prevails nationwide. Taxpayers in the central city and small rural towns tend to fare better in the tax-to-pupil-expenditure ratio than those in affluent suburbs.

Some reports go even further to cast doubt on whether the property tax is particularly regressive relative to other forms of taxation, as some of its critics have claimed. In state after state the principal leaders of the property tax "revolt" prove to be substantial homeowners and real estate agents rather than the proverbial "little people." Relatively well-to-do people would be the true beneficiaries of currently popular proposals for effecting massive property tax reductions.

But something different happened in Texas in 1973. In the Supreme Court's landmark decision in *San Antonio Independent School District v. Rodriguez et al.* one result is paramount: the High Court has recognized limits to its own power to effect social change. It could hardly have chosen a better case for the purpose. *Rodriguez* was very much a social case in that it was based upon the claim by Demetrio P. Rodriguez, a Mexican-American, and his neighbors that the Texas system for financing schools discriminates against the poor. This claim was upheld in a lower-court decision, which the San Antonio School District appealed to the Supreme Court.

The Supreme Court ruled five to four against Mr. Rodriguez and his co-complainants. Its majority opinion, written by Justice Lewis F. Powell, held that the Texas system discriminates against no definable "suspect class" and that thus there is no clear-cut violation of the equal protection clause of the U.S. Constitution. He wrote further that the Texas system does not interfere with the exercise of any fundamental rights or liberties implicitly or explicitly protected by the federal Constitution.

It would be hard to overemphasize the implications had the Court ruled the opposite way, in favor of the Rodriguez group. This was one of fifty-two cases in thirty-one states that challenged the validity of present methods of financing public schools, which in every state depend heavily upon local property taxes. The general complaint is that there are wide disparities among school districts in both the per capita tax rates and in the school expenditures and that the disparities favor the rich over the poor.

If the Supreme Court had upheld the Rodriguez group, it would, in effect, have required broad changes in long-standing methods of supporting and managing the public schools. It would have cast doubt on the principle that local officials have a large measure of responsibility and control over schools. And it is not inconceivable that this same "equal protection" attack on local management could have later been extended to other services, such as police protection, that traditionally have been largely local responsibilities. In other words, in the name of justice and an interpretation of the Constitution's insistence on equal protection, the Supreme Court could have effected sweeping changes in the nation's social and political structure that might even have been beyond the power of Congress.

It has always been a false generalization that present property tax systems invariably discriminate against the poor. It is quite true that there are wide disparities from district to district, but more often than not those disparities actually favor the people who live in central cities and who often are poorer than those who live in outlying suburbs. Central city property tax bases, relative to the number of students, tend to be stronger than average, not weaker.

There is, in addition, no clear-cut relationship between school quality and spending. In some central cities, spending is relatively high, partly because salaries and other costs are high. But by both subjective and objective measurements school quality in many of these city districts would have to be rated low. But the general social conditions of the city and the recent social dislocations of many of the inhabitants are more to blame for this than spending levels. A general statewide equalization would, in some cases, actually reduce spending in some of these troubled central city districts, thus running counter to the liberal thesis that such districts should have large measures of special help.

Also in 1973, the New Jersey Supreme Court struck down the state's system of financing public school education on the ground that it failed to fulfill an 1875 mandate in the state's constitution for equal educational opportunity. Although the court did not strike down local property taxes as unconstitutional, it did say that any system that continued to rely primarily on them for financing public schools, as New Jersey does, would be unconstitutional.

The state's highest court said that the legislature had warned of this in 1971, when it said that local property taxes could not be expected to provide "equal educational opportunity." Despite the warning, however, the state has saddled communities with 68% of the cost of operating public schools, thereby sending local property tax rates soaring in its decaying cities.

The decision came two weeks after the U.S. Supreme Court upheld local property taxes as the primary means of financing public education in the *Rodriguez* case in Texas. Given the same arguments, the New Jersey court indicated that it might have ruled the same. The key difference, however, was that the federal Constitution does not guarantee the right to an education, while the

New Jersey State Constitution does. The court did not give the legislature a deadline for adopting a constitutional system of school financing.

Virtually every state, under the pressure of the *Rodriguez* case and the earlier *Serrano* decision in California, has a study commission working on ways to make the property tax more equitable.

The *Serrano* case reached the Supreme Court but was returned to a state court, where it is being reargued.

Neither the *Serrano* nor the *Rodriguez* case produced a decision against the property tax itself. Both the California court and a federal court in Texas found that it was the systems used to administer the tax that were unconstitutional.

Still many people assumed that abolition of the local tax was the wave of the future after the *Serrano* decision in 1971. Abolition has been recommended in a number of studies by government and private groups going back to the early 1960's. One finding, though, was strong opposition in every part of the country to any suggestion that the local property tax be abolished in favor of state and federal financing.

Behind the opposition lie years of tradition and familiarity with the present system, the desire for local control of schools, and the realization that new sources of funding would be hard to come by.

BUILDING REGULATIONS AS ADDED COSTS

In the name of consumer protection we add to housing's cost at every turn. There is a long list of things that make new housing more expensive for today's and tomorrow's buyers, the oncoming generation. That list includes building codes, minimum property standards, zoning and ordinances, environmental impact statements, new environmental legislation which adds to a builder's cost of simply moving earth, the increasing fees we have to pay for utility tap-ons, building permits, and the like.

Stephen Seidel, a Rutgers University researcher, has compiled startling figures showing the effect of government regulations on construction time and housing costs. In 1970, 43% of the homes built took less than four months to go through the regulatory process, but in 1975, only 9% were making it in that time. In 1970, only 3% of the homes required longer than a year for preconstruction approval, but in 1975, over 50% did.

The Construction Industry Research Board says that for the six-year period beginning in 1970, increases in costs incurred as a result of government regulations rose 124.2%. This cost factor accounted for 12% of the average price of a new home or $8,000, in 1979.

As an example, the average construction project in California requires 118 different permits from various local, state, and federal agencies and may require as many as 150 on-site inspections after construction has finally begun.

It is virtually impossible to quantify the actual dollar increase in the price of new housing to the American consumer because of regulations, but it is substantial over the last two decades. Literally thousands of varying conditions, codes, rules, regulations, and government agencies across the country make any quantification of the cost of government interference almost meaningless if applied to a broad range of housing. Specific projects or houses may carry added costs from 5% to 25% for such interference, but each case is different and for different reasons.

In some places today it takes up to three years to complete all of the planning, environmental, and permit processes necessary to build a major subdivision, but it takes big builders only sixty-five days to build a house, and prefab builder-dealers not more than ten. Yet any quantitative study on the impact of regulations on housing costs does not show the ultimate market costs resulting from the delay and the lessened supply of housing.

The impact of delay is huge. A study done in 1976 by an ad hoc committee of builders and public officials in Orange County, California, found that for every month a residential project was delayed beyond its planned construction start date, the sales price of each unit increased by at least 1.1%. That's *per month*. The components of that increase are holding costs, construction financing, and cost increase of new housing due to inflation of land, materials, and labor at 11% per year. Delaying a $50,000 house nine months adds almost $5,000 to its price tag.

Delays are usually caused by:

1. The approval processes for annexation, zoning, subdivision, and platting

2. Special district formation or annexation for water, sewer, or recreation as well as school district, fire district, and health department acceptance

3. Mortgage insurance (FHA, VA) approval

4. Environmental impact statements for large subdivisions, measurement of indirect sources of air pollutants or of fugitive dust, and quality and disposition of waste-water effluent

5. Inspection of plans and the construction process

6. Financing, including loans for land, development, and construction

FHA processing includes appraisal, architectural considerations, cost estimating, inspections, and mortgage credit evaluation of the borrower. Subdivision analysis is the route to qualification for FHA financing. This process begins with a preapplication meeting, which must be scheduled at least one week in advance. Review of the subdivision concept with the builder and FHA planners and engineers results in setting the processing schedule, which requires four to six months. Considerations include land planning, drainage, market analysis, value determination, and impact studies—there is a checklist of twenty items.

The obvious presumption that some public agency, or agencies, can make more fruitful and rational decisions than the private marketplace is open to serious question. But we have seen governments grow by leaps and bounds over the last half century, and there is no reason to believe that the process will not continue.

Often led by zealots with a negative view of the development process, more than ten thousand governments today are involved in land-use regulation, even though much of the land is under no zoning restrictions. No growth, fortunately, is seen by most of them as no solution to our land uses in light of our still expanding population, our need for more energy, and our need for continued mineral development.

The question of how much building codes have added to housing costs over the last sixteen years, for example, is a tough one. The Douglas Commission determined in 1968 that building codes had added almost $2,000 over and above the FHA minimum property standards to the cost of detached single-family housing. A more recent Rutgers University study said that building codes, or overly stringent or outdated codes, have increased housing costs by somewhere between 5% and 10% of total unit costs.

In general, building codes have probably added roughly 10% to housing costs—just the structure itself, not the land—within the last sixteen years, allowing for variation from state to state and community to community. Certain additions to building codes, such as requiring life security items and smoke detectors, have an economic impact that presumably cannot be measured. Building-code bodies citing the health and safety of occupants (presumably the goal of all building regulations), can justify whatever measures they choose, thereby further increasing the cost of housing.

Chapter 24

A Summation—
Our Long-term Romance
With Our Homes

Your house is the most important purchase you will ever make. You'll probably buy more than one in your lifetime. Each purchase will be more important than the last, because each time you'll be able to put more of your own money, your equity, into the house as down payment. Upon retirement, if you're like most Americans, you'll be able to buy your retirement house for cash. Homeownership represents the greatest equity you will ever acquire; it will be the major portion of your estate over time. Your house is worth more than the total of everything you may have in stocks, bonds, life insurance policies, furnishings, savings accounts, jewelry and silver.

The meaning of homeownership to us is historical. Our forefathers came to this country with the expectation of a new and better life, including the opportunity to own their own houses, their own land, their own things. Most Americans could not participate in that dream until after World War II, but Americans have always had it.

There have been occasions when a lot of people in this country may have felt that the dream was fading. In the 1970's we had two severe recessions. Some houses lost value, and a lot of people were precluded from buying a house because they couldn't qualify for a high-priced mortgage, or they didn't have a large down payment. But Americans snapped back from those two recessions and continued to buy houses in record numbers after the recession of 1974–1975. Even more people will buy their own homes in this decade than in the last one.

That demonstrates that Americans are more serious about homeownership—having their own place, their own nest—than they are about almost any other material item. In fact, you might say that the home ranks right up there with spouses and children.

266

What has made all this possible, of course, is the restructuring of the money markets, starting in the Great Depression with the advent of the long-term fixed-rate mortgage. Most of us really couldn't take advantage of the mortgages until after World War II, when the economy was back on its feet and we could orient our attention toward domestic rather than wartime consumption.

The way we get our money to buy our houses was further improved in the 1970's by the secondary mortgage market, which did much to ensure a more even flow of mortgage money; fluctuating cycles in the number of house purchases were flattened out to a large degree.

The recession of 1979–1980, at the very height of inflation, made mortgage money almost impossible to pay for. Not that mortgage money wasn't available; there was a lot of money. But interest rates of 12% to 15% are a steep price to pay, and many lenders were unwilling to loan at that rate. As the rate of inflation slows in the 1980's, however, the interest rates on mortgage loans will drop.

Just as important as our ability to buy a house is the way we regard it. I believe that the homebuyer of today is a lot more sophisticated in what he wants and expects in a house than he might have been a generation or two ago. We are more acutely aware of how a house works—for instance, separating the sleeping zones from the living zones, or the bedrooms from the kitchen, dining, family-living area. We are more rational in the way we use our houses.

We are also a lot more sophisticated about how our house works. In this day and age of exceedingly high energy costs, we have to be aware of how much energy it is going to take to heat a house in the winter time, how much of our muscle it is going to take to keep the house well maintained.

In just the last third of a century the United States has become a nation of homeowners, the most sophisticated and capable homeowners in the world. We love our houses and are able to maintain them, to make them "live" better for us. And their value, like the value of gold, is a real asset that will not decline over time.

Go and buy that house, care for it, fuss over it, trade it in for a better one, and you'll be very happy in all your homes all your life.

GLOSSARY

The words and phrases listed here are common to the real estate and mortgage lending businesses but not common in everyday parlance. Many of these words and phrases are used in this book, but I've included some that are not because you may hear or see them during your search for your new house.

Abstract of title A document ordered by the buyer's attorney for a closing of sale, containing a list of all instruments, legal claims, and encumbrances on the property that occurred because of previous chain of titles.

Acceleration clause A clause in the mortgage contract that serves to make the entire outstanding balance due and immediately payable if there has been a breach of the mortgage contract by the purchaser.

Adjustments at closing The apportionment between the buyer and seller, as of the date of the closing of title, of expenses such as maintenance, taxes, prepaid charges, and oil.

Advance commitment A commitment by a mortgage lender to make or buy a mortgage loan for a stated amount on a specified property, existing or to be constructed, within a stated period of time, to an owner-occupant homebuyer whose credit meets the lender's approval.

Amortization The gradual repayment of a mortgage debt on a payment schedule, usually the same amount once per month.

Apartment corporation The corporation that supervises the operation of a cooperative building or project.

Appraisal An evaluation of a property to determine its value, usually its market value.

Architectural control board Committee of a homeowners' association which passes on any changes to the exterior of a condominium unit.

As-built drawings Drawings that show what actually has been installed in a house, such as sewer lines, electrical conduits, and so on.

Assessed value   The value placed on realty by an elected or appointed local official, usually reported as the value of the land and the value of improvements on the land. The assessed value is used to determine the taxes on the property.

Assessment   A proportionate share of the budgeted annual cost of maintaining the common areas and elements of a condominium and sufficient reserves to assure financial stability. The annual assessment is reduced to monthly charges payable to the home-owners' association. A special assessment is for special purpose or to cover inadequate budgeting of operating expenses.

Assumption of mortgage   Agreement of a purchaser of a property that is covered by a mortgage to pay the mortgage. Should the mortgage be foreclosed and the property sold for an amount less than the amount due, the purchaser who has assumed the mortgage is personally and primarily responsible for the deficiency.

Attachment   A seizure of a defendant's property as security for any judgment plaintiff may recover in a legal action.

Balloon mortgage   A not fully amortizing mortgage, the bulk of which is paid off in a lump sum at the end of a specified period.

Basis point   A unit of measure used to express interest rates and yields. One basis point is equal to one one-hundredth of a percent.

Binder   An agreement drawn up between the buyer and the seller of property which secures the sale until the parties can go to contract. Most often the binder is not refundable if the buyer decides not to go ahead with the purchase.

Blanket mortgage   A mortgage covering an entire property. In a con-dominium when an apartment is sold, the individual unit is re-leased from the overall lien of the blanket mortgage when a required payment is made to the owner of the mortgage. The individual unit then usually has its own mortgage.

Board of directors   The group of individuals chosen by the owners of a cooperative or condominium to supervise the affairs of the proj-ect.

Broker   One who for a commission or fee brings parties together and assists in negotiating contracts between them. In real estate trans-actions the broker usually brings together the buyer, the seller, and the mortgage lender.

Broker's agreement   A written agreement between the seller and the broker which specifies the commission to be paid and the length of time of the agreement. (1) Nonexclusive agency: The broker is not the only broker who shows the property and is able to earn the commission. (2) Exclusive right to sell: Regardless of who sells the property, the broker earns the commission.

Building code   The details of how a building is to be erected in a specific community. Since requirements vary, the ordinance is usually enforced by a local building inspector.

Building energy performance standards (BEPS)   Requirements of federal legislation enacted in 1976 to regulate and control building design and construction to conform to specified energy usages.

Bylaws   The constitution and working rules of the homeowners' association written and filed by the developer, along with the declaration or master deed.

Certificate of Reasonable Value (CRV)   The written amount that the VA guarantees as a home purchase mortgage loan for an eligible veteran.

Certificate of title   A document usually given to the homebuyer with the deed stating that title to the property is clear. It is prepared by a title company or an attorney and is based on the abstract of title.

Chain of title   A history of all prior owners of a property up to the present owner who have been recorded in public records.

Closing   The final completion of the sale of real property when the balance of money above the down payment is exchanged for the deed. In the case of a cooperative, there is assignment of stock and a proprietary lease to the purchaser.

Closing statement   A detailed presentation, drawn up by an attorney, that explains the details of a transfer of title (see Loan closing charges).

Cloud on title   A proceeding or instrument such as a deed, or deed of trust, or mortgage, or tax or assessment, judgment, or decrees which, if valid, would impair the marketability of title.

Cluster   A grouping of low-rise housing units to ensure maximum open space around the units.

Common areas   Property in a condominium held jointly by two or more persons.

Conditional commitment   A written document issued by FHA that designates the highest insurable amount of a loan to a qualified buyer.

Conditional sale contract   A contract of sale to be delivered to the buyer of a property to which the seller retains the title until the conditions of the contract have been fulfilled.

Condominium   A form of co-ownership of a multiple-unit property in which the owner-occupant has undivided ownership of the grounds and common areas with other unit owners. The purchaser of a condominium receives a separate deed for a specific dwelling unit and a prorated interest in the common property.

Contract of sale   A contract that fixes the obligations of the seller and purchaser for the transfer of title to real estate.

Conventional loan   Mortgage loan based on security of real estate, not guaranteed or insured by a government agency.

Conversion plan   The plan by which a building on an ordinary lease basis converts to cooperative or condominium ownership.

Conveyance Form used to transfer title to land from one person or class of owner to another.

Cooperative apartment The purchaser of a cooperative apartment buys shares of the apartment corporation which owns the building or project in which his or her apartment is located. Ownership of the prorated shares in the total project entitles the purchaser to a special lease of the apartment which is commonly known as a proprietary lease. As a shareholder, he or she has the right to vote annually for the board of directors, who conduct the affairs of the apartment corporation.

Covenant A promise, usually in the form of a recorded agreement when used as a part of real estate language.

Declaration The instrument that creates the condominium form of ownership. See also *Master deed*.

Deed The legal instrument that embodies ownership of property and passes title from the seller to the purchaser.

Deed of trust A conveyance of the title land to a trustee as collateral for the payment of a debt, with the condition that the trustee shall reconvey the title upon payment of the debt. The trustee may sell the land and pay the debt in the event of a default on the part of the debtor. Used instead of a mortgage in Colorado, Delaware, Mississippi, Tennessee, Virginia, West Virginia, and elsewhere.

Disintermediation The removal of funds from interest-bearing savings accounts at thrift institutions and commercial banks and reinvesting them at higher rates in market instruments such as corporate bonds or Treasury bills.

Down payment The amount of money required, together with the mortgage loan, but not including normal closing costs, to close on a home-purchasing contract.

Earnest money The deposit given to the seller by the potential buyer to show that he is serious about buying a house. If the deal goes through, the earnest money is applied against the down payment. If the buyer changes his mind and backs out of the deal, the seller generally keeps the earnest money. If a satisfactory mortgage cannot be obtained or the house turns out to be defective, the buyer may legally pull out and get his money back (but this contingency should be clearly written in the offer to purchase).

Easement The legal written right of one party to use the property of another. It is usually recorded at the courthouse.

Encroachment An unlawful extension of one's land use upon the land of another.

Encumbrance A claim or lien upon an estate.

Equity The money interest that an owner holds in a property. A house worth $80,000 on the open market and with a mortgage debt of $50,000 would have an owner's equity of $30,000.

Escalator clause A clause in a lease that provides for increased rental payments in accordance with an index such as the consumer price index.

Escrow   Securities, instruments, or other property deposited by two or more persons with a third person, to be delivered on a certain contingency, or the occurrence of a certain event. When used in the expression "in escrow," the state of being so held. The subject matter of the transaction is the escrow; the terms with which it is deposited with the third person constitute the escrow agreement; the third person is the escrow agent.

Escrow agreement   An agreement in which an agent, usually a bank, broker, title company, or attorney, holds earnest money or a down payment while the conditions in the contract of sale are being acted upon.

Estoppel   A statement from the holder or servicer of a mortgage outlining the remaining balance due on the mortgage as of a certain date, the amount of funds in escrow if any, and the insurance information if available.

Exclusive listing   A listing for the sale of a piece of property by the owner, giving the broker the exclusive right as against all other brokers to sell the property.

Exclusive right to sell   Same as *Exclusive listing* except that the owner agrees in writing that he will pay a full commission to the broker even if he himself sells the property.

Farmers Home Administration (FmHA)   Rural credit service of the U.S. Department of Agriculture that insures and guarantees mortgages and makes loans for housing, community facilities, and business and industrial development in rural areas.

Federal Home Loan Banks   A system of twelve regional banks established by the Home Loan Bank Act of 1932 to provide regulations, audits, and certain facilities for savings and loan associations.

Federal Housing Administration (FHA)   The Federal Housing Administration insures private loans for financing new and existing housing and for home repairs and improvements. The FHA promotes better housing and neighborhood standards and broader opportunities for homeownership. The FHA does not lend money, plan, or construct housing.

Federal National Mortgage Association (FNMA)   An organization created by the Reconstruction Finance Corporation on February 10, 1938, under provisions of the National Housing Act to provide supplemental liquidity for the secondary mortgage market by investing in mortgages originated by FNMA-qualified lenders. In late 1965 FNMA was transferred to the new Department of Housing and Urban Development, and in 1968 FNMA was partitioned into two corporations. One of these, the Government National Mortgage Association (GNMA), remained as part of HUD and retained the management, liquidating, and special assistance functions. The other, which kept the FNMA name, retained the secondary market operations and in late 1968 became a government-sponsored, privately owned corporation.

Fee simple   Outright ownership of land in the highest degree. The only limitations on this type of ownership are governmental limitations.

Financial statement   A listing of the income and expenses for a given year of operation of a cooperative or condominium, usually with accompanying notes explaining the details of all money flow.

Firm commitment   A document issued by FHA designating the amount of loan it will insure to a specific loan applicant.

First mortgage   A mortgage that is a first lien on property pledged as security.

Fixtures   Property that is attached to realty in a way that would cause substantial damage if it were removed.

Foreclosure   The legal process by which a mortgagor of real or personal property, or the owner of a property subject to a lien, is deprived of his interest therein, because of failure to comply with all terms and conditions of the mortgage or any other lien.

Freeholder   One who owns real estate.

Freehold estate   An estate that is to endure for an uncertain period and must, or at least may, last during the life of some person.

Going to contract   The formal signing of a written contract for sale of real property. All terms and conditions of the sale are specified in detail, and a date is set for a closing, when monies will be exchanged for the deed or other evidence of ownership.

Graduated payment mortgage (GPM)   A form of mortgage loan that provides for lower monthly payments in the early years, later increasing to a level-payment plan, usually after five years. During the early period, the outstanding principal balance of the loan increases by a low percentage amount.

Grantee   A person to whom real estate is conveyed; the buyer.

Grantor   A person who conveys real estate by deed; the seller.

Ground lease   A lease in which the land underlying a property is rented and an annual ground rent is paid for its use. Many cooperatives and condominiums are built on rented ground.

Guarantee sale   The written commitment by a broker that within a specified period of time he will, in the absence of a sale, purchase a given piece of property at a specified sum.

Homeowners' association (HOA)   An organization consisting of *all* condominium unit owners, established for the purpose of running the development. It is created through provisions filed with the condominium declaration.

Homestead   The home and property occupied by an owner which is protected by law up to a certain amount from attachment and sale for the claims of creditors. Rights are designated through state laws.

Homestead estate   The rights of record of the head of a family or household in real estate, owned and occupied as a home, which are exempt from seizure by creditors.

House rules   The rules adopted by the apartment corporation and contained in the proprietary lease of a cooperative or condominium. The owner is responsible for compliance with these rules as though they were part of a lease contract.

Indenture   A legal term for a formal, written instrument.

Institutional lender   A lender that invests its own funds in mortgages and carries a majority of such loans in its portfolio, such as saving and loan institutions, mutual savings banks, commercial banks, and life insurance companies.

Insurable title   A form of title on which a title insuring company is willing to issue its policy of insurance.

Insured loan   A loan on which an agency such as the FHA or a private mortgage insurance company insures the lender against loss of principal.

Joint tenancy   A form of ownership in which two or more individuals hold equal title to real property. If one owner dies, his or her interest goes to the surviving owner(s). There is personal liability for all expenses.

Junior lien   A lien placed on property after a previous lien has been made and recorded.

Junior mortgage   A mortgage second in lien to a previous mortgage.

Lease   A document allowing for the use of property without purchase in return for stipulated payment(s).

Lessee   The tenant in leased space.

Lessor   The landlord in leased space.

Lien   A legal claim on another property as security for the payment of a mortgage or other debt. If necessary, the property may be seized and sold to satisfy the debt.

Limited common elements   Elements that are attached to individual units, such as shutters, window boxes, or patios.

Loan closing charges   Costs that arise out of the closing of a loan and the compliance with all the instructions of the mortgagor and mortgagee.

Loan commitment   A letter from a commercial bank, savings and loan, or other lender stating that a mortgage loan has been approved under specified terms and conditions.

Low-balling   Low quotation, purposely given or not, by a salesperson of the costs of a housing unit, taxes, fees, and other charges relating to purchase.

Maintenance   The rent payable under a proprietary lease to the apartment corporation of a cooperative or to a condominium. Maintenance charges are a proportionate share of the cash requirements for the operation and maintenance of the building or project assigned to each unit in it.

Management agreement   A contract between the owners and an outside agent which outlines the obligations and compensation of the agent.

Marketable title   A title not completely clear but with minor objections that a well-informed and prudent buyer of real estate would accept; the usual form of title used in the transfer of real estate.

Master deed   The overall declarations of legal right, title obligation, and immunity for those who participate in condominium ownership, sometimes called the declaration.

Mechanic's lien   A legal claim on property by a person who furnishes labor and materials that have improved the property and not been paid for.

Minimum property standards (MPS)   Design and construction standards that a house must meet to qualify for an FHA-insured loan.

Monthly cash flow   The dollar amount needed to pay maintenance, taxes, mortgage, and other expenses in a cooperative or condominium.

Monthly expense schedule   A chart with a series of columns that indicate the number of shares assigned to each unit of a cooperative or the percentage of common areas assigned to condominium units, and the monthly charges that arise from common ownership. Financial information on mortgage financing is often included.

Mortgage   An instrument that pledges property to a financial institution or a person as security for a loan.

Mortgage banking   The lending of company funds for the purpose of improving land, building, and purchasing buildings secured by a mortgage loan, later sold to a permanent investor with servicing retained for the life of the loan at a specified fee.

Mortgage discount   An amount charged by a mortgage lender to increase the amount of interest received above that shown on the mortgage note.

Mortgagee   The lender of funds that are secured by a mortgage.

Mortgage insurance   Insurance provided by FHA or by a private company for a fee, that makes possible a lower down payment on a mortgage and repays the lender in cases of default.

Mortgage life insurance   A life insurance policy, usually offered by mortgage lenders, to pay a mortgage loan in full in case of death.

Mortgagor   The borrower of funds secured by a mortgage.

Multiple listing   The arrangement among real estate board members in which each broker brings his listings to the attention of the other members. If a sale results, the commission is divided between the broker bringing the listing and the broker making the sale.

Net monthly cost   The actual cost for maintenance, taxes, mortgage, and other expenses on a cooperative or condominium after all available tax benefits are subtracted from monthly cash flow.

Office of Interstate Land Sales Registration of HUD (OILSR)   The federal agency responsible for oversight of lot sales in recreational and retirement homesite projects.

Open-end mortgage   Mortgage, or deed of trust, written so as to secure and permit additional advances on the original loan.

Open listing   A listing given to a broker by an owner which may be in the hands of all brokers in the city. Whoever makes the sale gets the commission.

Originate   To provide a loan to a homebuyer—the basic function of the lender in the primary mortgage market—including such services as underwriting and processing the loan application.

Origination fee   Charge by a lender to cover the costs of originating a loan.

Permanent financing   A long-term mortgage granted to an owner of real estate.

Phase construction   Development planned in phases; a builder completes one phase before beginning construction on the next.

Phase-out   The time at which a developer relinquishes his control of a project.

Points   A one-time charge by the lender to the borrower for making a loan, enabling the lender to improve the yield of the loan so that it is competitive with the yield from other investments. One point is 1% of the face amount of the loan. Also known as discount points.

Preclosing   The collection of information and preparation of documents needed for the closing of a mortgage loan.

Prepayment penalty   Penalty to the mortgagor for the payment of a debt before it actually becomes due.

Prepayment penalty clause   A clause in a mortgage contract that requires the mortgagor to pay a penalty if the mortgage is prepaid prior to its maturity. Most mortgage contracts have such a dollar penalty in the first year of the mortgage.

Prepayment privilege   A clause in a mortgage that confers on the mortgagor the privilege of prepaying the mortgage debt. It recites the conditions under which the note may be prepaid.

Private mortgage insurance   Mortgage insurance provided by private companies enabling high-ratio conventional mortgages approximating the high-ratio government backed mortgages.

Proprietary lease   The document providing for occupancy of a unit in a cooperative which stipulates payment of maintenance, services, house rules, repairs, use of the premises, subletting, assignment, alterations, notices, and many other basic functions that affect a unit in a cooperative.

Pro rata   Divided or assessed proportionally.

Prospectus   The offering document in a condominium or cooperative which sets forth the terms for purchase of a unit.

Public offering statement   See *Prospectus*.

Purchase agreement   See *Contract of sale*.

Purchase money mortgage   A mortgage given by the seller at the time of closing which takes the place of cash due at the closing.

Quitclaim deed   A deed or release; an instrument by which all right, title, or interest that one person has in or to an estate held by himself or another is released or relinquished to another.

Real Estate Settlement Procedures Act (RESPA)   Law that requires a lender to give a good-faith estimate of settlement costs and an informational booklet at the time of submission of a loan application.

Real property   Land and generally whatever is erected on, or growing upon, or affixed to, land; real estate.

Realtor   A real estate broker who is an active member of a member board of the National Association of Realtors and as such is an affiliate member of the organization who is subject to its rules and regulations, who observes its standards of conduct, and who is entitled to its benefits.

Reasonable value   A valuation of land and its improvements given by the FHA and/or VA based upon an appraisal of the subject land and improvements.

Recording   Having a written instrument placed in the public records. Deeds, mortgage liens, easements, and other instruments are usually recorded in the county clerk's office or in the county courthouse.

Reserves   Funds that are accumulated on a monthly basis to provide a cushion of capital to be used for contingencies. There are general operating reserves and replacement reserves (used to replace common elements, such as roofs, as needed at some future time).

Restrictive covenant   A limitation in a deed that requires property to be used or not to be used in some stipulated manner.

Right of first refusal   A right that provides that prior to any transfer of shares in a cooperative, or deed in a condominium, to a prospective buyer, the shares or deed must be offered to the board of directors at the price that the prospective buyer is willing to pay.

Right of redemption   The right of the owner to reclaim title to his property if he pays the debt to the mortgagee within a stipulated period of time after foreclosure.

Right of way   Authority to use the lands of another for ingress and egress.

Sales agreement   An agreement by which one of two contracting parties, called the seller, gives a thing and passes title to it, in exchange for a certain price in current money, to the other party, called the buyer or purchaser, who agrees to pay such price.

Satisfaction   Settlement of a claim or demand; payment.

Satisfaction of mortgage   Evidence of payment of a mortgage in full.

Secondary financing   A loan secured by a second mortgage or deed of trust on real property.

Secondary mortgage market   The entire panoply of institutional and individual investors who purchase mortgage-backed securities.

Second mortgage   Placing a mortgage on property subsequent to an existing mortgage, thereby giving the holder of the mortgage an interest secondary to the holder of the first mortgage.

Security interest   The specified amount that a lender or lien holder has in the total value of a property. It is usually recorded.

Settlement costs   The costs paid at a closing to enable the completion of a sale, including legal fees, recording of mortgage fee, mortgage tax, cost of title search and title insurance, the purchaser's reimbursement of seller's prepaid taxes, and bank charges.

Special assessment   A special charge to the stockholders in a cooperative or owners in a condominium for a particular repair or improvement.

Sponsor-seller   The developer of a cooperative or a condominium building or project, sometimes the builder, sometimes an investor, who purchases an existing building and converts it into a cooperative or condominium.

Standby commitment   (1) Issued to a seller of real estate: A contract from a lender to process and close loans at a fixed price for a given period of time with a further provision to pay to the seller of the real estate any price received for the mortgage over the fixed price after the mortgage has been sold to a permanent investor. (2) From an institutional lender: A contract to accept delivery of a mortgage or group of mortgages within a specified period of time at a fixed price, usually considerably lower than market price, and requiring a commitment fee payable in advance. Loans may or may not be delivered under the commitment. There is no obligation to deliver loans to an investor under this type of commitment.

Stock pledge   The document that pledges the stock from a cooperative apartment as security for a loan.

Subject to a mortgage   Assumption by a purchaser of the mortgage obligation of the former owner of the property.

Survey   An engineering examination of property that identifies its boundaries and the location of structures on the property.

Tax assessment   A tax for a specific purpose such as providing paved streets or new sewers in a new development. The people who benefit from the improvement must pay the assessment.

Tenant-in occupancy   A tenant living in an apartment that is converted to cooperative ownership.

Tenants-in-common   A group of persons who acquire interest in real estate at the same time under a single deed. They need not all have equal interests, and there is no survivorship feature as in joint tenancy. All tenants-in-common are liable for their proportionate share of expenses and are able to dispose of their interest as they see fit.

Tenant-stockholder   An individual who is a shareholder in a cooperative housing corporation.

Three R's   Rules, regulations, and resolutions; the bylaws under which the homeowners' association functions. See Bylaws.

Title   Evidence of a person's legal right to the possession of property, usually in the form of a deed.

Title insurance policy   A contract to make good a loss arising through defects in titles to real estate, or liens or encumbrances thereon. (1) Owner's title policy: A title insurance policy usually issued to the landowner himself. The owner's title insurance policy is bought and paid for only once and continues in force without any further payment. Owner's title insurance policies are not assignable. (2) Mortgagee's title policy: Issued to the mortgagee and terminating when the mortgage debt is paid. In case of foreclosure or in case the mortgagee acquires title from the mortgagor in lieu of foreclosure, the mortgage policy continues in force, giving continued protection against any defects of title that existed at, or prior to, the date of the policy.

Title search   An examination of the title of the owner of real property in the public records to determine if it is free and clear of liens and other encumbrances. Such a search is usually necessary before title insurance may be obtained to guard against taking imperfect title from the seller.

Townhouse   An attached or separate house in a row of two or more. Most townhouses are two or three stories high, with the living area on the main floor and the bedrooms upstairs. In certain parts of the country they are called villas or town-home apartments.

Trust   A right of property, real or personal, held by one party for the benefit of another.

Trust deed   An instrument conveying property from the owner to a trustee for the accomplishment of the objectives set forth in the agreement. In many states, trust deeds are used rather than mortgages to secure loans on real property.

Underwriting   In the mortgage market, usually, the technical analysis by a lender of a prospective loan, including a credit check of the borrower's ability to repay the contemplated loan and of the property's propensity to either maintain or increase in value.

Undivided interest   In condominium law, joint ownership of common areas not owned individually.

Unencumbered property   Property that is free and clear of any assessments, liens, easements, or encumbrances of any kind.

Unsecured loan   A loan made without security or other legal claim upon specific property to satisfy the debt.

Usury   A rate of interest that exceeds the legal maximum set by state law.

Variable rate-mortgage (VRM)   A mortgage contract that allows the interest rate to slide up and down according to changes in a specified index that reflects the cost of money.

Veterans Administration (VA)   An agency of the federal government which, among other things, insures or guarantees mortgage loans for veterans in accordance with the provisions of the Servicemen's Readjustment Act of 1944.

Voting rights   The right of a stockholder in a cooperative or an owner in a condominium to determine matters concerning operation of the property.

Warehousing   Lending funds on a short-term basis with the permanent mortgage loan pledged as collateral. This form of interim financing is used until a mortgage can be sold to a permanent investor.

Warrant   A covenant whereby the grantor of an estate and his heirs are bound to warrant and defend title. See also *Deed*.

Warrantee   A person to whom a warranty is made.

Warranty   A promise that a proposition of fact is true.

Warranty deed   A deed that contains specific promises, called warranties, made by the seller to the purchaser.

Zoning   A legislative process by which restrictions are placed upon the use to which real property may be put.

Index